OCEAN MANAGEMENT
A New Perspective

OCEAN MANAGEMENT
A New Perspective

By
John M. Armstrong
Peter C. Ryner

ANN ARBOR SCIENCE
PUBLISHERS INC / THE BUTTERWORTH GROUP

Copyright © 1981 by Ann Arbor Science Publishers, Inc.
230 Collingwood, P.O. Box 1425, Ann Arbor, Michigan 48106

Library of Congress Catalog Card Number 81-66620
ISBN 0-250-40470-2

Manufactured in the United States of America
All Rights Reserved

Butterworths, Ltd., Borough Green, Sevenoaks, Kent TN15 8PH, England

FOREWORD

The ocean was once thought of as boundless; its resources infinite. Increased population, the explosion of technology after World War II, and diminishing land-based resources of hydrocarbons, minerals and physical space have proved these perceptions untrue. The ocean, like the land, is vulnerable to overcrowding, overexploitation and abuse.

Unlike the philosophy for use of public lands, however, a philosophy of multiple use, conservation, preservation and protection has been slow in developing for oceans. It was only 32 years ago that the U.S. Supreme Court declared that the federal government and not the states held title to the offshore waters. International doctrines based on seventeenth century concepts have further influenced national policies dealing with ocean space and marine resources. With the federal government and the states sharing responsibilities for jurisdiction over the ocean, the American governmental system further complicates developing a unified approach to administration of ocean programs.

Conflict among ocean uses in U.S. coastal waters is becoming more evident as oil and gas development accelerates on the Outer Continental Shelf, as oceanborne commerce increases, as fishing activities in the 200-mile Fishery Conservation and Management Zone expand and as more people clamor to use the ocean for recreation. Legislative solutions to these problems have been piecemeal. Single-purpose laws, administered on a case-by-case basis, are the hallmark of U.S. ocean policy aimed at allocating and protecting the marine resources.

Proposals for creating a system of "Ocean Management" have been advanced with greater frequency in recent years. Unfortunately, in the absence of conceptual framework, "Ocean Management" is a meaningless label. Furthermore, "Management" itself suggests to some the heavy hand of regulation, control and red tape, coupled with an unsavory hint of "government planning."

This book is intended as a point of departure for developing a theoretical construct for discussion of ocean management. It is not intended to be a treatise to promote the acceptance of the concept, but rather is intended to provide a historical discussion of the evolution of contemporary ocean policy, to explore current problems and programs for meeting these problems and to offer alternative means for dealing with the problems of allocating and protecting ocean resources in the future.

Some may find statements in this book to be contentious or controversial. Others will disagree with certain inferences and conclusions. To those persons who may be critical of this effort we would remind them that the U.S. Constitution itself was initially grounded in controversy and disagreement. Through debate and deliberation, however, the greatest living document of consensus emerged. We hope that this study will serve as a catalyst in the debate leading to better administration and stewardship of the ocean and its resources.

James W. Curlin
Former Deputy Assistant Secretary for
    Policy
U.S. Department of Commerce

PREFACE

This book is the result of a six-month study effort initiated by the U.S. Department of Commerce. The major intent of the study was to examine the subject of ocean management as an area of interest to the United States government. The principal approach was to view this question as one of management of a large, complex public resource, a resource with dynamic natural characteristics and a wide variety of uses and users.

Much has been said in the past about the issue of "ocean management" or "ocean policy." Most of this past discussion has been concerned with one of three subjects: (1) marine research and how to get support for more of it; (2) Law of the Sea negotiations and the attendant political/legal difficulties involved; and (3) administration of ocean management programs. Almost none of the many past efforts have been concerned with the actual management problems of our ocean resources, particularly with our ocean resources viewed as a total system. Marine science interests want to learn more about the characteristics of the various ocean subsystems that could be managed. Law of the Sea researchers want to learn how and when to negotiate a "good position." Ocean reorganization advocates want to tell us what agency or agencies should do something called ocean management. No one has really talked about ocean management in terms of where we have been, what we are doing now, and how we should think about the problems of controlling or managing even "our part" of this vast thing called the ocean.

Little has been written about the oceans as a resource management problem. This is, in part, because we do not really understand very well how the ocean works, how it responds to accelerating use, how its various subsystems interconnect and how they interact. There is a strong analogy between the problem of managing that other fluid body we live in, the atmosphere, and understanding and managing the fluid oceans. Further, we lack historic perspective on the impact of our use of the seas. In our management of other natural systems, such as public lands, forests and rivers, we have had the benefit of 200 years of living on and in these particular resource systems and, as a result, a strong sense of association has evolved. This is not the case with the oceans.

The United States does, however, have a long history of thought and action associated with ocean affairs. This awareness goes back further than one normally might suppose. Because past patterns of development can be so important in understanding present ocean management issues and possibilities, considerable attention has been directed to the evolution of ocean control.

The major objective of this study was to explore some of the basic factors that have brought about federal government involvement in the use, protection and development of ocean resources. In this light, two major comments are in order. First, there is an implicit assumption made in the study that the boundaries of the system under consideration are somehow "domestic" in scope, that is to say the study deals primarily with the territorial sea, coastal waters and possible future adjacent zones that might be established. The study was not directly concerned with international waters, high seas or other subjects related to international negotiations or treaty. It must be emphasized, of course, that these two areas are not fully separable or independent. The passage of maritime commerce from domestic waters to international waters, the development of seabed resources, the management of transient living resources all involve management issues that bridge both of these areas and others. Nonetheless, the focus is on issues, concepts and problems that relate more to domestic ocean resources than to international issues. As such, any implication created by the discussions in this book that bear on international ocean issues or problems must be recognized as beyond the scope of this work, even though they must eventually be accounted for in any future extensions. No conclusions should be drawn about the future international ocean policies of the United States from the discussion presented here. While there is an interactive relationship between so-called domestic ocean management issues and international issues, it is the "domestic system" that is the subject of consideration in this book. Thus, even while international considerations and events have had a significant impact on domestic ocean policy and programs, there is no intent in this presentation to encourage the reverse. In many instances, international considerations, law, or treaties may directly or indirectly influence "domestic" programs, even regulations. While domestic program objectives or operating characteristics may not always be in harmony with international considerations, it is not intended that "domestic ocean management" concepts or goals presented here would necessarily influence existing or future international agreements.

Second, the terms "ocean control," "control of ocean resources," "government control," etc., are used throughout this book in the broad sense of discussing the wide range of government actions that can guide, manage, regulate, influence or affect the use, nature and/or character of ocean resources or ocean space itself. Control, as used here, does not always imply jurisdictional control or jurisdiction itself. As presented in the introductory section, control is a generic term that implies a range of management functions that may result in more efficient or wiser use of ocean resources. It does not necessarily mean full and absolute control of resources or space in the oceans. Furthermore, control does not necessarily imply any direct action by the federal government in the international waters of the ocean.

The major purpose of this document is to stimulate renewed consideration of a very complex management issue. The purpose here is not to prescribe how ocean management should work but rather to describe the system as it has evolved to date, to offer some observations about future development alternatives, and, most of all, to encourage further examination of this increasingly important issue. The United States has not yet learned how to fully and effectively manage any of its large public resource systems. We have from time to time, however, successfully asked the right questions, formulated potential approaches, and established principles to guide our actions. If this can be done for the oceans, it will be a major step forward. And, if this study contributes to some further understanding, discussion and debate about the issues and problems associated with the wise use of the oceans, it will have been a success.

From our perspective, this study has been a necessary and important starting point, but there remains a great deal to be done. There is a need to understand better the conflicts in ocean use and the concepts and options related to the management of the ocean system. While there should be a reasonable tradeoff between study and action, we hope that the topic of "ocean management" will derive the benefits of further inquiry, study, and debate. If formal actions are needed before the problem is fully understood, we hope that those actions will allow the flexibility and spirit of further inquiry that are necessary to deal with this profound and fascinating problem.

John M. Armstrong
Peter C. Ryner

ACKNOWLEDGMENTS

The authors wish to express their thanks to those who assisted in the preparation of this book. Staff members of the Office of Coastal Zone Management and other offices of NOAA, the Office of Water and Hazardous Materials, Environmental Protection Agency, the Office of Ocean, Resource and Scientific Policy Coordination, U.S. Department of Commerce, reviewed and commented on various drafts of this book. The thorough reviews and critical comments of Captain L. C. Kindbom, United States Coast Guard, and James E. Brown, Office of Ocean Affairs, Department of State, were particularly helpful in clarifying and focusing discussion of several important matters. Mr. Harold Gortner, University of Indiana at Gary, also provided many helpful comments on both the style and substance of the study, and Patricia Spencer made substantial and valuable editorial contributions. We are, however, responsible for the work and its conclusions.

When we try to pick up anything by itself, we find it attached to everything in the universe.

John Muir

John M. Armstrong is Professor in the College of Science and Mathematics at the University of South Carolina. He is also Professor of Resource Policy and Management at the College of Charleston. He served as director of the Coastal Zone Laboratory at the University of Michigan and faculty member in the Civil Engineering Department.

Dr. Armstrong has been involved in coastal and ocean resource policy analysis during the past 14 years. He has researched and written extensively in the field and his previous book, *Coastal Waters: A Management Analysis,* with P. Ryner was the first comprehensive treatment of territorial sea management issues. He has served as consultant to government and to industry in coastal and ocean resource development issues both in the United States and abroad.

Peter C. Ryner, President of Peter C. Ryner and Associates, Bath, Maine, specializes in public policy analysis, environmental impact assessment and natural resources planning. He received his MS in resource planning and conservation from the University of Michigan, and has served on several local and state public policy boards. For several years he provided coastal planning services for the University of Michigan, and also served as Executive Director and Principal Planner of a coastal regional planning commission. Mr. Ryner has published numerous technical papers and reports in the areas of ocean/coastal policy and rural growth management. He is co-author of the 1978 Ann Arbor Science publication, *Coastal Waters: A Management Analysis.*

CONTENTS

CHAPTER ONE

INTRODUCTION

This book is an exploration of the origins, content, and structure of United States Federal efforts to control and/or influence the use of ocean space and ocean resources. This book does not prescribe how such efforts should be structured, but instead attempts to describe and analyze past efforts and present systems, and to discuss certain basic principles and ideas that may be important to think about when considering the subject of ocean resource management.

In recent years, the term "ocean management" has come into use and also has become a political issue. It is not the intent of this book to advocate "ocean management," and when possible that term is avoided because of its several contemporary definitions and interpretations. This book does not assume that some new form of "ocean management" is needed. Rather, a major objective is to develop a background for viewing, examining, and discussing "ocean management" in its various possible forms.

I. Definitions and Assumption

This effort to synthesize ocean-related programs and policies into a discussion of "management" has involved the consideration of a large number of issues and dynamics. Adding to the inherent complexity of this subject is a set of confusing and sometimes ambiguous or contradictory terms and concepts that have evolved within government, industry, and the academic community. For this reason, it was necessary to establish some specific definitions and make certain assumptions which may not reflect common usage. Some of these are presented at this point for definitional purposes and will be considered in further detail elsewhere in the text.

A. A Definition of "Management"

As used in this book, "management" refers in a general sense to a deliberate effort to direct or control conditions and actions, without suggesting that such efforts are necessarily successful. Such efforts can either be supportive, in the sense of attempting to encourage, promote, or assist some action or condition, or restrictive in the sense of attempting to prevent, diminish, or discourage.

1. Spectrum of control. In this book, "management" will also have a more specific use, suggesting a range of governmental intervention actions that can be imposed upon ocean space and ocean activities. At one extreme is full control, or at least an attempt at full control, which could involve direct governmental development of a resource or an assignment of what activities will or will not take place within a certain sector of ocean space. At the other end of the "management" spectrum is something akin to influence, with minimal exertion of governmental power. A totally laissez-faire situation would fall outside of this concept of "management;" some effort to control or direct must be involved for management to occur, as used here.

This concept of "management" is reflected in present United States ocean-related programs, which range from the provision of weather information and the publication of navigation charts, through fisheries "management" in which fishing "seasons" and total catch are allocated by the Federal Government for some species. At the far end of the control spectrum are certain national defense ocean zones where during certain periods all activities are monitored and controlled.

In this sense, the United States is already involved in "ocean management." Although the Federal Government has not yet presumed or attempted to "comprehensively" manage the ocean, it is "managing" or attempting to control or direct a variety of uses and/or users: ocean water quality, the disposal of materials and substances into the ocean, fishing activities within a 200-mile zone, the pattern of vessel traffic within certain waters, oil and gas production on the outer continental shelf, and many other matters.

2. A range of functions. "Management" involves not only different levels of control, but also various forms of governmental action or "functions." There is often a correlation between the amount of control desired and the number or type of functions utilized. Some of the present Federal ocean-related management functions are:

- research;
- information collection, storage, distribution;
- financial assistance;
- revenue collection;

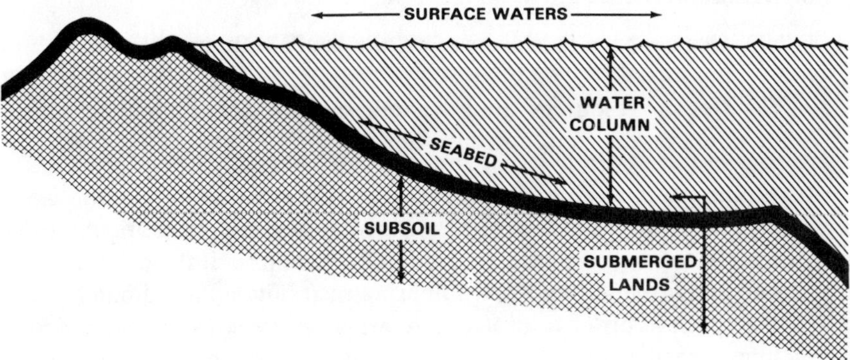

Figure 1: VERTICAL OCEAN PROFILE

On a vertical axis, ocean space can be divided into four components: the surface waters, water column, seabed, and subsoil. For purposes of this book, seabed and subsoil will usually be combined and referred to as either seabed or submerged lands.

- monitoring;
- enforcement;
- conflict resolution;
- policy setting;
- regulation (including permitting, zoning, licensing); and
- standard setting.

It is this combination of functions and degree of control which constitute "management."

B. Defining "Ocean"

In developing a concept of "ocean management," it is necessary to recognize several different aspects or components of the term "ocean." In this book recognition is given to physical components, management components and jurisdictional components.

1. Physical dimensions of ocean space. A conventional terminology has evolved to describe various components of ocean space. Figure 1 shows the vertical division of the ocean into its four components: the surface waters, the water column, the seabed, and the subsoil.

2. Management dimensions. In order to discuss Federal actions that are referred to as ocean management, it is important to recognize that there are three major components that must be dealt with:

4   OCEAN MANAGEMENT

    a. The natural ocean system, including:

        (1) **Ocean space** (surface waters, the water column, the seabed and the subsoil — see Figure 1).

        (2) **Ocean "resources" and dynamic systems** (thermal patterns, fish, mineral deposits, currents, tides, etc.).

    b. Ocean users and/or ocean activities. Federal ocean-related "management" or control efforts can involve sorting out competing demands for ocean space or resources, dealing with the impacts of one activity upon another, imposing restraints upon human uses of the ocean in order to protect natural ocean systems or to encourage human activities by providing financial support, information or physical protection.

    c. Government programs, agencies, and policies. As the number of ocean-related Federal management efforts has expanded, various mechanisms have been estabished to guide, direct, coordinate or "manage" these efforts. Ocean management entails not only ocean space, resources and activities, but also the collection of laws, programs, agencies, and policies which have been created in an effort to control. This aspect of ocean management contains two elements:

        (1) **Ocean related programs.** Since the establishment of several ocean-related Federal programs during the 1970's, a number of studies have concluded that the Federal Government should give more attention to how the growing number of ocean programs can or should interface and what the appropriate degree and mechanism of separation or coordination might be.

        (2) **Ocean vs. non-ocean programs.** It is administratively difficult to isolate "ocean" affairs totally from all other areas of national interest and Federal activity. The ocean is not a single unique system in the national or world order. Thus, ocean management has historically included consideration of how Federal ocean-related programs should be placed institutionally within the Federal Government system, and of possible linkages between ocean management efforts and other areas of national policy, such as national defense, foreign policy, and energy.

    3. Jurisdictional dimensions. On the basis of present United States ocean-related programs and policies, the ocean can be divided into four separate jurisdictional zones. For each of these zones, the Federal Government presently has a different degree of ability to control or manage, and thus a different management approach. With the exception of the

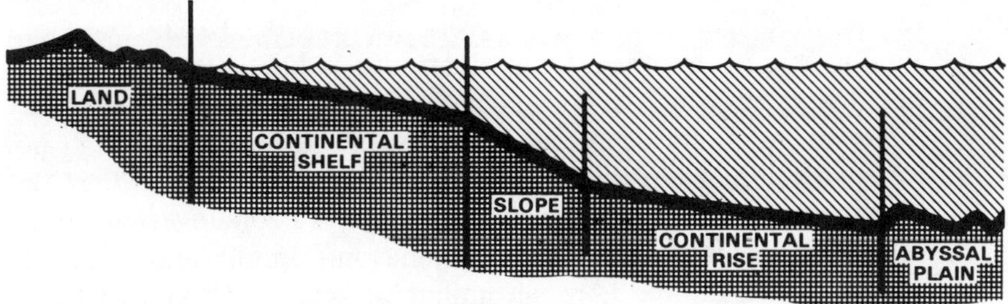

Figure 2: HORIZONTAL OCEAN PROFILE

The major components of ocean space on the horizontal axis are the continental shelf, the continental slope, the continental rise, and the abyssal plain. In this report primary attention will be limited to a portion extending to the outer edge of the continental shelf, which reflects the limits of the majority of United States ocean-related programs and policies. However, consideration is given to the interface between management efforts for this area and those management efforts extending beyond this relatively narrow band.

"territorial sea," these zones are not formally recognized either by government or within the literature, nor is it the intention of this report to propose the widespread adoption of the terminology developed here. These terms have been chosen in an effort to simplify what, in reality, is a complex issue, and in recognition of the fact that a uniform terminology may be emerging but has not yet been accepted.

a. **Teritorial sea.** This is a segment of ocean space over which the United States asserts full sovereign jurisdiction, although some residual international rights, such as the right of innocent passage, are provided in this area. While some nations currently claim "territorial seas" as wide as 200 miles,[1] the United States presently claims a territorial sea three nautical miles in width.

b. **Outer continental shelf zone.** This ocean zone extends seaward approximately 200 nautical miles, although the actual width of the shelf varies greatly. In terms of any Federal management efforts, it is an exceedingly complex zone, in which the United States claims full authority to manage or control the resources of the submerged lands of the continental shelf (see Figure 2), but less than full authority to control the waters and resources above the sea floor. Contained within this zone is the *Contiguous Zone* which the

---

[1] U.S. Department of State, "National Claims to Maritime Jurisdiction," *Limits in the Seas,* No. 36, 3rd revision. April 19, 1978.

United States currently recognizes as being nine miles wide, extending seaward from the outer edge of the territorial sea. The Contiguous Zone is another formal, internationally recognized jurisdictional area in which a coastal nation is perceived to have many interests and some degree of management authority, although not full ownership or jurisdiction. It should be emphasized that the Contiguous Zone is a part of the high seas and is a zone over which the U.S. exercises jurisdiction for fiscal, customs, immigration and sanitation matters only. Through unilateral action, the United States has extended the idea of partial management authority outward 200 miles, for fisheries, and some types of pollution control.

The degree to which the United States or other nations should exert control over resources or activities within this 200-mile zone has been a subject of debate since at least the 1930's. The United Nations' Conference on Law of Sea (UNCLOS) is currently considering the formal designation of this area as an "economic zone" over which a coastal nation would have certain management authority. (It should be noted that "jurisdiction" seems to pertain to resources in the water column and not on the water column itself as an element of ocean space.)

c. **International ocean zone.** As used in this report, this zone represents that portion of ocean space, usually seaward of the continental shelf, over which no nation claims or exercises direct control or jurisdictional authority. "Management," to the degree that it is attempted, is through bilateral, multi-national and international treaty or agreement. This segment of ocean space and the resources located there are principal areas of concern to negotiators at UNCLOS. It now appears that at least the submerged lands portion of this zone may eventually be established as a formal international management zone.

d. **Foreign ocean zone.** This refers to those portions of ocean space and resources under the jurisdictional control of some other nation, either as a "territorial sea" or through some other assertion of authority. Historically, the United States has had economic, transportation, defense, research, and in recent years, environmental interests in these foreign ocean areas and has attempted to influence through various means how they are managed.

While this book focuses upon the first two zones, and the emergence of Federal efforts within them, consideration will also be given to the importance of linking management activities within each of these zones.

C. The Concept of a Management Regime

Ocean management involves the extension of control over ocean space, resources, and/or activities, as well as over the individual governmental efforts to exert that control. To be considered are the degree of control needed, the objective(s) of government intervention, the number and type of functions which should be undertaken, the area of ocean space and type of resources or activities over which control is to be applied, and how multiple control efforts should be structured in relation to each other.

In several instances, the United States has formalized its ocean "management" efforts, establishing specific management boundaries, indicating the type and degree of control to be applied over specified portions of ocean space, resources or activities, and how a particular control or management effort will interface with other programs and policies. While these efforts are most often referred to as programs and/or policies, this book uses the term regime.

Regime. Regime generally refers to a manner, method, or system of rule of government, and in this report will be used to refer to the systems devised by the Federal Government to undertake ocean control efforts. In this usage, the *Submerged Lands Act of 1953* can be said to have established a management regime for the submerged lands and resources of a three-mile wide ocean zone. This regime is managed primarily by coastal states. It does not specifically include the living resources of this zone and is clearly differentiated from a separate management regime established for the submerged lands beyond three miles through the *Outer Continental Shelf Lands Act of 1953*. That regime is under Federal rather than state authority. Using this concept of "regime," the *Coastal Zone Management Act of 1972* can be seen as a Congressional revision of the earlier territorial regime established by the Submerged Lands Act, this time specifically including not only the waters of the territorial sea, but also adjacent shoreland. This new regime involves a combination of Federal and state authority.

Ocean management regimes can be comprehensive or narrowly defined, constructed with considerable detail and specificity or vaguely drawn. In the United States since 1945, the tendency has been to establish single purpose or narrowly defined regimes in what has often been referred to as a "functional" approach, although there are exceptions. Also, these "regimes" were at first not constructed in great detail. But as the number of regimes, programs, policies, and interest groups increased, early regimes such as that for the Outer Continental Shelf have been modified and given more detail, either administratively or by Congress, or in some instances by the courts. More recent management regimes, such as the coastal zone and deepwater port systems, have been constructed with a considerable amount of detail, indicating the linkages or methods of establishing linkages with other control efforts.

Importance of regime concept. The term "regime" is not normally used in discussions of domestic Federal ocean-related programs and policies, and the concept which it represents in this study is one more frequently discussed with reference to the law of the sea. Much of the present UNCLOS discussion could be characterized as a consideration of the establishment of new ocean management regimes and the codification and adjustment of presently recognized regimes. While the concept of regime is not usually used today in the context of domestic ocean programs, it has been used in the past in conjunction with U.S. domestic ocean program formulation. Depending upon the outcome of the UNCLOS negotiations and future national interests, this concept may well become a major issue again. In fact it may already be re-emerging through assertions of the need for some new type of ocean management programs and policies. These assertions will be discussed in Chapter Five.

II. Structure of Study

A brief discussion of the contents of each chapter is included here as an indication of the structure of this analysis. This first chapter has attempted to establish some basic terms and concepts and to indicate the approach of the book.

A. Chapter Two: Evolution of Federal Efforts to Control Ocean Space and Ocean Resources

This chapter traces the evolution of Federal efforts to control ocean space and resources from the 1930's until the present time. The analysis is divided into several parts, moving from an initial assertion of Federal authority over both the territorial sea and some distance beyond, through legislative resolution of conflicts which resulted from those assertions, to the present consideration being given to new national and international jurisdiction regimes since the late 1970's.

B. Chapter Three: An Analysis of Selected Ocean Control Programs

In Chapter Three, attention is directed to the *Deepwater Ports Act,* the *Marine Sanctuaries Provisions* of the *Marine Protection, Research, and Sanctuaries Act,* the *Coastal Zone Management Act,* and the *Fisheries Conservation and Management Act.* Discussion focuses upon the type and degree of control being attempted, the role of the Federal and state governments, the relationship with other ocean programs, and various issues or problems which these particular programs raise.

C. Chapter Four: Issues of Ocean Management

The efforts of the United States to exert control over the ocean have involved several basic national issues. Some of these issues continue to have relevance as future ocean management problems while others present new opportunities. Using the material in Chapters One, Two, and Three as background, Chapter Four describes the issues associated with: (a) the role of state and local government in Federal ocean management; (b) national security aspects of ocean management; (c) the national interests; and (d) the role of private industry.

D. Chapter Five: Some Management Aspects of Ocean Control

Chapter Five discusses Federal ocean control efforts in terms of degree and type of control, problems of coordination, principles for management, the variety of possible government actions, and alternative management "regimes."

E. Chapter Six: Future Considerations

This final chapter briefly considers the need for ocean management. It also discusses the concern over "creeping jurisdiction" and lists some issues that warrant further attention.

CHAPTER TWO

EVOLUTION OF FEDERAL EFFORTS TO CONTROL OCEAN SPACE AND OCEAN RESOURCES

I. Introduction

From the early days of the Republic, the United States had established ocean-related Federal programs and activities concerning commerce, navigation, and defense. Early ocean/coastal water concepts contained no Federal claims of national authority, beyond a three-mile territorial sea, other than for customs purposes and perhaps for defense. Within that territorial sea, it was commonly held by Federal and state government, and supported by the courts, that the submerged lands and resources were "owned" by the coastal states, and that most regulation or management was a state rather than a Federal function.

By the late 1930's, several factors led to a significant change in the way in which responsibility was viewed. Those factors included the growing economic importance of oil and gas; the ability to recover offshore oil and gas resources; a perception of serious overfishing in waters near our shores by foreign nations; and concern over the ability to detect and control hostile submarines near U.S. coasts. These disparate factors, combined with the personal interests and views of Secretary of the Interior Harold Ickes and President Franklin Roosevelt, resulted in the first major public statement of United States Federal ocean jurisdiction, and the first formal and significant articulation of state and Federal rights and authorities over ocean space and ocean resources.

This chapter discusses the various assertions and events that characterized the emerging Federal control over ocean space and ocean resources and provides a historical perspective and background for present Federal efforts to "manage" ocean space, resources, and activities.

II. National Jurisdiction Claims Prior to 1937

Prior to 1937, the Federal Government had not made any significant efforts to control or regulate the living or non-living natural resources of the ocean. Federal ocean-related policies and programs seemed to focus upon the use of the *water surface* as a means of conveyance rather than upon problems of ocean systems. Control was over commerce, revenue collection, harbor and port development, and preventing obstacles to navigation.

E. R. Bartley, in *The Tidelands Oil Controversy*[1], provides clear evidence that until the 1930's both state and Federal Governments assumed that the territorial sea was state, rather than a Federal domain; that the nature of authority was proprietary, (that is, the states owned the submerged lands and natural resources of the territorial sea). Typical of this attitude was the finding of the U.S. Supreme Court in the case of *Mumford v. Wardell* during the late 1860's:

> California was admitted into the Union September 9, 1850, and the Act of Congress admitting her declares she is also admitted on an equal footing, in all respects, with the original states. . . . Settled rule of law in this court is that the shores of navigable waters and the soils under the same in the original states were not granted by the Constitution to the United States, but were reserved to the several states.[2]

Offshore Oil and Gas as a National Ocean Resource Issue

By 1920 offshore deposits of oil and gas in California were being commercially developed, and in 1921 California enacted legislation[3] which reserved to the state all oil, gas, and other mineral resources in prescribed areas of offshore waters, and established rules for leasing those mineral resources. The right of the state to exert such control was challenged in state courts.[4] The U.S. Supreme Court refused to hear the case on the grounds that no substantial Federal issue was involved.[5] This serves as further indication of the degree to which state ownership and authority were accepted by both Federal and state authorities.

The first challenges to state authority over ocean resources were by private interests hoping for more favorable access to offshore oil under Federal authority rather than under the existing state system. In California a few major oil companies had managed to create what amounted to a monopoly through the state leasing system. These companies op-

---

[1] Ernest R Bartley, *The Tidelands Oil Controversy* (Austin: University of Texas Press, 1953).

[2] *Mumford v. Wardell*, 6 Wall 423, 435-36 (1867).

[3] *Calif. Stats.* 1921, c303, p. 404.

[4] *Boone v. Kingsbury*, 206 Calif 148 (1928).

[5] *Workman v. Boone*, 280 U.S. 517 (1929).

posed Federal control, since it represented a threat to their favorable position within the state leasing system.[6] Throughout the 1920's and 1930's, the Department of the Interior continued to receive requests for Federal mineral prospecting permits in waters off the California coast under authority of the Federal Mineral Leasing Act of 1920. Each of these requests was denied by the Department of the Interior on the grounds that the Federal Government had no jurisdiction over offshore oil, either within or beyond the territorial sea.

Proctor Letter

When the Federal Government attempted to gain control over ocean resources and submerged lands in the 1930's and 1940's, its previous policy of recognizing state authority was to cause a certain amount of embarrassment. One particular matter that became an issue in the subsequent debate was a letter written on December 22, 1933, by Harold Ickes as Secretary of the Interior to an applicant, Mr. Olin S. Proctor, for a Federal offshore exploration permit:

> As to the jurisdiction of the Federal Government over lands bordering on tidewater, the Supreme Court of the United States has held in the case of *Hardin v. Jordon* as follows:
>
>> 'With regard to grants of the government for lands bordering on tidewater, it has been distinctly settled that they only extend to high-water mark, and that the title to the shore and lands under water in front of lands so granted inures to the state within which they are situated, if a state has been organized and established there. Such title to the shore and lands under water is regarded as incidental to the sovereignty of the state, a portion of the royalties belonging thereto and held in trust for the public purposes of navigation and fishery and cannot be retained or granted out to individuals by the United States.'
>
> The foregoing is a statement of the settled law, and therefore no rights can be granted you either under the Leasing Act of February 25, 1920 (41 Stat. 437), or under any other public-land law to the bed of the Pacific Ocean either within or without the three-mile limit. Title to the soil under the ocean within the three-mile limit is in the state of California, and the land may not be appropriated except by authority of

---

[6] See Robert Egler, *The Politics of Oil* (Chicago: University of Chicago Press, 1961), pp. 86-95; Carl Solberg, *Oil Power* (New York: New American Library), Chapter Six, and Bartley, op. cit.

the state. A permit would be necessary from the War Department as a prerequisite to the maintenance of structures in the navigable waters of the United States, but such a permit would not confer any rights in the ocean bed.

I find no authority of law under which any right can be granted to you to establish your proposed structures in the ocean outside the three-mile limit of the jurisdiction of the state of California, nor am I advised that any other branch of the Federal Government has such authority.[7]

III. Federal Assertions of Authority (1937-1942)

A. Within the Territorial Sea

The Proctor letter of 1933 indicates that at that time Harold Ickes believed that the Federal Government had no authority over mineral resources or submerged lands within or beyond the three-mile territorial sea. By 1937 he had changed his opinion,[8] and using his considerable influence both as Secretary of the Interior and as a key official within the Roosevelt Administration, initiated a campaign to replace state authority with Federal authority over submerged lands and offshore oil and gas.

His first major action was to convince Senator Gerald P. Nye of North Dakota[9] to introduce legislation declaring the submerged lands of the territorial sea to be the property of the Federal Government (Senate Bill 2964, April 15, 1937). In Nye's original measure, Federal title to the submerged lands was claimed. However, in House amendments and later Senate bills, a different approach was taken. Rather than claiming ownership, subsequent bills claimed *paramount Federal interests,* especially national defense and protection of interstate commerce as a necessary justification for Federal rather than state control of the submerged lands and associated resources.

While Congress was debating what came to be known as the "tidelands" issue, Secretary Ickes used the authority of his office to adopt a new Department of the Interior policy regarding applications for Federal permits for offshore mineral exploration. After June 9, 1937, all such requests (such as that associated with the Proctor letter) were held in abeyance, rather than denied, as had previously been done.

---

[7] Bartley, pp. 128-129.

[8] The reasons for this change remain unclear and warrant additional research.

[9] Bartley indicates that Senator Nye was chosen because he came from a state in which oil was not a major economic or political force. Apparently Ickes felt that opposition from major oil companies to Federal control of offshore oil required this type of strategy.

This action severely retarded offshore oil and gas development; it had the effect of clouding title to the submerged lands, and its impact was not confined to the offshore oil industry. As an example, the General Counsel of the Port of New York Authority testified before Congress in 1946 that the New York Port Authority was unwilling during this period to undertake any improvements in its port facilities, fearing that they might be taken over by the national government.

State Response to the Federal Challenge

As the Federal Government attempted to assert full jurisdiction over offshore resources, the states responded with a counterattack that grew in intensity as both sides became more sophisticated regarding the potential implications of a shift from state to Federal control. Very quickly the issue extended beyond control over oil and gas, although that remained a principal interest. A wide variety of groups with interests that might be affected by Federal rather than state control became involved, including: port authorities, ship owners, fishermen, the Department of the Navy, as well as various segments of the oil industry. A basic tactic of the states was to expand the debate from a narrow consideration of submerged lands jurisdiction into a basic constitutional question of state versus Federal rights in the oceans, or at least in "coastal waters."

The states' primary argument was that they always had owned the submerged lands of the territorial sea, and that any effort on the part of the Federal Government to claim control of these areas would be unconstitutional. Second, the states argued that the legal position of the national government consisted of delegated powers only, and that there had been no delegation of jurisdiction or title in the submerged lands of the territorial sea.[10]

The coastal states, for the most part, did not argue that state ownership precluded all Federal interest or authority. Many states were willing to recognize certain Federal powers, especially within the waters of the territorial sea, for purposes of commerce, navigation, and national defense. The states did argue that these legitimate constitutional concerns of the Federal Government did not carry with them the tenet of ownership. This type of argument had been generally recognized in the courts, as reflected in a 1921 decision of the U.S. Supreme Court written by Justice Brandeis:

---

[10] Memorandum in Opposition to S.J. Res. 208 of the American Association of Port Authorities, *Hearings* before the House Judiciary Committee on S.J. 208, 75th Congress, 3rd session, 1938, pp. 84-85.

> In the navigable waters within the several states [the right of the United States] is limited to the control thereof for purposes of navigation. . . . The character of the state's ownership in the land and in the waters is the full proprietary right.[11]

Bartley has developed a convincing case that the states failed to understand fully the Federal strategy, which had quickly shifted from a claim of Federal ownership to an assertion of paramount constitutional rights, which according to the Federal claims, overshadowed any state interests, be they based upon ownership or otherwise. By failing to refute vigorously the paramount rights concept, the states were eventually to suffer significant jurisdictional losses.

This political and legal contest between state and Federal authority over ocean resources and submerged lands diminished with the onset of the Second World War and did not fully resume until 1945. But between 1937 and 1945, other major national ocean issues were being debated, and these issues were to have great impact upon the eventual form of United States "ocean management" programs.

B. Beyond the Territorial Sea

Offshore oil and state control of submerged lands were not the only ocean-related concerns of the Federal Government in 1937. By the mid-1930's, the United States was experiencing growing pressures on its offshore fishing stocks, especially from the Japanese who were involved in intensive salmon fishing in the Bristol Bay area off Alaska.

In what remains a little known series of events, in 1937 the United States, on the direct initiation of President Roosevelt, gave serious consideration to a significant extension of the United States jurisdiction and authority over ocean resources and ocean space beyond the three-mile territorial sea.

In a memorandum issued November 21, 1937, President Roosevelt wrote:

> . . . I suggest . . . the study of the possibility of adopting a new policy relating to offshore fishing in Alaska: The policy would be based on the fact that every nation has the right to protect its own food supply in waters adjacent to its coast in which its fish, crabs, etc., leave at certain times of the year on their way to and from the actual shoreline or rivers.
>
> . . . it occurs to me that a Presidential proclamation closing the sea area along the Alaskan coast to all fishing — Japanese, Canadian, and

---

11 *Port of Seattle v. Oregon and Washington R. Co.,* 255 U.S. 55, 63 (1921).

American — might be a way out — in other words a kind of marine refuge where one is essential to end depletion. I do not know what Japan could well say in the event of such a proclamation and I am reasonably certain that the Canadian government would approve and probably do the same thing along their British Columbia coastline.[12]

President Roosevelt indicated directly to Under Secretary of State Sumner Welles that what he had in mind was

> . . . an Executive proclamation by the President, declaring that on account of the peculiar scientific conditions which exist with regard to the habits of salmon and which consequently affect the salmon fisheries industry, the waters of the Pacific Ocean between the three-mile limit and that point of the ocean bed where the water reaches a depth of 100 fathoms, must be considered as territorial waters indispensable to the proper safeguarding of this important portion of the food supply of the American people. He stated that *he had under consideration the proclamation of these waters as territorial waters of the United States,* and as a national game preserve within which no fishing, whether American or of any other nationality, could be undertaken, except under the prior issuance of a license permitting such fishing, to be issued by the government of the United States.[13] (Emphasis added).

Thus, in 1937 President Roosevelt had considered issuing a Presidential Proclamation asserting United States Jurisdiction over ocean space and resources beyond the three-mile territorial sea to a water depth of 100 fathoms. In 1937, Roosevelt also had a rather fully developed concept of establishing a national marine fisheries management program, apparently quite similar to the one established through the Fishery Conservation and Management Act of 1976, almost forty years later.

For some reason, such action was not taken.[14] Instead the United States made a strong diplomatic protest which declared a United States interest in the Alaskan salmon fisheries and, in essence, asserted jurisdiction over this particular resource.

> It must be taken as a sound principle of justice that an industry such as described which has been built up by the nationals of one country cannot in all fairness be left to be destroyed by the nationals of other countries. The American government believes that the right or obligation to protect the Alaska salmon fisheries is not only overwhelmingly sus-

---

12 *The Right of the United States with respect to Fisheries in which its Nationals have Participation Off the Coasts of the United States,* undated. State Department file #811.0445/11-2844.

13 *Ibid.*

14 This is another area in which additional research is needed, especially within State Department files.

tained by conditions of their development and perpetuation, but that it is a matter which must be regarded as important in the comity of the nations concerned.[15]

These issues diminished in importance as the threat of war increased and did not again receive serious attention until 1943. However, in 1939 President Roosevelt did use Presidential authority to assert a degree of national jurisdiction over a large portion of ocean space by creating a 200-mile wide national ocean defense zone, which was not removed until after the Second World War.

IV. A National Marine Resources Policy Study (1943-1945)

In June of 1943, Harold Ickes proposed to President Roosevelt that a national marine resources policy study be carried out. He proposed, as the text below indicates, that the study consider the relative role of Federal and state governments in dealing with domestic territorial sea resources and also consider the possible extension seaward of Federal jurisdiction over ocean waters, submerged lands, and resources to a distance of from 100 to 150 miles. It is possible that he even contemplated a retention of the national ocean defense zone which at that time was still in effect, combining it in some fashion with natural resources management.

> The war has impressed us with the necessity for an augmented supply of natural resources. In this connection I draw your attention to the importance of the continental shelf not only to the defense of our country, but more particularly as a storehouse of natural resources. The extent of these resources can only be guessed at and needs careful investigating.
>
> The continental shelf extending some 100 to 150 miles from our shores forms a fine breeding place for fish of all kinds; it is an excellent hiding place for submarines; and since it is a continuation of our continent, it probably contains oil and other resources similar to those found in our states.
>
> I suggest the advisability of laying the groundwork now for availing ourselves fully of the riches of this submerged land *and in the waters over them.* The legal and policy problems involved, both international and domestic, are many and complex. In the international field, it may be necessary to evolve new concepts of maritime territorial limits beyond three miles, and of rights to occupy and exploit the surface and subsoil of the open sea. It may, therefore, be important to consider the matter in the negotiation of any treaties of peace which follow the war.

---

[15] Department of State, *op. cit.*

> In the domestic field, one of the perplexing questions would be that of the respective sovereign and proprietary roles of the Federal Government and of the several coastal states.
>
> I recommend, therefore, that this Department, in collaboration with the National Resources Planning Board, and the Department of State, and Justice now study the many aspects of such an undertaking and submit their findings and conclusions to you as expeditiously as possible. If you should agree, I would undertake to have these Departments and agencies designate representatives to undertake this joint study.[16] (Emphasis added.)

On June 9, 1943, President Roosevelt responded by sending a memorandum to the Secretary of State:

> I think Harold Ickes has the right slant on this. For many years, I have felt that the old three-mile limit or twenty-mile limit should be superceded by a rule of common sense. For instance, the Gulf of Mexico is bounded on the south by Mexico and on the north by the United States. In parts of the Gulf, shallow water extends very many miles offshore. It seems to me that the Mexican government should be entitled to drill for oil in the southern half of the Gulf and we in the northern half of the Gulf. That would be far more sensible than allowing some European nation, for example, to come in there and drill.
>
> Another case which we have all talked about relates to the shelf in the bend of Alaska. Japanese fishing vessels netted habitually for salmon and crabs twenty-five, thirty or forty miles offshore, catching them on their way to the shores and rivers of Alaska for the purpose of spawning.
>
> Would you agree to setting up a Board as he suggests, with representatives of the State Department, Interior Department, National Resources Planning Board, and the Department of Justice?[17]

As a result of this memo, a national marine policy study commenced, and the two principal participants were the Department of the Interior and the Department of State. During the next eighteen months, this study group attempted to develop proposals for a national marine policy, and by December of 1944, Interior and State had reached an agreement, which was subsequently approved by Roosevelt on March 31, 1945. The decisions reached during this policy formulation process were, at the least, major determinants of the basic structure of United States ocean programs and policies up to the present time and thus are of particular importance in understanding the direction and character of government activity in the ocean.

---

[16] *Ibid.*
[17] *Ibid.*

The policy study was marked by a series of major disagreements and even confrontations between the Department of the Interior and the Department of State, each of which had its own ideas about how to construct a national maritime or ocean management program.

A. Interior Department Concept

Harold Ickes conceived of a national marine resources management system that would include ocean resources, water, and submerged lands from the shoreline to the outer edge of the continental shelf. Using the terminology developed in Chapter One, he seems to have been supporting the equivalent of a single Federal management regime that would deal with oil and gas, fisheries, perhaps national defense (see his June memo above), and all other marine resource management issues. Although he may not have openly advocated it, one can assume that Ickes at least considered the possibility of placing this marine resources management program within the Department of the Interior.

B. State Department Concept

The Department of State strongly disagreed with the Department of the Interior concept. In *Ocean Space Rights*[18] the author, Lawrence Juda, suggests that the conflict which emerged at this time between Interior and State may have, to some degree, been a "turf" fight over which Department would have control of this new national marine program. It is difficult to sort out such dynamics after the fact, and it is unwise to place too much emphasis upon such factors. But it would appear that this was a significant element in the policy formation process and should be considered when evaluating the management approach that was finally adopted. Thus part of the conflict was about, even if not explicitly stated, which department of the Federal Government would have authority over and responsibility for national marine resources programs and policies.

The other part of the conflict involved a clash between domestic management concepts and needs and foreign policy factors, although at times it is difficult to fully separate conceptual differences from "turf" posturings. The Department of State urged that the United States not create a unified ocean management regime, and not extend its territorial sea outward beyond its present three-mile limit. The Department of State claimed that other nations might not accept a unilateral extension of na-

---

[18] Lawrence Juda, *Ocean Space Rights* (New York: Praeger, 1975).

tional jurisdiction over ocean space or resources, that other nations might retaliate by blocking the United States from ocean areas adjacent to their coasts, and that resource management could be accomplished without the need for a unified ocean regime.

One month prior to Ickes' memo to President Roosevelt, the Department of State had established a Departmental Committee on Marine Resources. This committee had been established in recognition of "pending bills in Congress (territorial sea), interest in the Interior Department, and increasing pressure of public opinion that something be done about such resources."[19] It appears to have operated as a policy committee.

The Department of State and the Department of the Interior had widely different perspectives on national marine resources interests and appropriate policies, and the issue was resolved by dividing the jurisdiction between Interior and State and using elements of the philosophy of each.

C. Segmenting the Ocean and its Resources

By December of 1944, the Departments of Interior and State had worked out a mutually agreeable approach. The essence of this agreement follows:

1. Ocean space. For purposes of United States policy and management programs, ocean space would be divided into two components: *submerged lands* and *ocean water*.

The *submerged lands* of the continental shelf would be incorporated into what shall be referred to in this report as a single management "regime." It was agreed that the United States would declare authority to manage these submerged lands and the resources through the mechanism of Presidential Proclamation.

Ocean waters above these submerged lands would be explicitly isolated from this submerged lands regime and would not be structured as a management unit or regime. Instead, the unit of management for this portion of ocean space would be the individual resources or activities taking place within ocean waters. The waters themselves would be considered as "high seas" with no assertion of national interest or appropriation.

---

[19] *Summary Report on Department Fisheries Committee and Informal Discussions with Canada and New Foundland,* September 9, 1944, Department of State file #811.0145/11-2844.

2. Ocean resources.

- **Oil and gas** and other resources on, in, or under the submerged lands were to be claimed as being under the sovereign *control* (in contrast with ownership) out to a depth of 600 feet and would be managed through the submerged lands "regime."
- **Fisheries** would be managed separately from the submerged lands program and would not be controlled within the context of an ocean water management effort. This aspect of the agreement did not deal explicitly with management of the water component of ocean space.

In keeping with these two different approaches, it was agreed that the Department of the Interior would prepare a draft proclamation on the submerged lands management regime, and the Department of State would prepare a draft proclamation on marine fisheries management.[20] On March 31, 1945, President Roosevelt approved both proclamations.

It should be remembered that the concept of "management of ocean space" and/or ocean resources for purposes other than national defense beyond a three-mile territorial sea was, at this time, a new idea. It is therefore understandable that aside from any interdepartmental maneuvers, the Department of State insisted upon consulting with Great Britain, U.S.S.R., Mexico, France, Denmark, Canada, and Norway to see what their reaction would be to such an action before actually issuing the proclamation. This caused delay, and then on April 12, 1945, President Roosevelt died. By early May, President Truman had agreed to the two proclamations, but their issuance was further delayed by additional international consultations and the appointment of a new Secretary of State.

A final delay occurred when the U.S. Senate Foreign Relations and Public Lands Committees expressed some concern that the proclamation on submerged lands might prejudice the claims of the states regarding the territorial sea. Whether Ickes had intended such an effect or not, he agreed to the insertion of language which explicitly declared that the question of state/Federal ownership of the territorial sea would not be affected.

Finally, on September 28, 1945, Presidential Proclamations on the Continental Shelf (No. 2667) and on Fisheries (No. 2668) were issued. They constitute a unilateral claim to the resources of the continental shelf

---

[20] *Memorandum on the Meeting in Assistant Secretary of State Long's Office,* July 25, 1944, State Department file #811.0145/7-2644.

and the right to establish a fishery conservation zone in waters above those submerged lands.

The Truman Proclamation on the Continental Shelf, September 28, 1945, stated in part:

> Having concern for the urgency of conserving and prudently utilizing its natural resources, the government of the United States regards the natural resources of the subsoil and seabed of the continental shelf beneath the high seas but contiguous to the coasts of the United States as appertaining to the United States, subject to its jurisdiction and control. . . . The character as high seas of the waters above the continental shelf and the right to their free and unimpeded navigation are in no way thus affected.

The Truman Proclamation on Fisheries, September 28, 1945, said:

> In view of the pressing need for conservation and protection of fishery resources, the government of the United States regards it as proper to establish conservation zones in those areas of the high seas contiguous to the coasts of the United States wherein fishing activities have been or in the future may be developed and maintained on a substantial scale. Where such activities have been or shall hereafter be developed and maintained by its nationals alone, the United States regards it as proper to establish explicitly bounded conservation zones in which fishing activities shall be subject to the regulation and control of the United States. . . . The right of any state [nation] to establish conservation zones off its shores in accordance with the above principles is conceded, provided that corresponding recognition is given to any fishing interests of nationals of the United States which may exist in such areas. The character as high seas of the areas in which such conservation zones are established and the right to their free and unimpeded navigation are in no way thus affected.

The full text of each Proclamation is in the Appendix.

V. Achieving a Legislative Basis for Governmental Control in the Oceans: 1946-1953

It had taken approximately eight years for the initial concepts and efforts of Ickes and Roosevelt to be translated into a national statement of authority over some portions of ocean space and ocean resources beyond the three-mile territorial sea. It was to take another eight years to resolve the issue of state and Federal jurisdictional interests within the territorial sea and to obtain legislative support for the continental shelf management regime which Truman had proclaimed by Executive Order.

A. Congressional Action

Many coastal states perceived the Truman Proclamation as evidence of a new, major effort on the part of the Truman administration to wrest control of the submerged lands of the territorial sea from the states. The "tidelands oil" issue had escalated to a basic confrontation over state versus Federal authority, and by 1945 many states were demanding Congressional action, declaring the submerged lands within three miles of shore to be the property of the states. During the 79th session of Congress, 19 bills were introduced attempting to block what many states saw as a Federal attempt to steal state lands. By 1946 both the House and Senate had passed legislation which removed any Federal claim, interest, right or title to the submerged lands of the territorial sea.

B. Executive Branch Action

President Truman appears to have been personally interested in the issue of territorial sea jurisdiction, and during his administration, efforts to assert Federal authority were intensified. As indicated previously, there had been, until the 1930's, a uniform assumption of state control over submerged lands. In the late 1920's, the U.S. Supreme Court had found no reason to challenge the California offshore leasing program. However, on May 29, 1945, the U.S. Department of Justice filed a suit in the U.S. district court in Los Angeles challenging ownership of the mineral deposits in the tidelands of the territorial sea. In September of that same year, Truman issued the proclamations on the continental shelf and fisheries, and in August of 1946 he vetoed the territorial sea "quitclaim" legislation which had been passed by both the House and Senate.

Resignation of Harold Ickes

There were many individuals and interest groups, both within government and the private sector, who were concerned about the outcome of this dispute over territorial sea jurisdiction. As will be discussed in Chapter Four, the Navy was concerned because it saw offshore oil as a national resource, as an important supply of Naval fuel, and wanted it under Federal, and specifically Navy, control. Another group with an obvious and strong interest was the oil industry, especially in California which at this time remained the principle location of offshore oil production. The major companies felt that the state leasing system was workable and favorable to their interests, and they were strongly opposed to the establishment of Federal authority.

In January of 1946, Truman proposed Edwin Pauley as Under Secretary of the Navy. According to Robert Donovan in *Conflict and Crisis,*[21] Truman wanted to assert more Presidential control over the Navy and other military departments and thought that Pauley was strong enough to assist him in these efforts. However, it would appear that Truman miscalculated how vulnerable Pauley would be, especially in light of Navy opposition to his nomination, for Pauley was well known to have significant business connections with the California oil industry. The Teapot Dome scandal, in which naval oil reserves had been diverted to private industry, was still a sensitive national issue, and Pauley was soon opposed by those who thought that someone with major oil interests should not be given administrative authority over national naval oil reserves.

In February of 1946, Harold Ickes was called to testify regarding Pauley's nomination, and Ickes accused Pauley of having asked him shortly after the death of Roosevelt to quash the Federal court action against California. According to Ickes, Pauley had promised major campaign contributions from California oil companies to the Democratic Party, if the Federal attempt to gain control of offshore oil would be dropped. Such accusations were politically embarrassing to Truman, but he continued to support Pauley's nomination. Ickes resigned on February 13, 1946, contributing to a growing Senate concern over Pauley's possible conflict of interest, and Pauley finally removed his name from consideration. This incident emphasizes the intensity of the debate over the tidelands issue and may have served to strengthen Truman's resolve to gain Federal control over this portion of ocean space and ocean resources.

C. The United States Supreme Court

The Federal challenge of California's ownership of offshore oil, which Ickes accused Pauley of having attempted to stop, eventually reached the U.S. Supreme Court. In 1947 the Supreme Court ruled in *United States v. California* that the states did not own submerged lands of the territorial sea and that the Federal Government had full authority over these resources.

> We decided for the reasons we have stated that California is not the owner of the three-mile marginal belt along its coast, and that the Fed-

---

[21] Robert J. Donovan, *Conflict and Crisis* (New York: W. W. Norton and Co., 1977), pp. 177-184.

eral Government rather than the state has paramount rights in and power over that belt, an incident to which is full dominion over the resources of the soil under that water area, including oil.[22]

Ownership versus Authority to Control

Although the Supreme Court determined that California did not own these submerged lands, and that the Federal Government had full authority to control them, it did not say that the Federal Government owned these lands or resources. Justice Frankfurter in a minority dissent, observed that finding California did not own the tidelands was a long way from saying that the United States actually did own them, and Justice Reed felt that California did own these resources, but that state ownership need not prevent necessary Federal control or regulation.

> Ownership in California would not interfere in any way with the needs or rights of the United States in war or peace. The power of the United States is plenary over these undersea lands precisely as it is over every river, farm, mine and factory of the nation.[23]

In an effort to obtain a clear statement of Federal ownership from the court, the United States submitted a proposed decree to the Supreme Court on September 13, 1947, which read in part:

> The United States of America is now, and has been at all times pertinent thereto, possessed of paramount rights *of proprietorship* in, and full dominion and power over, the lands, minerals, and other things underlying the Pacific Ocean lying seaward of the ordinary low-water mark on the coast of California, and outside of the inland waters, extending seaward three nautical miles. . . .[24] (Emphasis added.)

When the final order and decree were handed down on October 27, 1947, the words "of proprietorship" had been removed, thus emphasizing that the Court was specifically not declaring title to be held by the Federal Government, perhaps "inviting" Congressional action on the issue.

● Congress/White House Deadlock

After the *United States v. California* case, the Attorney General of the United States held that the Federal Mineral Leasing Act of 1920

---

[22] 332 U.S. 19, 38-39 (1947).
[23] 332 U.S. 19, 42 (1947).
[24] Bartley, p. 190.

was not a sufficient basis for the Department of the Interior to assert administrative authority over oil production in the territorial sea. Thus, new legislation would be needed. However, Congress supported state control of the submerged lands and would not pass such legislation unless Truman would accept state control of the territorial sea. Unable to gain legislative authority, the Department of the Interior claimed authority to control the resources of the outer continental shelf under direction of an Executive Order issued for that purpose by Truman.[25]

● **Texas and Louisiana**

By the 1940's California was no longer the only state with recoverable deposits of offshore oil and/or gas, and the Gulf of Mexico had become a "frontier" area for offshore exploration and production. On December 21, 1948, the United States filed motions for leave to file complaints against Texas and Louisiana, challenging their ownership of offshore minerals, and the cases were argued before the U.S. Supreme Court in March of 1950 (*United States v. Louisiana* and *United States v. Texas*). In both cases the Court again held that because of Federal authority over foreign affairs, interstate commerce, the waging of war, treaties, and defense of the shore, it was necessary that the Federal Government have physical control of the submerged lands of the territorial sea, precluding state ownership. Thus Justice Douglas, writing the majority opinion in *Louisiana* stated that:

> . . . protection and control of the area [territorial sea] are indeed functions of national external sovereignty. . . . The marginal sea is a national, not a state concern. National interests, national responsibilities, national concerns are involved. The problems of commerce, national defense, relations with other powers, war and peace focus here. National rights must therefore be paramount in that area.[26]

However, as Bartley suggests, the Court never clearly demonstrated why these constitutional authorities warranted or allowed the removal of state ownership. Justice Reed stated this opinion in a dissent to the majority decision in the *Texas* case:

> The needs of defense and foreign affairs alone cannot transfer ownership of an ocean bed from a state to the Federal Government any more than they could transfer iron ore under uplands from state to Federal ownership.[27]

---

[25] Executive Order 9633 (10 Fed. Reg. 12305), 1945.
[26] 339 U.S. 699, 704 (1950).
[27] 339 U.S. 707, 721 (1950).

Rather than having resolved the issues involved, these three Supreme Court decisions served to intensify both the debate and Congressional resolve to secure control by the coastal states through national legislation. In his dissenting comments upon the *United States v. Texas* decision, Justice Frankfurter echoed the feelings of those who supported control by the states, apparently including the majority of Congress.

> . . . the submerged lands now in controversy were part of the domain of Texas when she was on her own. The Court now decided that when Texas entered the Union she lost what she had and the United States acquired it. How that shift came to pass remains for me a puzzle.[28]

D. Increased Pressure for Resolution

By the early 1950's the debate over the submerged lands of the territorial sea was a major national problem. President Truman refused to accept state ownership or control. Legislation assigning full control to the Federal Government could not get out of committee. The Korean conflict had begun, Iranian oil became scarce, and the United States had major energy commitments to Europe and Japan. Because of the uncertainties caused by the continuance of this debate, offshore production in California was down and also declined in the Gulf of Mexico.

Submerged lands legislation became entangled in debates as to whether or not to admit Hawaii and Alaska as states, but by May of 1952 both the House and Senate had again passed legislation which declared that the states had full authority over the submerged lands of the territorial sea. In a change from previous legislation, Congress now gave recognition to the authority of the Federal Government over outer continental shelf (OCS) lands beyond the territorial sea. Characterizing this legislation as "corruption" and "robbery in broad daylight - and on a colossal scale."[29] Truman vetoed the measure on May 29, 1952.

E. Resolution of the Dispute

The issue of state versus Federal control of offshore lands and resources was an important issue in the 1952 Presidential campaign, although the degree to which it influenced the outcome is difficult to determine. Adlai Stevenson was strongly opposed to state ownership, and Dwight D. Eisenhower was strongly in support of it. In some of the oil

---

[28] 339 U.S. 707, 724 (1950).

[29] "President Assails Offshore Oil Bill," *The New York Times,* Vol. CI No. 34,448, p. 1.

states such as Texas, this issue may have been a decisive factor.

President Truman had strongly opposed state jurisdiction over ocean resources and was annoyed by Congress' refusal to provide his administration with a legislative mechanism for OCS mineral leasing. After Eisenhower was elected, and it became clear that Congress would soon be able to get Presidential agreement for a tidelands quitclaim law, Truman used his Presidential authority, but it only added more confusion to the issue. On January 16, 1953, as one of his last Presidential actions, Truman issued Executive Order 10426, which transferred authority and control over OCS lands and resources from the Department of the Interior to the Department of the Navy.[30] It was to take many months and legislative action by Congress to undo that action.

Soon after taking office, Eisenhower signed the *Submerged Lands Act of 1953* and by the fall of 1953 had signed the *Outer Continental Shelf Lands Act* which represented a legislative implementation of the Truman Proclamation of 1945, the legislation which Truman had unsuccessfully attempted to obtain for eight years. Thus after fifteen years of debate, public authority over ocean space and ocean resources was detailed for the first time in national legislation. The coastal states retained most, if not all, of the authority they had exercised prior to the debate. However, for the first time in history, the United States claimed full control and authority over the resources and lands of the outer continental shelf. Although the United States had previously established ocean defense zones during time of war and had claimed revenue collection authority as far as 60 miles to sea, this new claim over submerged lands was the equivalent of a unilateral extension of national territory into a portion of ocean space that had theretofore been considered as international "high seas." The Federal Government was also now involved in a major natural resources management effort, through its assumption of authority over oil and gas resources of continental shelf lands.[31]

The Submerged Lands Act

The provisions of the Submerged Lands Act reflect the debate which had preceded its passage and emphasized that the primary concern of the coastal states at that time was in control of offshore minerals and fisheries. The Submerged Lands Act is quitclaim legislation to the extent that any Federal claim to ownership or to the authority to manage or lease

---

[30] See Chapter Four for further discussion of role of Navy in this debate.

[31] Lawrence Juda, in *Ocean Space Rights* (supra, 18) provides a good description of how these conflicting interests interacted during this period.

resources or submerged lands is removed. Clear title is assigned to the states. However, the Federal Government retains authority over *commerce, navigation, international agreements, and national defense.* These "paramount" authorities are extensive, and to a certain degree, constitute a pervasive control over the waters of the territorial sea, conflicting with or overshadowing state authority to manage natural resources or the submerged lands.

The distribution of authority between Federal and state government contained in the Submerged Lands Act is shown in Table I. The complete text of the Act is contained in the Appendix. The OCS Lands Act is a major element of the existing U.S. domestic ocean management regime and the reader is encouraged to review it in its entirety.

VI. Trying Out the System: The Intervening Years (1954 to the 1970's)

Once the Submerged Lands Act and the Outer Continental Shelf Lands Act were enacted, the jurisdictional systems they created remained basically unchanged for twenty years. The only major events involving national authority to control ocean space and resources were the conclusion of the Geneva Convention on the Law of the Sea in 1958 and the establishment of a 9-mile U.S. fisheries management zone beyond the territorial sea in 1966. But it was not really until the 1970's that this system was significantly modified.

By the 1950's, general international support had emerged for an international agreement on a regime for the high seas, and this support was to lead to the 1958 Geneva Conference on the Law of the Sea. The need to define national interests and strategies for this conference helped to add more detail to United States ocean-related programs and policies, and the basic result of the Geneva Conference was to gain temporary international acceptance (although it was far from unanimous) of the ocean "regime" which had evolved in the United States between 1937 and 1953. It should be noted that the 1958 Geneva Conference was marked by a failure to agree on three important ocean matters:

(1) exclusive coastal state jurisdiction over fisheries;
(2) an outer boundary of the continental shelf; and
(3) the extent of the territorial sea.

By means of the Truman Proclamation of 1945 and the Outer Continental Shelf Lands Act of 1953, the United States had greatly extended the amount of ocean space and resources over which it claimed territorial rights. However, as described above, in an effort to minimize the adverse impacts upon United States interests if other nations should extend

Table I

The Submerged Lands Act of 1953

Distribution of Authority between State and Federal Government

State	Federal
• Ownership of submerged lands of territorial sea.	• During time of war, or when necessary for national defense Federal Government has first refusal to purchase any or all of the natural resources of the territorial sea, or to acquire and use any portion of the submerged lands.
• Ownership of natural resources of both waters and submerged lands of territorial sea, including, but not limited to; — oil, — gas, — all other minerals, — fish, — shrimp, — oysters, — clams, — crabs, — lobsters, — sponges, — kelp, — other marine animal and plant life.	• The Federal Government retains control of the waters and lands of the territorial sea for purposes of *navigation, flood control, and the production of power.*
• The right and power to manage, administer, lease, develop, and use the submerged lands and natural resources of the territorial sea.	• "The United States retains all its *navigational servitude* and rights in and powers of regulation and control of said lands and navigable waters for the constitutional purposes of *commerce, navigation, national defense,* and *international affairs,* all of which shall be paramount to, but shall not be deemed to include, proprietary rights of ownership or the rights or management, administration, leasing, use, and development of the lands and natural resources which are specifically recognized, confirmed, established, and vested in and assigned to the respective states. . . ." (Sec. 6 (a)). Emphasis added.

their territorial seas outward in a similar fashion, the United States laid full jurisdictional claim only to the resources of the submerged land and not to ocean waters. This pattern of jurisdictional authority, or ocean regime, is depicted in Figures 3, 4 and 5.

A. Seeking International Acceptance

Although the distinction between jurisdiction over submerged lands and that over the ocean water might serve the interests of a major mari-

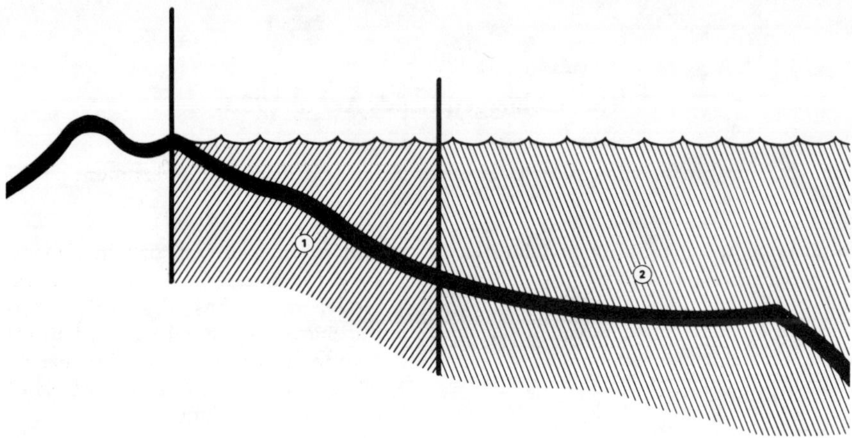

Figure 3:

Until the 1930's there was general international recognition of two types of ocean space. First, there was a territorial sea (1) which included submerged lands, waters, and resources out to a distance of three miles. Beyond these national territorial seas was the international "high seas" (2). This portion of the ocean was controlled by customary use and certain provisions of international law and multinational agreements of treaties.

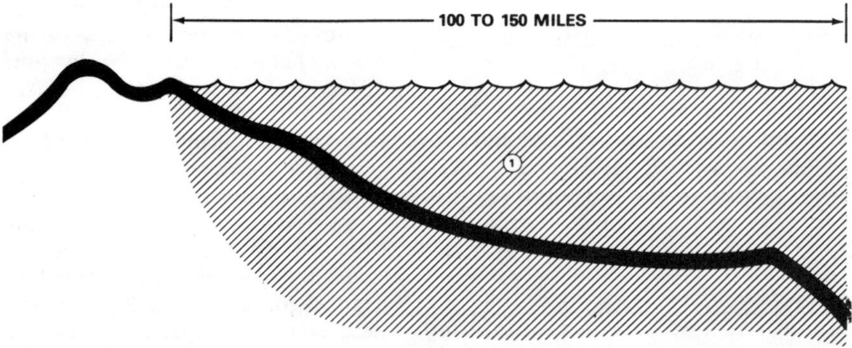

Figure 4:

In 1937 the Roosevelt Administration considered the creation of a national ocean management "regime" which would incorporate but extend beyond the three-mile territorial set to include the submerged lands, waters, and resources of the ocean out to a distance of 100 to 150 miles from shore. Roosevelt contemplated the use of an Executive Order to establish this zone, one of the primary purposes of which would be the regulation of fisheries.

time power, such as the United States, there were many nations which had no large navy, no large deepwater fishing fleet, no advanced offshore drilling technology. For these nations, national ocean interest was in the

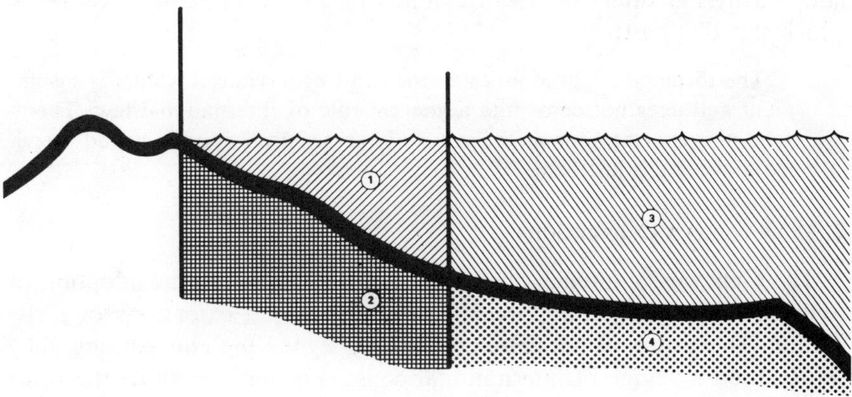

Figure 5:

In 1945 the United States established two ocean management systems or regimes, both by Presidential proclamation. These included a continental shelf regime (4) extending from beyond the territorial sea to a water depth of 100 fathoms, and a fisheries management zone (3) extending the same distance.

In 1953 jurisdiction over the submerged lands and resources of the territorial sea was legislatively assigned to coastal states (2), although control over the water of the territorial sea was not specified. (1) The Outer Continental Shelf Lands Act followed the earlier 1945 Truman OSC proclamation. Legislation was not established for a fisheries management zone or for ocean waters above the continental shelf.

collection of revenues, the development of offshore resources, and the military protection of national territory. For these nations, particularly those in South America, there was little reason to treat ocean waters separately from ocean submerged lands. The "territorial seas" proclaimed by some Latin American States during this era did not conform to traditional territorial sea claims, but were more, in effect, economic zones. Also, many of these claims were made for negotiating leverage in international forums and had little practical effect.

1. Southern Hemisphere Conflicts

During the early 1950's, the Organization of American States and the Inter-American Council of Jurists initiated a series of conferences and meetings on the subject of territorial waters and related matters. The issue was highly controversial.[32] Typical of the debate was a resolution

---

[32] Juda, pp. 2-36.

adopted by the Inter-American Council of Jurists in January of 1956, which stated in part:

> The distance of three miles as the limit of territorial waters is insufficient and does not constitute a general rule of international law. Therefore, the enlargement of the zone of the sea traditionally called "territorial waters' is justifiable.[33]

2. 1958 Geneva Conventions

The Geneva Conference on the Law of the Sea led to the adoption of four conventions regarding ocean use and national extensions of jurisdiction. While not all nations agreed to or signed the conventions, they represented a degree of international consensus and constitute the basis of the international ocean regime in force today, although the UNCLOS negotiations underway could in time lead to significant shifts. The approach at Geneva reflected the United States system developed for the ocean space and resources adjacent to its shores:[34]

a. A *three-mile territorial sea* over which a coastal nation had sovereign rights but would allow innocent passage of ships;

b. A *nine-mile contiguous zone* in which coastal nations were recognized as having certain authorities to exercise national control, especially over customs, fiscal, immigration, and sanitation matters;

c. A *high sea* which included the surface waters and water column extending beyond the territorial sea over which no country could claim jurisdiction and all nations were free to utilize;

d. A *convention on fishing and conservation of living resources* on the high seas which recognized both national and multinational authorities and responsibilities; and

e. A *continental shelf* over which a coastal nation could exert exclusive resource jurisdiction extending from shore to a depth of 200 meters or beyond that limit to where the depth of the superjacent water admits of exploitation of the natural resources of the said area.

B. The Beginnings of a New Direction

The Geneva Conventions were by no means a final solution to the problems of national efforts to control ocean space and resources. As an

---

[33] *Ibid.*, p. 3.

[34] *Ibid.*, p. 34. Also note that the word nation has been substituted for the word state to avoid confusion between individual states of the United States and foreign nations which are often referred to as states.

example, by the 1960's several nations were exerting heavy fishing pressure upon fisheries near U.S. shores. Reflecting the concept developed by Roosevelt in 1937 and proclaimed by Truman in 1945, the U.S. Congress in 1966 established a 12-mile contiguous fishery zone (P.L. 89-658) within which the United States asserted the right to control all fishing activities. This was in accord with the actions of other nations which likewise had established 12-mile fishery zones and in some instances 12-mile territorial seas as well. Such actions could be seen as a shift away from the spirit of the 1958 Geneva Conventions.

During the 1960's several other nations also began to exert increased control over ocean space and resources, and it became increasingly clear that the provisions of the Geneva Convention pertaining to living resources were not being adhered to. During this period, ocean use greatly increased, with more fishing, more offshore oil and gas production, more vessel traffic, and more military activities and facilities. By the late 1960's interest developed within the United States to take some new action in order to keep some portion of the ocean free of national claims and to insure an orderly and workable international ocean regime, one that would regulate the exploitation of seabed resources beyond areas of national control for the benefit of developing nations, as a "common heritage"[35] of mankind.

C. The Nixon Proposal

In May of 1970, President Nixon proposed to the United Nations that:

> . . . all nations adopt as soon as possible a treaty under which they would renounce all national claims over the natural resources of the seabed beyond [a depth of 200 meters] and would agree to regard these resources as the common heritage of mankind.[36]

Under the Nixon proposal, the idea was not that coastal states would renounce "control" per se, but rather that they would act as a "trustee" for the international community over the non-living resources of the continental shelf beyond a 200-meter depth, and would contribute substantial resources to the international community resulting from exploitation in that area. Nixon also proposed the establishment of an "international regime for the exploitation of seabed resources" beyond areas of national control.

---

[35] It is believed that this term was coined in the Johnson Administration which was quite active in ocean matters, emphasizing particularly the importance of ocean resources to the U.S. and the need for international cooperation.

[36] Juda, pp. 202-4.

The regime should provide for the collection of substantial mineral royalties to be used for international community purposes, particularly economic assistance to developing countries. It should also establish general rules to prevent unreasonable interference with other users of the ocean, to protect the ocean from pollution, to assure the integrity of the investment necessary for such exploitation, and to provide for peaceful and compulsory settlement of disputes.[37]

Many nations were surprised by this proposal. The surprise resulted not so much from the concepts presented, since these had been developing for several years, but from the fact that the United States would so strongly support them, at the Presidential level. As Juda related, this national ocean policy did not have unanimous national support, with several interest groups objecting to the United States giving up all claims over ocean space and resources beyond the 200-meter depth.

The concept supported by President Nixon in 1970 is, with some modifications, currently being considered by the United States and approximately 150 other nations at the Third International Conference on the Law of the Sea (UNCLOS). While it is not possible to determine what the outcome of those negotiations will be, it would seem possible that certain changes in how the United States structures its ocean policies and programs could result. For example:

- The territorial sea may be extended from three to twelve miles, immediately raising the issue of what shall be the role of state and Federal Government within this expanded zone.
- The 9-mile contiguous zone concept could be extended to form a 200-mile wide "economic zone" which might include submerged lands, water, and resources in a management regime subject to national control but partially responsible to an international set of rules, thus not being under complete national control.

At present, Article 33 of the Informal Composite Negotiating Text (ICNT), provides that the contiguous zone may be extended up to a maximum distance of 24 nautical miles from the baselines from which the territorial sea is measured. The concept of the economic zone would mean in terms of present negotiation that the coastal state has sovereign rights over resources out to a distance 200 miles from its shore, with residual rights reserved for international users. In addition, the continental shelf or "submerged lands" would be recognized as extending beyond 200 miles in cases where this applies. There is also a provision (Article

---

[37] *Ibid.*

2 of the ICNT) for revenue sharing to the international community with respect to the exploitation of the shelf beyond 200 miles.

But perhaps most important, no matter what the outcome of the UNCLOS negotiations, it appears that the United States will be increasingly constrained in the future in its ocean programs and policies, not only by the attitudes and actions of individual foreign nations, but also by an increasingly organized international community of ocean users.

CHAPTER THREE

AN ANALYSIS OF SELECTED OCEAN CONTROL PROGRAMS

I. Introduction

Federal Ocean Activities in the 1970's

We have seen that early efforts of the Federal Government from the late 1930's until the early 1950's were to assert its authority over the territorial sea and the submerged lands of the outer continental shelf. After 1953 the issue of jurisdiction was, at least temporarily, resolved, and the actual Federal ocean, "management" efforts which ensued were almost entirely confined to outer continental shelf oil and gas leasing. There were some ongoing programs related to expansions of navigation, the merchant marine, and national security. Considerable amounts of Federal money were also spent in ocean-related research. However, it was not until the 1970's that Federal Government programs began to have the variety and degree of *control* or regulation of ocean space, resources, and activities which now exists.

During the 1960's several studies had attempted to define the national interest in the ocean and the role of the Federal Government in carrying out that interest. Several are summarized in the National Interest section of Chapter Four. These studies advocated in various ways an increase in Federal ocean-related activities, and this effort accounted in part for the increased Federal ocean involvement of the 1970's. In addition, the decade of the 1960's was a period of new and increased ocean and coastal use: the amount of oil transported by tanker into the United States increased significantly; several foreign nations developed modern fishing fleets which by the mid-1960's were exerting heavy fishing pressure upon ocean waters near the United States; major public and private recreational developments modified the shore, removing wetlands and increasing human pressure upon the coastal environment; more power plants, roads, and homes were constructed near the shore, changing the amount and quality of runoff and further reducing the number of beaches and wetlands; a growing amount of dredge spoil; sewage sludge and other material was dumped offshore. Storm hazards and erosion became public management issues as more shoreline property was threatened by these developments.

Extensive ocean research undertaken in the 1960's combined with several national studies and a growing public concern to create a demand for new Federal management programs dealing with these matters. As a result, programs were established, dealing with air quality, water quality, endangered species, flooding, wetland protection, marine mammals, fisheries, ocean dumping, deepwater ports, vessel traffic control, and coordinated planning of coastal areas. And as the number of Federal programs increased, so did the difficulty of fitting them together in some reasonable way, both in terms of national policy and of operation. Thus the management *process,* the designing and administering of multiple public policies, goals, regulations and procedures, to the extent that they are individually effective and collectively compatible, has become an important part of federal "ocean management" discussion and effort.

For the purposes of this study, the major Federal ocean-related management programs established since 1970 are for:

— deepwater ports,
— marine sanctuaries,
— fisheries conservation and management, and
— coastal zone management.

Collectively these programs typify the kind of degree of action that the Federal Government is presently attempting to exercise upon ocean resources, activities, and space within 200 miles of shore. In the discussion which follows, an effort is made to identify the following elements in each of the programs considered.

- Why action is being attempted.
- What specifically is being managed.
- How the control effort is structured.
- What mechanisms exist for coordinating policies and programs.
- How the particular program fits within the ocean management "regimes" established by the United States in 1945 and 1953.

II. Deepwater Ports

A. Background

During the late 1960's and early 1970's, the United States became increasingly dependent upon tanker shipments of oil. During this same period of time, a new class of "super-tankers" with a capacity of from 100,000 to 500,000 deadweight tons became the prevalent means of long distance oil transport. However, most United States ports and waterways are too shallow to accommodate these deepdraft vessels. By the early 1970's, U.S. ports had become inaccessible to more than 55% of world tanker capacity, due to the increasing size of these vessels.

By the 1970's, there was strong commercial interest within the United States in the construction of deepwater ports, which, as their name implies, would provide tanker mooring and off-loading facilities in deep water, to accommodate the modern class of large tankers. Both industry and the Federal government believed that some form of regulation or control over deepwater ports would be needed. The primary objectives in establishing federal management of deepwater ports beyond the territorial sea were, as stated in the Deepwater Port Act of 1974 (P.L. 93-627) to:

1. Authorize and regulate the location, ownership, construction, and operation of deepwater ports in waters beyond the territorial limits of the United States;
2. Provide for the protection of the marine and coastal environment to prevent or minimize any adverse impact which might occur as a consequence of the development of such ports;
3. Protect the interests of the United States and those of adjacent coastal states in the location, construction, and operation of deepwater ports; and
4. Protect the rights and responsibilities of states and communities to regulate growth, determine land use, and otherwise protect the environment in accordance with law. (Sec. 2(4)).

However, the United States faced a basic problem in attempting to establish formal governmental management options for deepwater ports because most ocean locations of sufficient depth to accommodate supertankers are beyond the three-mile territorial sea.

B. National Control of Ocean Waters

Since the mid-1940's, the United States has refrained from claiming the authority to manage ocean waters beyond the territorial sea and has also attempted to discourage other nations from doing so. This policy in particular reflects the concerns of the Department of the Navy and the American distant-water fishing industry; its objective is to retain the maximum amount of ship and aircraft access to ocean space and superjacent air space in international and foreign ocean areas.

During the 1970's when national deepwater port legislation was being considered, the United States still advocated restraint in extending national controls beyond the three-mile limit and attempted to make a strong case for international adoption of that approach, as exemplified by the following 1975 declaration by Secretary of State Henry Kissinger:

> Within two hundred miles of the shore are some of the world's more important fishing grounds as well as substantial deposits of petroleum, natural gas, and minerals. This has led some coastal [nations] to seek full sovereignty over this zone. These claims . . . are unacceptable to the United States. To accept them would bring 30 percent of the oceans under national territorial control—they very areas which most of the world's shipping travels.[1]

While the United States wanted other nations to refrain from claiming national ownership or full sovereign control over ocean waters beyond a narrow territorial sea, the United States has itself found it desirable or necessary to establish selective management functions over ocean activities beyond its own territorial sea.

The problem faced by the United States in the 1940's and in the 1970's when the Deepwater Port Act (DPA) was enacted, was how to establish some degree of control over ocean waters without undermining its insistence that other nations not exert full sovereign control over ocean waters adjacent to their coasts. The solution for the United States has been, since 1945 and as mentioned in Chapter Two of this report, to treat ocean waters and ocean submerged lands as two separate entities, and to assert authority and undertake management in two different ways for each of these entities.

During the period from 1937 until 1944, Ickes had advocated establishment of a 150 mile wide national ocean control concept that combined ocean waters, resources, and submerged lands in a single regime.[2] Instead, the submerged lands beyond the territorial sea were established as a national resource management zone through the Outer Continental Shelf Lands Act of 1953, but the superjacent waters were deliberately not treated as a management unit.

This approach has not proven to be fully effective in discouraging other nations from extending national jurisdictional claims over both

---

[1] Cited in Lawrence W. Kaye, "The Innocent Passage of Warships in Foreign Territorial Seas: A Threatened Freedom," *San Diego Law Review,* Vol. 15, No. 3, p. 587.
[2] See Chapter 1 for the use of "regime."

water and submerged lands to distances ranging from 12 to 200 miles,[3] and several observers have criticized what they perceived to be "visible hypocrisies" in American ocean policy.[4] Nonetheless, the United States has persisted in this approach, and it is within this context that the Deepwater Port Act and the other programs to be discussed were established.

C. Single Purpose Programs and Multi-Program Coordination

Reflecting the foreign policy mentioned above, Congress treated the deepwater port regulatory system in legislation as a single purpose ocean control effort. The Deepwater Ports Act seems to have been established as a narrowly defined exercise of national jurisdiction, and an effort was made to avoid having this assertion of control over ocean waters beyond the territorial sea appear to be a violation of the United State's own foreign policy. Thus the Act contains a specific disavowal of territorial claims.

> The Congress declares that nothing in this Act shall be construed to affect the legal status of the high seas, the superjacent airspace, or the seabed and subsoil, including the continental shelf (Sec. 2(b)).

D. Fitting Mechanisms

For the reasons explained above, the Deepwater Port Act is legislatively isolated from other ocean-related programs, including the Outer Continental Shelf Lands Act. Yet deepwater ports, in their location, construction and/or operation have the potential for affecting a variety of ocean resources, ocean activities, and interest groups. A deepwater port represents the long-range commitment of a fairly large portion of ocean space to a single activity with a need for ancillary shore facilities. A deepwater port could affect fishing activities, merchant shipping, migration patterns of marine life, submerged lands mineral leasing, or shoreside patterns of growth. As the Act recognizes, there is a need to link, coordinate, or "fit" deepwater ports into the growing web of national coastal and ocean programs, policies and interests. Yet as a matter of long-standing national policy, the United States has avoided treating the ocean waters themselves as an element of management.

Given these constraints, necessary coordination is to be achieved through the Secretary of Transportation. In fact, the coordination re-

---

[3] As of April, 1978, 67 nations claimed a 12 nautical mile territorial sea and 14 claimed a territorial sea of 200 nautical miles. *National Maritime Claims,* Office of the Geographer, Department of State. April 19, 1978.
[4] Kaye, p. 594.

quirements contained in the Act are rather extensive, certainly far more so than in earlier legislation such as the Outer Continental Shelf Lands Act of 1953. Several avenues for coordination are part of the Act.

Prior to issuing a license for a deepwater port, the Secretary of Transportation must determine:

- that its construction and operation will be in the national interest and consistent with national security and other national policy goals and objectives, including energy sufficiency and environmental quality;
- that it will not unreasonably interfere with international navigation or other reasonable use of the high seas;
- that it will be constructed and operated using best available technology so as to prevent or minimize adverse impact on the marine environment;
- that the Administrator of the Environmental Protection Agency has found that the project will be consistent with the Clean Air Act, the Federal Water Pollution Control Act, and the Marine Protection, Research and Sanctuaries Act;
- that the Federal Trade Commission and the Attorney General judge that the project will not adversely affect competition, restrain trade, promote monopolization, or otherwise contravene the antitrust laws;
- that he has consulted with the Secretary of the Army, the Secretary of Defense, and the Secretary of State; and
- that the governor of the adjacent coastal state or states has approved.

Additional coordination is achieved through requirements that an environmental impact statement be prepared, with the Secretary of Transportation acting as lead agency, and that prior to the establishment of any safety zones, the Secretary of the Interior, the Secretary of Commerce, the Secretary of State and the Secretary of Defense must be consulted.

E. Coastal State Interests

The Deepwater Port Act acknowledges that a deepwater port will require the utilization of the territorial sea including, not only surface movement but pipelines as well, and may have significant landbased impacts upon traditional ports, local communities and coastal regions, especially if ancillary facilities are constructed.

Coastal states are recognized as having a legitimate interest in activities taking place beyond their coastal zone and are included at several points in the deepwater port decision process. All interested states are allowed to comment upon any deepwater port proposal. In addition, the governor of an "adjacent" coastal state can prevent the issuance of a Federal license (Sec. 9(b)(1)). As defined in the DPA, "adjacency" results from being directly connected by pipeline with the port, or by being within 15 miles of the proposed port. States can also petition the Secretary of Transportation for an adjacency designation, which can be granted if "there is a risk of damage to the environment of such state equal to or greater than the risk posed to a state directly connected by pipeline to the proposed deepwater port." (Sec. 9(a)(2)).

In 1976, Florida requested designation as an adjacent state with regard to proposed deepwater ports off the coasts of Texas and Louisiana (SEADOCK and LOOP). Florida expressed concern that, if either of these deepwater ports were approved, significant additional tanker traffic would be drawn through the straits of Florida increasing the chance for oil spills. Therefore, Florida wished to participate in the Federal licensing process to a degree which only an adjacency designation would allow. The Federal Office of Coastal Zone Management felt that Florida's claim had merit, but the U.S. Coast Guard determined that it was not a valid request, and the Secretary of Transportation denied the petition. In response, Florida initiated litigation but withdrew it after formal assurances were made that in granting deepwater port licenses all or most of Florida's concerns would be accounted for.

F. Degree and Form of Control

Although the United States has avoided comprehensive controls over ocean waters, it has established extensive controls over specific individual activities or resources located within ocean waters. The Deepwater Port Act establishes Federal control over the location, ownership, construction and operation of deepwater ports beyond the territorial sea, and upon vessels operating in connection with or in the vicinity of such deepwater ports:

- Construction, operation, or transfer of oil through a deepwater port must be licensed under authority of the Deepwater Port Act.
- Vessel movement, loading and unloading procedures, designation and marking of anchorage areas, maintenance, law enforcement, and the equipment, training, and maintenance required to (a) prevent pollution of the marine environment, (b) to clean up any

pollutants which may be discharged, and (c) to otherwise prevent or minimize any adverse impact from the construction and operation of a deepwater port, are all subject to federal regulation. (Sec. 10(a))

- Regulations for lights and other warning devices, safety equipment, and other matters relating to the promotion of safety of life and property are required. (Sec. 10(b))
- A safety zone around and including any deepwater port must be designated. Within this safety zone all installations, structures and uses will be regulated for compatibility with the operation of the deepwater port. (Sec. 10(d)(1))
- The United States claims the right to inspect records, files, papers, processes, controls and facilities. (Sec. 13(b))
- The discharge of oil into the marine environment from vessels within the safety zone or from the deepwater port is prohibited.
- The Federal Government requires the collection of two cents per barrel of oil handled by the deepwater port for the maintenance of a $100,000,000 deepwater port liability fund which will pay for administrative costs and for cleanup costs and damages which may result from the operation of the deepwater port. (Sec. 18(f))

G. International Considerations

The Deepwater Port Act in effect declares U.S. authority to establish ocean water regulatory zones over which the United States will assert full jurisdiction for the specific purpose of regulating and protecting deepwater ports. However, since the United States does not consider these ocean waters to be under the territorial control of the United States, these extensive regulations have no force under international law. In recognition of this, the Act requires that the Secretary of State be consulted with reference to regulations and specific license regulations and specific license requests. The Act authorizes the Secretary of State to seek international action and cooperation in matters such as the acceptance of and adherence to *safety zones.*

However, the Act does not rely entirely upon voluntary compliance by ships of foreign nations with the controls established under the authority of the Act. Section 19(c) specifies that a vessel registered in or flying the flag of a foreign nation will not be allowed to call at or utilize a deepwater port unless the foreign nation involved has agreed to recognize the concurrent jurisdiction of the United States over the vessel and its personnel while the vessel is within the safety zone.

H. Summary

The Deepwater Port Act establishes control over an ocean activity (deepwater ports) and also asserts the right of the United States to impose jurisdictional control over a portion of ocean space within the vicinity of deepwater ports.

Since the construction and operation of a deepwater port requires the dedication of some portion of ocean space to a single primary use, the decision process by which a proposed deepwater port is approved involves a large number of consultations with agencies, programs, and interest groups that might be affected.

Coastal states whether directly connected to the deepwater port by pipeline, within 15 miles of the port site, or significantly impacted by the port, can specify conditions which must be met. These states have then the ability to block granting of a license.

While the Act is limited to a single activity and to rather small portions of ocean space (at least at this time), it nevertheless constitutes a major exertion of Federal control or management over the ownership, location, construction, and operation of a deepwater port and over all ocean activities taking place within the vicinity of such ports. It is interesting to compare this management program with the Marine Sanctuaries Program, both in terms of similarities and differences.

III. Marine Sanctuaries

A. Background

Several reports of the late 1960's and early 1970's called attention to growing problems of wetland destruction and ocean dumping.[5] These reports and strong public reaction to the Santa Barbara oil spill of 1969 gave impetus for new Federal programs for protection and management of certain ocean resource systems.

During this time, the concept of establishing ocean or marine preserves or sanctuaries re-emerged. The basic concept was to set aside certain portions of ocean space as preserves, protected from the pressures and impacts of increased ocean use. Several reasons were advanced as justification for such sanctuaries.[6] Supporters of the sanctuaries concept

---

[5] *Our Nation and the Sea; National Estuarine Pollution Study; National Estuary Study; Ocean Dumping—A National Policy.*

[6] See Virginia Institute of Marine Sciences, *Marine and Estaurine Sanctuaries.* Report No. 70, 1973, for additional background information.

wanted to establish ocean areas in which offshore oil and gas production would be prohibited, reflecting concern over the Santa Barbara spill. Another purpose suggested was to assure the preservation of some natural ocean areas for continued scientific research and monitoring. In addition, there was some concern on the part of Congress as to the potential ocean impacts of pending federal clean water legislation. This new national program would require major increases in sewage treatment, producing large amounts of sewage sludge. There was concern that this sludge might be dumped into the ocean, in effect, transferring water quality problems from nearshore to offshore areas.

After considerable discussion and debate, authorization for the establishment of estuarine sanctuaries was provided in Section 312 (now 315) of the *Coastal Zone Management Act of 1972,* and provisions for the establishment of marine sanctuaries was included as Title III of the *Marine Protection, Research, and Sanctuaries Act of 1972* (MPRSA).

B. Ocean Waters as Wilderness

Title III of the Marine Protection, Research, and Sanctuaries Act authorizes the Secretary of Commerce with the approval of the President, to designate areas of ocean waters as marine sanctuaries for the purpose of:

> Preserving or restoring such areas for their conservation, recreational, ecological, or esthetic values. (Sec. 302(a))

Aside from this provision, there is no indication as to the purpose or objective of a national marine sanctuaries program. As discussed previously, several reasons were given for creating such sanctuaries, but no unified set of objectives or purposes emerged in Congress, and there seems to be no detailed statement of objectives, purpose or need contained in the authorizing legislation.

The idea of setting aside a portion of the ocean for special protection is not new, having been considered by President Franklin Roosevelt in 1937 for the Bristol Bay area of Alaska and by President Theodore Roosevelt in 1908 in the N.W. Hawaiian Islands Reserve area.[7] Wilderness areas and game preserves have been a part of public lands management at both the state and Federal level for many years. However, setting aside a portion of ocean water as a preserve or sanctuary involves some different or additional considerations from those on land.

---

[7] See Chapter 2 for additional discussion of this issue.

Conceptually, it is difficult to determine which portions of ocean waters can be preserved or restored by designation as a sanctuary. Unlike similar areas on land, any given volume of ocean water is not fixed in time or space. Impacts from thermal change, as well as noise and chemical pollutants tend to migrate across boundaries and through food chains. If the purpose of a marine sanctuary is to maintain some segment of the ocean in its present form, it is difficult to determine with precision what activities and parameters need to be controlled. There is much that remains unknown about how the ocean reacts to human activities. In fact, Title II of the Marine Protection, Research, and Sanctuaries Act directs the Secretary of Commerce to initiate:

> . . . a comprehensive and continuing program of research with respect to the possible long-range effects of pollution, overfishing, and *man-induced* changes of ocean ecosystems. (Emphasis added.)

Until more research is completed on this topic, it is not clear that portions of marine ecosystems can be successfully protected or restored or that regulations for such purposes can withstand challenges of being arbitrary or capricious.

Another potential management difficulty of the marine sanctuary concept is that in many instances a fixed zone will not provide a significant degree of management control over ocean dynamics, natural systems and human activities, each of which have complex spatial and temporal dimensions. There may be some clear value to protecting a special breeding ground or gathering site for marine mammals. But habitat within the ocean tends to include large portions of ocean space. Thus to protect baleen whales, there would be a need to protect not only specific breeding sites, but also a need to protect the quality of water through which they pass, over thousands of miles each year. There would also be a need to ensure the quality and amount of plankton available as food. These requirements imply the need to control oil spills, land based discharge and surface runoff, ocean dumping, atmospheric sources of water pollution, as well as other factors. The kind of protection implicit in the marine sanctuaries program may require major restrictions over most, if not all, ocean activities over a fairly large portion of ocean waters. From this perspective, marine sanctuaries might be most effective as a tool to help implement objectives established in some larger system-wide context.

Another problem not unique to marine sanctuaries is that in the absence of some type of specific national ocean development plan, it is impossible to evaluate the long-range consequences of dedicating a particular segment of ocean space to a single use. The various objections raised by wilderness designations on public lands throughout the United States would certainly apply as well to ocean matters. Those wishing to avoid marine sanctuary restrictions can be expected to argue that the nation cannot afford to preclude development and use of any portion of the ocean, and/or that specific ocean uses will not impart any significant damage and are compatible with the sensitives of the ocean environment, thus not warranting a sanctuary program.

Perhaps to a greater degree than with most Federal ocean management efforts, the Marine Sanctuaries Program raises basic questions of what the national interest in the ocean is, and to what degree the Federal Government can or should attempt to control how, the ocean is used. By the very act of setting aside a portion of ocean space for protection, every other Federal ocean program and all ocean activities are affected. In at least a limited sense, the Marine Sanctuaries Program is perhaps a portent of the future in ocean management. In this new program we are trying to set aside a volume of ocean space and manage it when we really don't have a management *process* yet established that is able to transcend the various physical, political and economic factors that strongly affect ocean management.

The Marine Sanctuaries Program is also an example of seeking a unified approach to ocean resource management without obtaining absolute control over resource development and/or preservation decisions. It is seeking to carry out a rather broad scale mandate in the absence of any unified policy on ocean management. In this sense, it may prove to be a microcosm example of how ocean space and resource management approaches must be evolved in order to achieve a degree of comprehensiveness that, at least some groups feel, is needed in building an ocean management process. How good an example it is remains to be seen.

As shall be discussed further in considering the specific provisions of the Marine Sanctuaries Program, there is not yet a clear articulation of where marine sanctuaries fit within the broad range of possible ocean activities, or among the growing number of Federal ocean management programs.

C. Foreign Policy Considerations

As discussed in the preceding section on deepwater ports, any effort to establish national control over ocean space, resources, or activities beyond the three-mile territorial sea raises a special series of issues or problems. Since 1945 the United States has attempted to persuade other coastal nations to refrain from extending national jurisdiction beyond a narrow territorial sea. And, although the United States has not only established management actions but also asserted full sovereign authority over the resources of the outer continental shelf, it has not claimed a similar degree of authority over ocean waters beyond the three-mile territorial sea.

Each time a national management program has been proposed which involves ocean waters beyond the territorial sea, a debate has ensued as to whether such controls should be attempted, and if so, what kind or how. As discussed previously, the primary concern has been that by establishing ocean water management programs, the United States might weaken its ability to prevent other nations from extending jurisdiction beyond a narrow territorial sea.

The above OCS rights are balanced however by the provision in Article 5(1) of the 1958 Convention on the Continental Shelf. This Article states that exploration and exploitation activities on the shelf "must not result in any unjustifiable interference with navigation, fishing or the conservation of the living resources of the sea, nor result in any interference with fundamental oceanographic or other scientific research carried out with intention of publication." In turn, freedom of the sea activities must be conducted with reasonable regard for other legitimate uses of the seas, i.e., resource exploration and exploitation.

When a marine sanctuaries program was proposed in the U.S. Senate, this topic, as might have been predicted, was actively debated. The principal objection raised by Senator Hollings and the Commerce Committee was that such sanctuaries would constitute the kind of "creeping jurisdiction"[8] which the State Department has resisted since Harold Ickes proposed the establishment of a comprehensive ocean management regime in the 1930's and 1940's. As Hollings observed:

> The issue is not the usefulness or desirability of marine sanctuaries . . . the issues are how to establish them, to whom they will apply, and with what ramifications on other interests of the United States.[9]

Senator Hollings labeled as a "fatal flaw" the fact that these sanctuaries would be located in high seas waters beyond the territorial limits of three miles. He suggested that, if the purpose of these sanctuaries was to protect certain areas from offshore oil and gas drilling, that this objective could be accomplished through the Outer Continental Shelf Lands Act, and that for other purposes international agreements should be sought, but that unilateral legislation would compromise our position at the UNCLOS negotiations. Supporters of the marine sanctuaries program declared that the Outer Continental Shelf Lands Act could not be used to

---

[8] See discussion in Chapter 6 on creeping jurisdiction.
[9] Vol. No. 17 Part 33, *Cong. Rec.* 72 (November 24, 1971), p. 43057.

establish sanctuaries and that the proposed legislation would apply only to Americans and would not impair the freedom of navigation of vessels of other nations. Eventually, the advocates of this program prevailed, and language was included in the legislation declaring that the regulations for marine sanctuaries would apply primarily to United States citizens and that any regulations affecting ocean waters beyond the territorial sea would be negotiated with other nations as necessary or appropriate by the Secretary of State.

The final marine sanctuaries provisions of the MPRSA are quite different from the Deepwater Port Act, with respect to the assertion of United States control over vessels or citizens of other nations. As discussed previously, in the Deepwater Port Act Congress declared that the regulations established for the Deepwater Port facility and for the safety zone surrounding it would apply to any vessel wishing to land at the Deepwater Port. If some vessels were subjected to strict regulations and others were not, the potential for collision or other accident in the vicinity of a deepwater port would be immense, and it is thus patently necessary to extend control over all vessels. Given the lack of specificity as to what marine sanctuaries will be and what regulations will be applied, it is not clear as to whether marine ecosystems can be protected or restored within international high seas if protective regulations apply only to American citizens and vessels. It is a curious situation which will undoubtedly require and receive additional attention by Congress.

D. Degree of Control

Unlike the Deepwater Port Act, Federal control of marine sanctuaries is not limited to ocean waters beyond the territorial sea. The MPRSA authorizes the Secretary of Commerce, with the approval of the President, to designate marine sanctuaries as far seaward as the outer edge of the continental shelf, within the territorial sea, and in the Great Lakes and their connecting waters.

Once a sanctuary has been approved, no permit, license, or other authorization issued pursuant to any other authority shall be valid unless the Secretary of Commerce certifies that the activity is consistent with the purposes of Title III of the MPRSA and the specific regulations for that sanctuary.

This is an extraordinary provision, in that it declares that a marine sanctuary shall have priority over all other programs and activities, once it is established. There is no provision for mitigating circumstances, or for compliance "to the maximum extent practicable" as is the case in other legislation.

E. Coordination

Since all other Federal ocean programs are required to be consistent with marine sanctuary regulations, and since marine sanctuaries can be established within large portions of ocean space both within and beyond the territorial sea, the process by which specific sanctuaries are established and regulations for them formulated becomes one of the most important administrative mechanisms in the Federal ocean management effort.

Title III of the MPRSA requires that any sanctuary must be approved by the President prior to designation. Furthermore, the Secretary of Commerce is required to:

- Consult with the Secretaries of State, Defense, Interior and Transportation, the Administrator of the Environmental Protection Agency, and the heads of "other interested agencies" on regulations for, as well as establishment of, sanctuaries. Section 302(a) indicates that "consultation" shall include an opportunity to review and comment upon specific proposed designations.
- Work through the Secretary of State to obtain agreements with other nations as necessary or appropriate.
- Consult with and give consideration to the views of any state whose waters are to be included in the sanctuary. The governor of any such state has sixty days after notice of designation to certify any or all of the proposed sanctuary within the territorial waters of his state as being unacceptable. Thus, coastal states have veto authority over the establishment of that portion of a marine sanctuary within coastal waters under their authority.
- A public hearing is to be held in the coastal areas most likely to be directly affected by a sanctuary designation.

F. Utilization of the Act

For reasons that are not fully clear, the Marine Sanctuaries Act has not really been used, although subsequent to its passage two sanctuaries were established through Presidential Executive Orders. In 1977, however, it was decided to take a new initiative in establishing sanctuaries in association with accelerated OCS leasing. In his May 23, 1977, Environmental Message to Congress, President Carter stated:

> I have . . . asked [the Secretary of Interior] to work closely with the Secretary of Commerce as she identifies potential marine sanctuaries in areas where leasing appears imminent.

> . . . existing legislation allows the Secretary of Commerce to protect certain estuarine and ocean resources from the ill effects of development by designating marine sanctuaries. Yet only two sanctuaries have been established since 1972, when the program began.
>
> I am, therefore, instructing the Secretary of Commerce to identify possible sanctuaries in areas where development appears imminent, and to begin collecting the data necessary to designate them as such under the law.[10]

Since that time more than 160 nominations have been submitted to the Secretary of Commerce for consideration as possible marine sanctuaries. Certain issues have emerged subsequently as the Department of Commerce began to implement some of these suggestions.

A proposal was made to declare all of Georges Bank as a marine sanctuary. This proposal was not well received, and in part stimulated Congressional efforts to amend the basic legislation. The issues which emerged from the Georges Bank proposal emphasize some of the difficulties of establishing marine sanctuaries that have been discussed previously in this section.

First, Georges Bank is already being administered as a special management area under the Fishery Conservation and Management Act of 1976, through the New England Regional Fishery Management Council and the National Marine Fisheries Service. Georges Bank is also a "frontier" area of new oil and gas leasing under the Outer Continental Shelf Lands Act, and it is an area of heavy merchant vessel traffic. Because of the heavy use of this area, there is an inherent difficulty in attempting to establish a preserve or sanctuary for the purposes of conservation, recreation, esthetic values or ecological protection. There is a very real danger that such efforts might disrupt intensive fishing efforts and complex fisheries management programs, commercial navigation, or OCS minerals leasing. It would also be administratively difficult to structure a marine sanctuaries program that would satisfactorily link all of the existing private and public activities and management efforts for the Georges Bank area.

Second, this proposed marine sanctuary seemed to reveal a certain interpretation of the Marine Protection Research and Sanctuaries Act which caused concern both within Congress and in various Federal agencies with ocean programs. There is a suggestion through the Georges Bank proposal that the "consistency" authority provided in Section 302(f) might be used by the government to attempt to establish a com-

---

[10] Office of the White House Press Secretary, *Presidential Message to the Congress of the United States,* May 23, 1977, pp. 9 and 14.

prehensive ocean management regime within the boundaries of a marine sanctuary, using Title III authority to assert control over all Federal ocean programs and activities within a specified geographic portion of ocean space. Subsequent testimony by representatives of NOAA before Congress confirmed that there was some tendency on the part of NOAA to see the Title III provisions of the MPRSA as a mandate to establish comprehensive ocean management programs over selected portions of the oceans, through the process of sanctuary designation.

By the fall of 1978, two marine sanctuaries were in existence and a third was officially proposed. It is reported by NOAA officials that none of the three marine sanctuary efforts constitute a comprehensive ocean management scheme. Further, it was indicated that the activities regulated within the sanctuaries are limited to those necessary to protect resources and the process of designation and development of regulations has involved extensive consultation with affected Federal and state agencies, public interest groups and industry.

G. Modifications of the Marine Sanctuaries Program

In May of 1978 the Senate Committee on Commerce, Science and Transportation submitted committee report S. 95-886 to accompany S. 2767, a bill to extend authorization of the Marine Sanctuaries Program and other portions of the Marine Protection, Research and Sanctuaries Act. In this committee report several important changes to the Marine Sanctuaries Program are suggested. Although the law has not been amended, as of this writing, many of the suggested changes have, in effect, been accepted by incorporating them into regulations or agency practice and policy.

1. Purpose. The Committee emphasized that the intention of the Marine Sanctuaries Program is *not* to establish comprehensive ocean management programs, but rather to preserve, protect, and restore specific ecologically important ocean areas. One recommended amendment was to delete "esthetic values" as a reason for sanctuaries designation and the Committee emphasized that, while recreation is important, it is a secondary concern and should not be construed as a primary purpose of sanctuary designation.

2. Coordination. The Committee suggested that, for marine sanctuaries of more than 1,000 square miles, both the House and Senate must give their approval, along with that of the President. Congress would, under these amendments, also be informed of any proposed sanctuary designation, no matter what its size. Furthermore, the Secretary of Commerce would be directed to consult with the chairman and members of any regional fishery management council having jurisdiction over living resources in the waters included in a proposed sanctuary. These proposed amendments appear to indicate a growing appreciation of the potentially widespread impacts of a marine sanctuary designation, and the need for special consideration of its administrative design if such designations are not going to disrupt a number of national interests and programs.

3. Degree of control. Ever since the Georges Bank marine sanctuary proposal, there has been concern that the original language of Title III of the MPRSA might require modification. In the original legislation the Secretary of Commerce was given what appeared to be total authority over all activities and programs within the sanctuary, once it had been approved by the President. Although the Senate Committee report may actually say that "all other statutes may be superceded," marine sanctuary regulations cannot legally supercede a Federal law or statute; they may only supercede the "permits, licenses, or other authorizations" issued under conflicting regulations. As the Senate Committee report further observes:

> One problem with the original Title III is that in designating a sanctuary the Secretary of Commerce automatically and perhaps inadvertently may assume authority to regulate all activities within a sanctuary; all other statutes may be superceded within the designated site. . . .
>
> All permits, licenses, and other authorizations issued pursuant to any other law or other authority *shall remain valid* unless these sanctuary regulations provide otherwise. . . . If the terms of the designation and the regulations implementing them do not provide for the regulation of a given activity, that activity within the sanctuary continues to be regulated under other applicable law.[11]

An additional modification proposed by the Senate Committee would be that, at the time of proposing a marine sanctuary, the Secretary of Commerce would be required to list the proposed regulations, so that the implications of designation would be clear to all interested parties. The Secretary would be required to list

> . . . not only the geographic area to be included and the characteristics of the site which give it conservation, ecological or recreational value,

---

[11] Senate Committee on Commerce, Science and Transportation, *Marine Protection, Research and Sanctuaries Act Amendments of 1978.* May 15, 1978, 95th Cong. 2nd sess., S. Report No. 95-886, p. 5.

but also those specific activities which the Secretary proposes to regulate in order to protect those characteristics.[12]

The Marine Sanctuaries Program is particularly important because of the degree of control over ocean activities implicit in the concept of a sanctuary. If the primary objective of a particular sanctuary is to preserve a specific submerged lands formation from the possible disruption of offshore oil and gas drilling activities, the necessary type and degree of control may not be major, and the Marine Sanctuaries Program could be viewed as a supplement to the Outer Continental Shelf Lands Act. However, if the features or conditions to be preserved or protected require control over additional activities, as seems to be the case, then the marine sanctuary becomes, in effect, a national designation of key values within some portion of ocean space and a national dedication of an area to that key value.[13]

If the area to be protected is of little value for other purposes such as mineral production, commercial fishing, vessel transit, offshore facilities siting, ocean energy production, or national security purposes, then preservation should be relatively simple. But as pressures for access to ocean space and ocean resources build, the administrative difficulties of monitoring and regulating a preservation or sanctuary area of any size may become serious, and the basic concept of setting aside a portion of ocean space as a preserve may come under serious challenge.

There is one other major ocean management program of the United States which involves a concept of ocean control even greater in type and degree than that of the Marine Sanctuaries Program. In contrast to the Marine Sanctuaries Program, in which there was some initial confusion as to Congressional intent, the Coastal Zone Management Act explicitly calls for the comprehensive coordination of all Federal, state and local activities and programs within the territorial sea.

IV. Coastal Zone Management

A. Introduction

The three-mile territorial sea, as part of the sovereign territory of the United States, is not encumbered with the degree of foreign policy constraints encountered in ocean space beyond the three-mile limit.[14] For

---

12 *Ibid.*

13 See Chapter 5 for additional discussion of key value concept.

14 It is assumed, however, that no portion of ocean space is totally devoid of foreign policy ramifications.

this reason, the United States could combine water, submerged lands, and resources into a single management unit without extensive concerns over subsequent international consequences which have so strongly influenced the structure of U.S. ocean programs beyond three miles. Nevertheless, the territorial sea has been divided into two parts for purposes of management, reminiscent of ocean space beyond the territorial sea, but for quite different reasons.

In 1937, Secretary of the Interior Ickes attempted to remove traditional state control of the submerged lands of the territorial sea and to replace their authority with a Federal ocean management regime that would include not only the waters and submerged lands of the territorial sea, but also a significant portion of ocean space beyond. As recounted in Chapter Two, it was not until 1953 that this domestic debate was at least temporarily resolved, through the passage of the *Submerged Lands Act of 1953*. Figure 3, Chapter Two, displays the management regimes established in 1953.

B. Waters versus Submerged Lands and Resources

Coastal states were recognized as having ownership of and authority over the submerged lands and the living and non-living resources of the territorial sea. However, the Submerged Lands Act (SLA) is not as specific regarding the *waters* of the territorial sea. The purpose of the SLA was in part to "provide for the use and control of said lands and resources." States were not recognized as having either ownership or management authority over the waters of the territorial sea, and most, if not all, of the then-conceivable governmental management interests in territorial waters were explicitly reserved for the Federal Government. Table I, page 31, indicates the division of authority between Federal and state governments over the waters, resources and submerged lands of the territorial sea which resulted from the Submerged Lands Act.

Thus the Submerged Lands Act did two things: (1) it split authority, or sustained an existing division of authority, over the territorial sea between Federal and state governments, and (2) it recognized resources and submerged lands as a management unit, without explicitly assigning authority over territorial waters. It focused instead upon water-related activities such as commerce, water power, navigation, and national defense. It is significant that this distribution of authority and lack of specificity over waters of the territorial sea were, for the most part, left unchanged by the Congress when it passed the Coastal Zone Management Act in 1972, establishing a new Federal-state territorial sea management effort.

C. The Coastal Zone Management Act of 1972

During the late 1960's, there emerged growing concern over the loss of wetlands and estuaries, overfishing, oil spills, erosion, major new proposals for large facilities located in coastal areas, water quality problems, crowded navigational fairways, and other issues described in studies and reports of that period such as *Our Nation and the Sea.*[15]

In 1967, Vice President Humphrey advanced the concept of "coastal zone management," and in 1969 the Stratton Commission suggested the formation of a comprehensive management regime for the territorial sea and adjacent coastline under state leadership, with an associated Federal coordinated effort directed by a single national ocean agency (NOAA). In 1972 Congress enacted several important environmental protection and resource management programs, including the Coastal Zone Management Act of 1972 (P.L. 92-583).

A Territorial Sea Management Program

Even though the Submerged Lands Act of 1953 had attempted to establish a legislative mechanism that would allow the "use and control" of the territorial sea, few states had established many controls. The Coastal Zone Management Act is based on the conclusion of Congress that "present state and local institutional arrangements for planning and regulating land and water uses [in the territorial sea] are inadequate."[16]

Because the Submerged Lands Act recognizes that coastal states own the submerged lands and resources of the territorial sea, it would be both politically and legally difficult to force states to establish some new type of territorial sea management. Congress chose instead to attempt to encourage states to undertake a new level of management and planning, by providing legislative authorization, through offers of financial assistance, and with promises of some new degree of influence or control over Federal activities within the territorial sea.

1. Objective: The concept of coastal zone management. In Section 302(c), the Coastal Zone Management Act (CZMA) identifies the major issues of concern:

---

[15] Commission on Marine Science, Engineering and Resources (Stratton Commission), *Our Nation and the Sea: A Plan for National Action* (Washington, D.C., January 1969).

[16] Sec. 302(g). "In light of competing demands and the urgent need to protect and give high priority to natural systems in the coastal zone, present state and local institutional arrangements for planning and regulating land and water uses in such areas are inadequate. . . ."

The increasing and competing demands upon the lands and waters of our coastal zone occasioned by population growth and economic development, including requirements of industry, commerce, residential development, recreation, extraction of mineral resources and fossil fuels, transportation and navigation, waste disposal, and harvesting of fish, shellfish and other living marine resources, have resulted in the loss of living marine resources, wildlife, nutrient-rich areas, permanent and adverse changes to ecological systems, decreasing open space for public use, and shoreline erosion.

The objective of the CZMA is to encourage coastal states in cooperation with Federal and local governments and private interest groups to develop land and water use programs for the territorial sea and adjacent shoreland, which would include

> unified policies, criteria, standards, methods, and processes for dealing with land and water use decisions of more than local significance. (Sec. 302(h))

The CZMA could be viewed as an evolutionary step in the formation of American ocean programs and policies, and it represents the most ambitious and comprehensive effort to exert public control over some portion of the ocean. However, it is essential to remember that while the concept is ambitious, it is also based upon voluntary participation by coastal states, and in terms of Federal authority, the Act must be placed at the low end of the management spectrum discussed in Chapter One; it is a program of encouragement rather than full control.

The Act calls for the formulation of management programs for the territorial sea and adjacent shore that include:

- A determination of which land and water uses will be permissible within this management zone;
- An identification of areas of particular national concern:
- Broad guidelines on priority of uses in particular areas, including uses of lower priority;
- Plans and policies to protect and provide access to public beaches and other coastal areas of environmental, historical, esthetic. ecological or cultural value;
- Programs for the anticipation and management of impacts created by energy facilities located in or which may significantly affect the coastal zone;
- Programs for the assessment of shoreline erosion and development control strategies to lessen the impact of erosion and restore areas adversely affected by this process; and

- Plans and policies for the siting of major facilities within this management zone.

In broader terms, coastal states are charged with determining and achieving "wise use" of the territorial sea and assuring that, in both the territorial sea and adjacent coastal lands, the broad web of national interests is accommodated and/or reconciled with local and state interests, as well as with the sensitivities and basic capacities of the natural ocean environment.

Considering the scope of this mandate and the emphasis it places upon national interests which need to be protected and reconciled, it is surprising to note how little substantive guidance the states have been provided, either by the Executive Branch of the Federal Government, the Office of Coastal Zone Management within NOAA, or by Congress through the provisions of the Act. States are asked to balance human needs and interests against natural system capacities and to accommodate those needs and interests which are diverse and sometimes conflicting, in a number of ways. Not only is minimal guidance given, as shall be discussed further, but very little explicit authority is provided to achieve such balancing. As one observer noted:

> What makes this essential problem of 'balancing' even more important is the almost total silence of the Act as to how the substantive balance is to be struck. On its face, the Act places states in this position, with the assessment process by (the Office of Coastal Zone Management, NOAA), mostly silent on its criteria for deciding the merits of the claims.[17]

2. Authority to manage the coastal zone. The basic premise of the CZMA is that:

> The key to more effective protection and use of the land and water resources of the coastal zone is to encourage the states to exercise their full authority over the lands and waters in the coastal zone. . . . (Sec. 302(h))

This raises the question of what the "full authority" of the states over the waters and lands of the territorial sea is. It should be remembered that in the late 1940's the U.S. Supreme Court ruled that on Constitutional grounds the states do not have management authority over the

---

[17] Timothy Alexander, *The Intergovernmental Balancing Act: State-Federal Interests in Coastal Zone Management.* Internal Document (1977), (available from author), p. 51.

territorial sea and that Federal interests should have paramount authority:

> . . . protection and control of the [territorial sea] are indeed functions of national external sovereignty . . . the marginal sea is a national, not a state concern. National interests, national responsibilities, national concerns are involved. The problems of commerce, national defense, relations with other powers, war and peace focus here. National rights must therefore be paramount in that area.[18]

Bartley and others have argued that such decisions run counter to 150 years of previous legal history and may not constitute good law,[19] but as a result of those findings, the only clear expression of state authority over the territorial sea is the Submerged Lands Act. This Act is not clear as to who might have authority over the water itself as contrasted to activities or national resources contained within it.

When the Submerged Lands Act was enacted, multi-purpose, comprehensive resource management such as envisioned in the Coastal Zone Management Act was obviously not a totally alien thought, but it did not seem to be the primary objective of the legislation. To the degree that Congress did address broad planning and management authorities over territorial waters, it tended to favor Federal rather than state authority, specifically in the areas of:

- navigation,
- flood control,
- power production,
- national defense,
- commerce, and
- international affairs.

Considering the encompassing and expanding nature of "commerce," "navigation," "national defense," and "foreign affairs," "power", and the unclear but potentially pervasive authority over the use of ocean waters "for the production of power," an argument can be made that states have very little authority over the waters of the territorial sea. As an example, consider the finding in *U.S. v. Wrightwood Dairy Company* which concluded that

> no form of state activity can constitutionally thwart the power granted by the commerce clause to Congress.[20]

---

[18] *U.S. v. Louisiana,* 339 U.S. 699, 704, (1950).
[19] Bartley, *op. cit.*
[20] *U.S. v. Wrightwood Dairy Company,* 319 U.S. 110 (1941).

In those instances where states have initiated regulatory or management efforts over ocean waters, they have experienced mixed receptions in the courts, with Federal paramount or preemptive interests or authorities often cited as constraints upon state action.[21]

Rather than resolving these areas of ambiguity or conflict, the Coastal Zone Management Act incorporates them whole: the states are to achieve comprehensive coastal management through the exercise of their full authority, whatever that may or may not be, and in concert with an unclear degree of Federal consistency or in compliance with other state efforts. In fact, the CZMA seems to obscure further just what authority coastal states can use to achieve the purposes of the Act. Section 307(e) declares that no Federal or state rights or laws are to be diminished, superceded, modified or repealed by the Act or by state coastal management programs.

> Nothing in this title shall be construed - (1) to diminish either Federal or state jurisdiction, responsibility, or rights in the field of planning, development, or control of water resources, submerged lands, or navigable waters; nor to displace, supercede, limit, or modify any interstate compact or the jurisdiction or responsibility of any legally established joint or common agency of two or more states . . . nor to limit the authority of Congress to authorize and fund projects. (Sec. 307(e))

At first glance, this rather extraordinary provision would seem to exempt virtually every governmental authority, including Congress itself, from any coastal management programs which might actually attempt to exert some degree of control or management.

This paradox is almost the antithesis of the Marine Sanctuaries Act, which provides, as discussed previously, that once a sanctuary has been properly designated, as prescribed in the Act, that the Secretary of Commerce will have full and direct control over all other Federal programs affecting that area:

> After a marine sanctuary has been designated under this section . . . no permit, license, or other authorization pursuant to any other authority shall be valid unless the Secretary shall certify that the permitted activity is consistent with the purposes of this title and can be carried out within the regulations promulgated under this section. (Sec. 102(f))

---

[21] See for example *Kossick v. United Fruit Company,* 365 U.S. 731 (1961); *American Waterways Operators,* 411 U.S. 325 (1973); and *Ray v. Atlantic Richfield Company,* 435 U.S. 151 (1978). For additional citations and discussion of this point, see Armstrong and Ryner, *Coastal Waters: A Management Analysis* (Ann Arbor: Ann Arbor Science, 1978), Part II.

3. Coastal zone consistency. Regardless of certain confusions or conflicts contained within the Act as to the authority of the states over the coastal zone, the CZMA at first reading appears to provide the same type of control to the states as has just been cited with reference to sanctuaries:

> Each federal agency conducting or supporting activities, directly affecting the coastal zone shall conduct or support those activities in a manner which is, to the maximum extent practicable, consistent with approved state management programs. (Sec. 307(c)(1))
>
> Any federal agency which shall undertake any development project in the coastal zone of a state shall insure that the project is, to the maximum extent practicable, consistent with approved state management programs. (Sec. 307(c)(2))

These and additional provisions of the CZMA provide a rather strong and detailed directive to Federal agencies to comply with the contents of approved state coastal management programs. However, there is a very real and significant limitation upon the effectiveness of these provisions in the phrase "to the maximum extent practicable." Formulation of regulations to implement this section of the CZMA required approximately 18 months and was surrounded with controversy. Basic disputes as to the degree to which Federal agencies should have to comply with state management efforts could not be resolved even at the Cabinet level among department heads, and intervention by the Executive Office of the President was necessary to achieve some degree of consensus.

Stratton Commission

Many of the provisions of the Coastal Zone Management Act follow recommendations contained in the Stratton Commission's report on national ocean programs, *Our Nation and the Sea.* One point at which there is wide divergence between the Commission's concept of territorial sea management and the final CZMA is in this specific area of degree of state control over Federal activities.

The Commission foresaw that without some actual redistribution of authority among states and the Federal Government, above and beyond that specified in the Submerged Lands Act, the coastal states might not be able to function as a coordinating agent for the territorial sea.

> . . . it may be desirable to delegate to the state coastal zone authorities certain regulatory functions of Federal agencies, such as reviewing proposals for construction in navigable waterways and advising Federal construction agencies.[22]

---

[22] *Our Nation and the Sea,* p. 59.

The Commission furthermore suggested that this delegation of Federal authority could be used to ensure proper performance of state coastal programs, by withdrawing that authority if necessary.

> The federal government should not make decisions for the state authority, but it should oversee the authority and withdraw funding support and delegation of specific federal functions if the authority performs inadequately.[23]

Congress chose not to delegate Federal authorities. It relied instead upon the utilization of existing authorities and the sharing of responsibilities in a spirit of cooperation. It is too early to tell if the territorial sea can be managed under state direction without some additional explicit authority. However, it is also not clear that actual delegation of authority would be constitutional, and it is certain that Federal agencies and their constituents would in most instances vigorously oppose any transfer of authority. The issue of state authorities and interests in ocean management is considered further in Chapter Four.

4. Federal role. As envisioned in the Coastal Zone Management Act, states are to have the lead in formulating "wise use" plans for the coastal zone, and Federal agencies are supposed to be supportive participants. The relationship might be described as a partnership. In terms of formulating rules, objectives, or policies for the management programs, Federal agencies are supposed to work with states during the program development process and to react to and comment upon those programs prior to final approval. The importance of such participation and comment follows from the facts that:

a. Since states are not given full authority over the territorial sea, they must devise programs which rely to some extent upon Federal authorities and which are acceptable to Federal agencies so that they will comply; and
b. Once coastal management programs are approved, Federal agencies are under a strong directive to comply with their provisions, and thus each agency does well to make sure that such programs are workable and acceptable prior to approval.

This idea of a joint Federal-state management effort is reflected in other management programs such as clean air management and clean water management.

---

[23] *Ibid.*

It is interesting that while states are urged to coordinate all of their state programs as well as local ones into a focused, comprehensive state management effort, there is no equivalent Federal effort to coordinate Federal programs in fisheries management, navigation, national defense, water pollution, offshore mineral leasing, and other ocean-related activities.

The Stratton Commission had envisioned a strong Federal management effort, complementing state programs in areas beyond state jurisdiction, both physically and in terms of policy.[24] The Commission wanted coordination among Federal agencies in this planning and management effort to be achieved through the establishment of a Federal ocean agency. A partial explanation for the lack of any unified Federal coastal water management effort may be that Congress thought it appropriate to avoid the many issues associated with the creation of a Federal ocean agency. However, through its decision to structure the Coastal Zone Management Act to avoid any national coordination of Federal coastal programs and policies, Congress has created an inherent fragmentation into 30 parts of the national territorial sea management effort.

D. Fragmentation of Territorial Sea Management

As the coastal zone management program is currently structured, each coastal state is encouraged to establish a coastal management program. The inland boundary of each state's coastal management "zone," as well as the structure for administering that zone and the priorities of use within it, is left up to the discretion of each state. To gain coordination between these state management programs and Federal ocean programs, each state is left to negotiate with each Federal agency as to the relationships that will or should exist. Each state establishes its own policies, and the degree of consistency between state and Federal interests and programs varies from segment to segment of the territorial sea. Because the Act relies upon voluntary participation by the states, there may be some segments of the territorial sea for which there are not comprehensive coordinated planning and management efforts, which are directly adjacent to segments with an approved program in place.

Obviously, fragmentation is inherent in state rather than Federal control, and that does not necessarily imply a problem. There are regional

---

24 "The Commission believes it important that the Congress assign planning, coordination, and management for coastal zone (sic) beyond state jurisdiction to a single federal agency. The federal planning and management role would be analogous to that exercised within the limits of state jurisdiction by the coastal zone authorities." *Our Nation and the Sea*, p. 62.

variations in current, temperature, bottom topography, historical patterns of use, political structure, and legal systems, and it may be essential to allow for a wide degree of variation in coastal management programs if they are to meet successfully the diversity of state interests and needs.

The point to be made is that there is no mechanism within the Coastal Zone Management Act to achieve any greater degree of coordination within the territorial sea. While there is encouragement, there is no requirement for internal consistency *between* state programs. Users of ocean space and ocean resources already face a variety of changing laws as they pass from the jurisdiction of one state to the next. The Coastal Zone Management Act represents a whole new level of controls, regulations and policies, including public determinations of which activities should have priorities of access to the various segments of the territorial sea and adjacent shore.

In its decision to allow individual state programs in contrast to a uniform national territorial sea management system, Congress has supported a program which may possibly increase the time, cost, and confusion of attempting to use the territorial sea. Figure 6 portrays this situation.

E. Management of Coastal Waters

> 'Coastal zone' means the coastal waters (including the lands therein and thereunder). . . . The zone . . . extends seaward to the outer limit of the United States territorial sea. The zone extends inland from the shorelines only to the extent necessary to control shorelands, the uses of which have a direct and significant impact on the coastal waters. (CZMA, Sec. 304(a))

Examination of this definition of coastal zone contained in the CZMA seems to indicate that the Act focusses heavily upon the *water* and submerged lands of the territorial sea. The Coastal Zone Management Act in a sense could be viewed as a territorial sea management program. Yet while a few states have done some interesting water-related planning, no coastal state has achieved or even attempted the degree of comprehensive planning and management for coastal waters suggested by the CZMA.[25]

Oregon has developed a general management goal for the ocean waters of its coastal management zone, which while general, provides a fairly clear statement of what the priorities of ocean management use will be:

---

[25] *Supra,* 16.

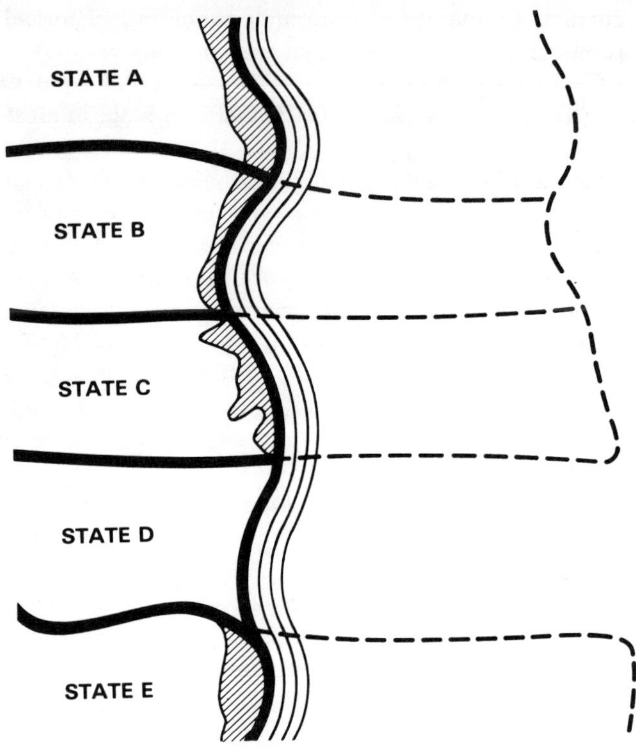

Figure 6:

The Coastal Zone Management Act of 1972 gives each state the authority and responsibility for determining the landward boundary of its coastal management "zone". Permissible uses, priorities of use, area of special concern, provisions for energy facilities, and programs for coastal access as well as other management components for the waters, submerged lands, and shorelands of the coastal zone may differ radically from state to state. There is a probability that Federal ocean programs will be administered in a less uniform fashion than before, as a result of the requirement of the CZMA that Federal ocean programs be administered in a fashion that is consistent with state coastal management programs as much as possible.

An additional interesting feature of the CZMA is that there may be some segments of the territorial sea for which there is no management program, if one or more coastal states are unwilling or unable to participate.

Since renewable ocean resources and uses, such as food production, water quality, navigation, recreation, and esthetic enjoyment, will provide greater long-term benefits than will nonrenewable resources, such plans and activities shall give clear priority to the proper management and protection of renewable resources.[26]

Few states have achieved comparable clarity in policy for coastal water use, nor have they established clear procedures by which territorial sea decisions will be made and conflicts resolved. Most states have approached coastal management as shorelands management and have not given detailed consideration to the adjacent territorial sea.

There are several Federal programs, left intact by the Coastal Zone Management Act, which will have major impacts upon state coastal waters as well as shorelands. The Ports and Waterways Safety Act, the Fisheries Conservation and Management Act, the Deepwater Port Act, the Outer Continental Shelf Lands Act and the Marine Protection, Research and Sanctuaries Act represent a series of public management decisions over which coastal states could have a significant degree of influence, if not control, through the provisions of the Coastal Zone Management Act. Without their own coastal *waters* management programs, states may not be able to interact effectively with these and future Federal ocean programs.

There are many explanations for the limited coastal water management efforts at the state level, not the least of which are insufficient time, money, and personnel, and pressing shoreland issues requiring immediate attention. Also, several states have become increasingly involved in offshore oil and gas leasing, and the associated shore impacts within the territorial jurisdiction of the U.S. These states have their own concepts of how the territorial sea should be used, at least in terms of energy transportation and production. But the limited number of state coastal water management efforts, combined with an ambiguous or conflicting distribution of responsibility and authority, leaves unsettled the issue of whether or not national management of the territorial sea can or will be achieved through the approach contained in the existing Coastal Zone Management Act.

F. Conclusion

From the 1930's through the 1950's, much of Federal ocean management entailed the establishment of authority to manage. In the 1970's the Federal Government exercised its recently asserted jurisdiction over ocean resources and activities through the enactment of a variety of separate ocean management programs.

---

[26] Oregon Land Conservation and Development Commission, *Statewide Planning Goals and Guidelines* (Portland, 1976).

In waters beyond the territorial sea, the United States has continued to use caution in imposing controls, primarily in an effort to instill a similar degree of caution in other coastal nations.

Within the territorial sea, states continue to hold authority over submerged lands and resources, and the Federal Government retains most authorities over the waters. In 1972 Congress began an effort to establish a comprehensive management program linking these two separate authorities through the enactment of the Coastal Zone Management Act. For both the territorial sea and the ocean beyond, the United States has, since 1972, attempted to impart a new level of control over the ocean and activities taking place within it, which begins to approach the control now commonly asserted on land.

V. Fisheries Management

A. Introduction

Federal regulation of ocean fishing is a relatively new concept, which appears to have been first stated nationally in the late 1930's. Before that time most, if not all, governmental regulation or control was at the state level within the territorial sea and the United States claimed no authority to regulate fisheries or other resources beyond the three-mile limit.

President Roosevelt's idea of establishing a fisheries game preserve in the northern Pacific Ocean waters and extending U.S. jurisdiction over ocean space and resources far beyond the three mile limit was not implemented. However, because of continued concern over foreign fishing pressures within traditional American fishing grounds, President Truman established by proclamation in 1945 what might be interpreted as a Federal ocean fisheries management "regime," at the same time that an outer continental shelf lands management regime was formed. But as with Roosevelt's earlier idea, this proclamation was not translated into actual controls, and the 200-mile fisheries management idea remained no more than an assertion of Federal ability to control.

By the mid-1960's the amount of fishing being done by sophisticated foreign fleets near U.S. shores was so extensive as to spur Congress to enact P.L. 89-658, which established a 12-mile wide contiguous fishing zone in which the United States declared the right to exclude fishing activities of other nations.

However, this action proved insufficient to deal with the issue. Foreign fishing pressure continued, and even expanded, beyond the new 12-mile regulatory area. U.S. fishing activities, both commercial and recreational, were also extensive. These fishing activities, as well as increased pollution and some habitat destruction, contributed to a noticeable and, in some instances, sharp decline in various fish stocks.

Finally, in 1976, Congress enacted legislation which imposes Federal control over all ocean fishing within 200 miles of shore and beyond the territorial sea. This system echoes to a considerable extent the earlier concepts of Roosevelt and Truman, but marks the first time for the U.S. that actual Federal regulations and controls over ocean fishing have been established beyond 12 miles and the first time that a Federal legislative basis for such control has existed.

B. The Fishery Conservation and Management Act of 1976 (P.L. 94-265)

Purpose

There are several declared purposes included in the Act (Sec. 2(b)), but the two major objectives are to prevent foreign fishing within 200 miles of shore except when there is an "excess" amount of fish that cannot be utilized by American fishermen and to establish a comprehensive fisheries management program that will or may regulate all recreational and commercial fishing within this 200-mile management zone. It is noteworthy that the Fishery Conservation and Management Act (FCMA) is concerned not only with the protection and conservation of fish stocks, but also, to some degree, with the protection and conservation of commercial and recreational fishing as major ocean activities.

1. Type of control.

Access by nationality. The Act declares that American fishermen will be given preferential access to all fish stocks within 200 miles of American shores and that fishing by other nations will be allowed only if there is a surplus.

> The total allowable level of foreign fishing, if any, with respect to any fishery subject to the exclusive fishery management authority of the United States, shall be that portion of the optimum yield of such fishery which will not be harvested by vessels of the United States, as determined in accordance with the provisions of this Act. (Sec. 201(d))

Securing preferential access to American fishermen and extending controls over foreign vessels were perhaps the principal reasons why United States commercial fishing interests supported the enactment of this legislation, but as shall be discussed below, attempting to do so raises certain basic issues and various administrative problems.

Amount of catch. Management plans are to be established for each fishery existing within the 200-mile management zone. These plans may include:

- Designation of zones and time periods when fishing shall be limited or shall not be permitted or shall be permitted only by specified types of fishing vessels or with specified types and quantities of fishing gear;
- Limitations on the catch of fish (based upon area, species, size, number, weight, sex, incidental catch, total biomass, or other factors).

As a result of this program, individual commercial fishermen are or may be told how many fish, of what size, and what type they can catch during a given year; in effect each species of fish now may be allocated, with the Federal Government determining, for example, how many yellowtail flounder will be caught, and to some degree, by whom. While this type of allocation, as well as restrictions upon number of vessels or type of equipment used, has in the past been used at the state level, this approach constitutes significant extension in the exercise of Federal power.

2. Regional Fishery Management Councils. The FCMA calls for the establishment of eight Regional Fishery Management Councils (Regional Councils) which comprise a unique institutional arrangement for a Federal ocean management effort. The Councils represent a partnership of Federal, state and private interests, requiring membership by the principal state official with marine fishery management responsibility and expertise in each member state, as well as the Regional Director of the National Fishery Service (Sec. 302(b)). The actual degree of control over this program by the Regional Councils is not clear from the language of the Act, because final regulations are pending approval by the Secretary of Commerce. However, the Councils do have clear responsibility for preparing and updating comprehensive fishery management plans for their regions, subject to departmental approval.

3. Federal/State linkages. The FCMA contains several provisions to ensure that state interests are considered, including the requirement that state governors determine or recommend most of the members of the Councils. Also, Section 306 of the Act declares that state jurisdiction over fisheries in coastal or territorial waters is not to be diminished by the Act.

Section 306(b) stipulates, however, that the Secretary of Commerce can, under certain conditions, assume management responsibilities of a specific fishery within the boundaries of a state if and as long as that state's management program fails to meet with Department of Commerce approval.

4. Coastal zone management. While the Act assures state participation in the Federal fishery management program, it does not discuss or require linkages between regional Federal fishery management plans and state coastal fishery management plans. While state fishery personnel are to be included on the Regional Councils, state coastal zone management personnel are not required to be included; and while there are opportunities for coordination and cooperative management, there is no requirement or assurance of it. As a result, there are two separate national fishery management systems: one for a 200-mile zone, administered by the eight Regional Councils and the other within the territorial sea, administered by each coastal state.

Coastal states and local communities could be affected by Regional Councils' plans if they induce increased fishery pressure or suppress a local fishing industry; and state or local actions could destroy important fish habitats, hamper the construction of necessary fish processing facilities, or fail to provide necessary commercial fishing vessel access.

On the other hand, there is a considerable opportunity for mutual support, if the plans of the Regional Councils were coordinated in a positive fashion with the coastal management efforts of the states. The Office of Coastal Zone Management has established a Fisheries Assistance Program to address these opportunities.

C. Foreign Fishing within the Management Zone

As described in Chapter Two, the main reason this kind of national control over ocean fishing had not been established until 1976 was the concern that such action on the part of the United States would lead to an exclusion of American fishermen from foreign waters or result in other limitations upon public and private American interests in foreign ocean space and ocean resources. In fact, some commercial fishermen within the United States had resisted Federal fishery management programs until the 1970's, because of commercial interest in foreign water fisheries and because of a widespread dislike among commercial fishermen of governmental control in general. However, the opposition to

Federal control by distant-water fishermen was increasingly matched by demands for protection from foreign fishing activities by coastal fishermen.

The FCMA contains an elaborate mechanism for the regulation of foreign fishing within the new United States ocean fisheries management zone. Title II, Foreign Fishing and International Fishery Agreements, begins with a declaration that after February 28, 1977, no foreign fishing will be allowed within the 200-mile fishery conservation zone without a permit from the United States.

Problems with Foreign Exclusion

Mexico and other nations have in recent years increasingly restricted United States access to fish resources adjacent to their coasts, just as the United States has done in this Act. In some instances the restrictions may have been an effort to increase revenue collections from use of their ocean resources by foreign nations, and in others they represent an effort to protect and develop a strong domestic commercial fishery. One of the problems that has resulted from United States restrictions upon foreign fishing is that foreign nations have also restricted American fishermen. Since other nations face many of the same domestic aspirations and concerns as the United States regarding ocean fisheries, it is difficult to perceive how such actions could be prevented. Nonetheless, Federal fishery management actions may have accelerated or intensified the trend by other nations toward nationalizing offshore fisheries.

The United States has a complex series of interests and relationships with other nations, beyond the concerns of fisheries or the ocean. Japan is a particularly appropriate example. Since the 1930's the United States has been attempting to control Japanese fishing near U.S. shores. Yet Japan is dependent as a nation upon ocean fishing for a significant portion of its national food supply and views with concern the increasing exclusion of its vessels from various fishing grounds. The United States has strong military, economic and political ties with Japan and during the late 1970's has been attempting to establish a major shift in the pattern of trade between the two nations. If the United States restricts the amount of fish protein which Japan can obtain from important fishing grounds such as the Bristol Bay area in Alaska and Georges Bank in the Atlantic Ocean, major problems may result in other vital areas of national interest. Other nations can "retaliate" for being excluded from the 200-mile fishery conservation zone in several ways other than excluding or restricting American fishermen from their coastal waters. For this reason, this aspect of fisheries management, the control of foreign fishing, cannot be treated as an isolated resource management issue and may involve major national strategic and economic considerations.

Co-Ventures

An additional complication in attempting to deal with the foreign policy aspects of fisheries management is a growing practice of many nations, including Japan, of gaining access to United States fish stocks through partnership with American commercial fishermen, either by contracting for their catches, or through co-ownership of vessels and/or processing facilities. Basic questions arise about the long-range implications of foreign ownership of U.S. vessels or facilities, and these issues are only now being considered.

Foreign Registration

When U.S. fishermen find themselves restricted either under the provisions of the FCMA or other Federal ocean programs such as the Marine Mammals Protection Act, they have in some instances shown an inclination to avoid those restrictions by removing themselves from U.S. jurisdiction or changing their regulatory status by registering their vessels under the flags of other nations. This is of particular importance with the American deepwater tuna fleet subjected to increasing restrictions upon incidental catches of porpoise. Under present U.S. law, they can avoid those restrictions by registering their vessels under the flag of Mexico or other nations not subject to American control, but they cannot sell the catch to the U.S. if porpoise kills are involved.

While these are major complexities in Federal efforts to establish and maintain a national fishery management program, they are in some ways secondary to the central purpose of the Act, which is to limit the total amount of fishing allowed, not to determine which fishermen have access to fish stocks.

D. Management of Fishing Versus Management of Ecological Systems: What Needs to be Controlled?

A basic premise of the FCMA is:

> If placed under sound management before *overfishing* has caused irreversible effects, the fisheries can be conserved and maintained so as to provide optimum yields on a continuing basis. (Emphasis added.) (Sec. 2(a)(5))

Starting with this premise, the major thrust of "management" efforts is to control fishing pressure exerted by both American and foreign fishermen. However, there is growing evidence that shellfish and finfish are being seriously affected by other factors. In 1973, swordfish were found to contain sufficient amounts of mercury to warrant concern for public health, and human consumption of swordfish was actively discouraged. In a growing number of cases fishermen have had areas of shellfish production closed to them because of the presence of contaminants in the water.

Such problems suggest that the ability to maintain sustained yields of various fish populations may require water and atmospheric water quality control as much as control over the amount of fishing pressure exerted by fishermen.

1. Chlorine. Chlorine was introduced in the early 1900's for the disinfection of water supplies and has remained an important part of water quality management. However, until recently little consideration was given to possible effects that chlorine might have upon fish and other aquatic organisms, and many industrial and municipal treatment plants have proceeded on the assumption that the more chlorine, the better. Some Federal and state standards require or encourage the use of large amounts of this substance, and it is estimated that more than 5,000 tons are released into coastal and inland waters each year.

Chlorination of water for drinking and of wastewater prior to discharge from treatment plants can result in the formation of halogenated organic compounds which may be toxic to man, and chlorine can be displaced by bromine in salt water, forming harmful brominated hydrocarbons. Research noted by the Environmental Protection Agency reported the following:

> Available data, though limited, indicates that chlorine at concentrations in excess of 0.01 mg/liter poses a serious hazard to marine and estuarine life.[27]

Chlorine at levels commonly contained in treated effluent from power plants, vessels, and sewage outfalls can lead to reproductive failures and respiratory or filtering failures in fish, phytoplankton destruction, and perhaps is in part responsible for a growing number of neoplasms on oysters, clams, and mussels. An EPA task force recently recommended that alternatives to chlorine treatment be vigorously encouraged.

2. Air pollution. Research indicates that in the Great Lakes PCB con-

---

[27] Environmental Protection Agency, *Disinfection of Wastewater: Task Force Report.* EPA-430/9-75-012. March, 1976, p. 3.

tamination of fish results to a significant degree from atmospheric transport of that compound from the land into the water. In a similar fashion, sulfate pollutants released into the atmosphere are increasingly leading to the formation of "acid rain" with a pH as low as 2.1 and 3.0. The Environmental Protection Agency reports that the effects of this acidic precipitation upon aquatic and terrestrial ecosystems are numerous and complex:

> These effects include the elimination of fish populations inhabiting acidified waters and the decline of populations of aquatic invertebrates.[28]

The sulfate pollutants may be transported hundreds or even thousands of kilometers from the original source of emission, and with increased use of fossil fuels and possibly nitrate-containing fertilizers, the acidic conditions "will probably increase."[29] Thus air quality emission standards set by state and Federal Government in areas as far away as the Midwest may seriously affect finfish or shellfish stocks in the Atlantic Ocean. The nation's choices regarding alternative energy policies may likewise determine available fish stocks in the ocean, depending upon the amount of fossil fuel used.

3. Impingement and entrainment. Intake pipes placed in ocean or freshwater areas to obtain water for power plant cooling or other purposes not only draw in water, but also fish, invertebrates, larvae, and juvenile fish. This aquatic life can either be impinged against screen covering the mouth of the intake pipe or entrained in the water drawn through the pipe. The amount of aquatic life lost is now a subject of concern at both the state and Federal level. There are some who suggest that the problem is so severe that new technologies for cooling must be developed to replace those requiring constant water intake.

For problems such as aquatic damage to the northeastern United States induced by the burning of coal to produce power in the Midwest, the tradeoffs involved are technically, politically, and legally difficult to deal with. Given that these are real problems with very real effects upon fisheries, it must be pointed out that they are not presently being considered as part of fisheries management. Under the present policy and institutional arrangements, it may be that optimum yield will, in effect, be determined by the Environmental Protection Agency or the Department of Energy, rather than the Department of Commerce or the Regional Councils.

---

[28] Environmental Protection Agency, *Research Highlights* (June, 1978), p. 23.
[29] *Ibid.*

E. The Purpose of Fisheries Management

The Fishery Conservation and Management Act approaches various species of finfish and shellfish as "resources" that are to be harvested and consumed; a marketable commodity that should be extracted at such a rate so as to allow a sustained "yield." However, the United States has other management programs which treat various forms of ocean life differently. The Marine Mammals Protection Act assumes that it is in the national interest to protect certain species of ocean life. The Endangered Species Act contains as a basic premise that no species of life should be destroyed. There is also an emerging concept of "natural diversity" which would seek to maintain the present diversity of plants and animals, at least for some special protected areas. In combination with the Marine Sanctuaries Program, these national management efforts suggest a concept of living resources management in which the population size and types of ocean life-forms are determined by or strongly influenced by national policy.

Systems versus Species

At the present time each species or "fishery" tends to be treated separately. However, in some instances these individual species are interlinked biologically. And for each target species, there is a complex web of food chains and environmental conditions which will influence how many fish exist at any one time.

If it is, or were to become, national policy to maintain certain species of ocean life, not so that they would be caught and consumed, but to maintain natural ocean systems, fisheries management might require different types of control. For example, international consideration is now being given to Antarctic krill populations in developing a new commercial fishery for that form of ocean life. However, the present abundance of krill is in part the direct result of the destruction or severe diminution of several marine mammal species, including baleen whales and seals. If krill is harvested for human use, it may result in the permanent suppression of the maximum population levels of various forms of ocean life directly or indirectly linked to krill consumption. In a similar fashion, anchovies in California can be harvested and used for both food and nonfood purposes, or anchovies can be managed as forage for various species of fish which function as predators upon anchovies.

In one sense, man is in direct competition with various forms of ocean life, not only for krill and anchovies but also for water, wetlands, migratory routes, or offshore reefs. If the nation decides to protect some forms of ocean life, it will almost certainly require major constraints upon the United States' use of fish stocks, the oceans, adjacent shorelands, and the atmosphere as well. If interest in the ocean is limited to its use as a source for food or products, air quality, water quality, land use and ocean dumping will have to be administered as part of living resources management, if the supply of these living resources is to be maintained or increased.

F. Conclusion

The Deepwater Port Act, the Marine Sanctuaries Act and the Coastal Zone Management Act each recognize the need to exert some type or degree of control over activities that might affect the purpose of that particular management effort. Activities taking place within the safety zone of a deepwater port are to come under the deepwater port regulations. However, vessels simply transiting these zones, for example, are not subject to the regulations of the DWPA. All programs and activities by American citizens within the area of a designated marine sanctuary are to comply with the various regulations for that sanctuary. All Federal, state, and local programs and activities taking place within the coastal zone are to be consistent with the management plan formulated for that zone.

The Fishery Conservation and Management Act does not attempt to control power plants, wetland development, or water quality, all of which can affect finfish or shellfish populations. What it really attempts to control is the activity of fishing, through regulation of who can fish, how often they can fish, what equipment can be used, and how much can be harvested. This is really "fishing" management. If it were fish management or living resources management, then the uses of ocean space, the quality of air and water, and policies regarding marine mammal protection and diversity of life forms would become a direct part of the control system. This review of existing efforts would seem then to indicate that we are still not viewing the ocean and its resource system as a complete problem.

CHAPTER FOUR

ISSUES OF OCEAN MANAGEMENT

I. Introduction

Since the 1930's, a variety of ocean-related national issues have emerged which might be appropriately discussed in a study of national ocean management. This chapter focuses upon four of those issues. They have been chosen because collectively they illustrate the complexities of ocean management and because they appear to be central to any future efforts at ocean control.

The issues discussed include:
- The role of state and local government,
- Considerations of national security,
- The role of private industry, and
- The national interest.

Within the context of this study, discussions of these issues are, of necessity, brief. An effort is made to indicate why these issues are important to management of the ocean, how they have been dealt with in the past, and what their present and/or future relevance to national ocean programs appears to be.

II. The Role of State and Local Government in Ocean Management

A. The Role of the States

The first debate over the role of state governments in the management of ocean space and ocean resources arose over the control of offshore oil in the late 1930's. Just as the Department of State was to argue during that time that Federal declarations of jurisdiction beyond the three-mile territorial sea should intrude on the high seas only in certain cases, so the states argued that Federal interests within the territorial sea should only be expressed on a limited, single-purpose basis, and without an im-

81

pairment of the basic ownership interests and management authorities of the states.

With the passage of the Submerged Lands Act of 1953 an initial resolution of this issue was achieved, but that legislation is both ambiguous and incomplete in its assignment of rights and authorities. Now, with greatly expanded ocean activity taking place in the context of a new governmental regulation and interest in the oceans, the weaknesses of this earlier resolution become more apparent and more important.

B. The Scope of State Interests

The interest of states in the ocean does not stop at the outer edge of the territorial sea, any more than the interests of the Federal government stop at the outer edge of the continental shelf.

States are responsible for the health, safety and general welfare of their citizens. In addition, coastal states are held by Act of Congress to own the submerged lands and resources of the territorial sea. As public trustees of these resources, they have additional responsibilities which grow apace with the increasing value and importance of the ocean. Not only do states have extensive interests in the ocean, but they also have responsibilities over a variety of programs and activities which can have a direct and significant impact upon the ocean. States, in most instances, are administering clean air and water quality programs, park development, licensing of major facilities, approval of sewer and water projects, transportation planning, and environmental review. The state government is the principal entity through which these programs can be linked with ocean programs, and it is a link that has begun to receive increased attention.

1. Outer continental shelf oil and gas development. In the OCS Lands Act of 1953, the interest and importance of coastal states in offshore oil and gas development were not acknowledged. Given the bitter antagonism between state and Federal government, which developed prior to the enactment of the Submerged Lands Act and the OCS Lands Act, and the pressing interest at that time in obtaining a legislative framework for OCS leasing, it is understandable that little attention was given to the broader questions of how offshore oil would be brought to land or what effects outer continental shelf development might have upon the submerged lands and resources of the territorial sea.

In the 1970's, however, when the Federal government attempted to accelerate offshore oil and gas development through increased leasing in "frontier" OCS areas, these questions could no longer be avoided. State governments, in cooperation with local units of government, effectively demonstrated an ability to influence, delay, and in some instances prevent, oil and gas development. Of great significance is that in 1978 Congress modified the Outer Continental Shelf Lands Act to acknowledge the interests of the states in the Federal leasing program and to allow states a considerable degree of participation in the Federal decision process. As early as 1976, when Congress amended the Coastal Zone Management Act, the problems and interests of states in OCS development were being more fully considered. As the result of administrative changes made by the Department of the Interior and legislative changes made in the Coastal Zone Management Act and the Outer Continental Shelf Lands Act, coastal states now have a considerable degree of access to the OCS leasing process. However, there are other areas of Federal ocean activity where the role of the states is either disputed or ill-defined.

2. Dredge spoil disposal. Most coastal states have some form of regulation over the water disposal of dredge spoil. An example is legislation enacted by Massachusetts in 1976[1] in an effort to prevent the U.S. Army Corps of Engineers from establishing a regional dredge spoil disposal site within Massachusetts waters.[2] This law declares that the Massachusetts Department of Environmental Quality Engineering has exclusive authority to issue permits for waste disposal in Massachusetts waters.

However, Federal legislation affecting this activity contains certain language which brings into question whether states can legally regulate ocean disposal of dredge spoil, even within the territorial sea. The Marine Protection, Research and Sanctuaries Act of 1972 assigns permitting authority to the Corps of Engineers, using criteria developed by the Federal Environmental Protection Agency. Sec. 106(d) of the Act states that:

> After the effective date of this title, no State shall adopt or enforce any rule or regulation relating to any activity regulated by this title. . . .

States could certainly argue that they must have authority to regulate such activities in order to protect the resources and submerged lands which Congress has agreed are in state ownership. Furthermore, the Coastal Zone Management Act would seem to encourage state consideration for all coastal water activities and does not specify dredge spoil disposal as something that is not to be considered.

---

[1] Massachusetts General Laws, Chapter 347, Acts of 1976.
[2] See Armstrong and Ryner, pp. 80-81.

However, the CZMA also declares that States must use their existing authority, and the Submerged Lands Act is silent on the regulation of dredge spoil disposal. If Congress did intend to preempt state regulation of this activity, then how does that affect state efforts to undertake comprehensive coastal zone management? The location and manner of disposal of dredge spoil could affect a number of activities within state waters and would seem to be necessary part of coordinated management of the territorial sea.

3. Navigation. There has been a continuing debate between state and Federal governments regarding the degree to which states have or should have authority over the regulation of navigation and marine transportation. The Submerged Lands Act and many U.S. Supreme Court decisions clearly favor Federal control. Perhaps the most recent major case is *Ray v. Atlantic Richfield Company.* Effort by the State of Washington to establish construction, size, operational, and equipment standards for tankers in Puget Sound were in large measure rejected by the Supreme Court, with the additional suggestion that state authority may in the future be further diminished if Congress should enact additional Federal legislation.

The *Port and Waterways Safety Act of 1972* (**P.L.** 92-340) authorizes the establishment of quite comprehensive vessel traffic control systems by the U.S. Coast Guard. While local or state regulations can be utilized as part of these control efforts, the Act contains little recognition of state ocean management interests and programs which might be affected by vessel control programs, nor is there provision for the level of participation by coastal states in the designing of port and waterway management plans as is provided in the Marine Sanctuaries and Deepwater Port Programs. Conflicts have arisen, not only about the degree to which states should be able to participate in such ocean management efforts, but also about the states' ability to establish regulations over the transportation of liquefied natural gas or other hazardous substances.

In many instances there is cooperation in the area of marine transportation, but as a rule the degree to which state and local government can participate in such programs is a matter of choice on the part of the Federal government, and there is no clear national acknowledgment of, or provisions for, an expression of state needs and concerns. As states have attempted to formulate coastal management programs, they have often encountered the attitude that navigation is clearly a Federal concern and that it is up to the state to accommodate Federal interests. An example of this attitude which emerged during the formulation of the

Culebra, Puerto Rico, coastal management program, is found when the Coast Guard indicated its interests in Culebra's coastal zone.

> . . . for all existing and future Coast Guard operations, navigation aids, and communications, we would like to reserve the same rights to *uncontrolled, non-monitored* ingress and egress, by whatever means we deem practical . . . . The [coastal] management plan should *not attempt to regulate* the legitimate exercise of interstate or international maritime activity, an authority specifically reserved for the national government. (Emphasis added.)[3]

When such attitudes prevail on the part of either state or Federal government, it is difficult to conceive of a workable management by partnership of the territorial sea. At issue is not whether the Federal Government has primary responsibility or authority, but how legitimate and necessary interests of both Federal and state government on the same issue can be accommodated. At the present time, there are many areas of Federal ocean activity from which the state is virtually excluded.

4. National security. National security is an additional area in which the Federal Government has clear responsibility and authority, but it is one in which important interests and concerns of states have often gone unrecognized. On the other hand, national security has not always been understood or supported by the states.

The discussion of national security included in this chapter details some of the legislative provisions which attempt to ensure that national security interests have priority over all other ocean concerns. Traditionally, military use of the oceans has been the largest element of Federal ocean activity, in terms of organization, research, and expenditures, and it remains a critical national interest. Yet many coastal states have been largely unfamiliar with national security interest in their coastal management zones; and, in what must be deemed a failure on the part of both the Navy and the State of Washington, the first coastal program for that State was strongly objected to by the Navy, because U.S. Navy interests had not really been considered.

> . . . the Navy has interests in 32 separate geographical areas in Washington's coastal zone. These areas include installations, shipyards . . . mooring piers . . . combat maneuver and general operating areas, [and] gunnery ranges and testing areas. . . . Some prominent installations [include] the Trident Submarine Base, where $75 million of new construc-

---

[3] *Supra.*, Chapter Three Footnote 18.

tion is taking place. Further, the headquarters of the 13th Naval District is in Seattle. Yet Washington [state] did not contact the Navy until after the State submitted its [coastal management] program to NOAA.[4]

If states have been insensitive to national security needs, the same lack of sensitivity seems to exist at the Federal level where it often is perceived that the role of state governments in national security use of the ocean is to accommodate whatever the national government claims to be necessary. Consider the following Navy document excerpt:

> Regardless of the legislative jurisdictional status of the property involved, the United States may exercise in all places whatever jurisdiction is essential to the performance of its constitutional functions *without interference from any sources.*
>
> Thus no state may exercise any authority which would in any way interfere with or restrict the United States in the use of its property or obstruct it in the exercise of any of the powers which the states have relinquished to the United States under the Constitution. One of the powers expressly surrendered by the States under the Constitution is the power to provide and maintain a Navy. It follows that enforcement of a state law may not be permitted to interfere with any authorized naval functions.[5] (Emphasis added.)

C. The Role of Local Government in Ocean Management

If the authority of states is unclear and constrained, the authority and opportunity for local units of government in national ocean management programs is almost non-existent. With the important exception of the Coastal Zone Management Act amendments of 1976, most ocean programs and policies pay little attention to local government.

"Local" government includes a wide variety of governmental structures, from that of villages with 100 people to that of San Bernardino County, California, which is larger than several foreign nations. Every citizen lives with a local unit of government, and major ports, offshore pipeline landfalls, naval bases, power plants, and coastal access sites are located in the jurisdiction of local governments. Local government is particularly important as the focal point of most land management; the responsibilities for zoning and planning and the provision of basic public service are most often at this level of government. For offshore management to be successful and to protect local units of government from un-

---

[4] General Accounting Office, *The Coastal Zone Management Program* (Washington, D.C., 1976), p. 58.

[5] Naval Facilities Engineering Command, Department of Defense, *Naval District Washington Coastal Land Use Study, Part I* (July, 1976).

due impacts, there must be better coordination between local and off-shore planning and management.

As an example of the problem, the Coast Guard is in the process of upgrading its vessel traffic control system for the New York Harbor area. Part of this control system involves the installation of large microwave towers. In the spring of 1978, the City of New York, at least temporarily, blocked their installation over fears that the microwave radiation emanating from these towers might constitute a health hazard to city residents. Similarly, local and state governments were able to obtain an initial order against offshore leasing in the Baltimore Canyon area in 1977 when they declared that they would refuse to allow pipelines to enter into their areas of jurisdiction, and a Federal judge declared the OCS leasing environmental impact statement inadequate because it had failed to consider that possibility.

1. Coastal zone management. When the Nation adopted a national goal of energy independence (Project Independence), it became increasingly evident that local units of government should receive attention in relation to ocean management programs. In 1976, Congress amended the Coastal Zone Management Act to recognize a strong role for local units of government in national ocean programs.

Section 306(c)(2)(B), CZMA, 1976 Amendments

(i) [The State] management agency is required, before implementing any management program decision which would conflict with any local zoning ordinance, decision, or other action, to send a notice of such management program decision to any local government whose zoning authority is affected thereby.

(ii) Any such notice shall provide that such local government may, within the 30-day period commencing the date of receipt of such notice, submit to the management agency written comments on such management program decision, and any recommendation for alternatives thereto, if no action is taken during such period which would conflict or interfere with such management program decision, unless such local government waives its right to comment.

(iii) Such management agency, if any such comments are submitted to it, with such 30-day period, by any local government—
   (I) is required to consider any such comments,
   (II) is authorized, in its discretion, to hold a public hearing on such comment, and
   (III) may not take any action within such 30-day period to implement the management program decision, whether or not modified on the basis of such comments.

These provisions augment what are already fairly extensive requirements contained in Section 306(c)(1) and 306(c)(2)(A) and (B). For example, the latter requires that prior to approval a state program must be found to have

> coordinated its programs with local, areawide, and interstate plans applicable to areas within the coastal zone . . . which plans have been developed by a local government, an areawide agency designated pursuant to regulations established under Section 204 of the Demonstration Cities and Metropolitan Development Act of 1966, a regional agency, or an interstate agency; and
>
> established an effective mechanism for continuing consultation and coordination between the management agency designated pursuant to paragraph (5) of this subsection and with local governments . . . and agencies in carrying out the purpose of this chapter; . . . .

This is a somewhat unusual provision for any Federal legislation and reflects as much a pragmatic recognition of the political and legal power of local government as any philosophical support for their interests. In fact, there is often a Federal distrust, if not hostility, toward local government, and the Coastal Zone Management Act is premised in large part upon the alleged inadequacies of local institutional arrangements for planning and regulation (Section 302(g)), and a belief that local government has a tendency to advance parochial interests over those of the nation (Section 306(c)(8)).

Few states have yet to develop a workable system for achieving the objectives established in the 1976 CMZA amendments, and many local units of government remain unaware either of the degree to which state coastal planning may impact their interests or of the opportunity which the 1976 amendments provide them. But the measure of the effect of these provisions will come after several states have actual experience in administering coastal management programs. In the meantime, local government remains largely apart from other national ocean management programs and is either opposed or insensitive to state or national projects.

D. Cooperative Management

Given the fact that the shore and various components of the ocean are under the control of multiple authorities, cooperative management is very reasonable. In the Coastal Zone Management Act and in the 1978 amendments to the Outer Continental Shelf Lands Act, a cooperative approach to ocean management is suggested. There seems to be a move in this direction, and legislation, such as the Deepwater Port Act, provides additional evidence that both state and Federal Government are more aware of the need for coordination and cooperation.

However, many times this cooperation does not take place, and it is even resisted. There remains a tendency to resort to assertions of jurisdictional authority, which in most instances are not relevant. While the presumption within the Federal courts may be in favor of the Federal government, there comes a point at which the most basic of local and State rights and authorities require some degree of recognition and accommodation by the Federal government, no matter what the determined distribution of "authority."

E. Limits to Development

As more coastal areas become extensively developed and subject to comprehensive planning, such as under the Coastal Zone Management Act and the Clean Air Act, there are going to be increasing difficulties in finding any acceptable coastal site for large-scale development, particularly energy development. At times, project sponsors, faced with opposition at the state or local level, have charged these units of government with being selfish or failing to understand that a national interest is involved. In the growing frustration, proposals appear from time to time for making the accommodation of major facilities mandatory, although it is not clear how that could be done.

In some instances, local or state resistance may be based upon the lack of sensitivity to regional or national interests. But often at issue, instead, is the future of the local community or the state. It is at the local level where the "costs" of accommodating coastal development must be absorbed, and in a growing number of instances, as coastal and ocean areas have become more developed and water and air quality standards more stringent, these costs are perceived as being too high to be acceptable. Programs such as the Coastal Energy Impact Program, devised by Congress in 1976, may make some states or local units of government more interested in accommodating energy-related development. But quality of life is sometimes a non-negotiable commodity. If wetlands and water quality are to be protected, if recreation, fishing, aquaculture and residential development are to take place in coastal areas, and if national standards for air and water quality are to be attained, then, in time, there will be no room for large power plants, refineries, chemical plants, or other major facilities in coastal areas. This is already a national problem, and, unless some resolution can be achieved, it will eventually become a crisis. But a solution, if there is one, will require moving beyond a historical conflict among all three levels of government.

F. Conclusions

With the passage of the Submerged Lands Act the role of state and local government in ocean management may have been considered resolved. Yet problems remain. Local and state governments receive literally billions of dollars in federal assistance each year, and, in many instances, the expenditure of those funds can have major impact upon shore and ocean resources and activities. And other billions of dollars are spent each year directly by the Federal government in ocean programs and activities, often uncoordinated with, often unaware of, the programs of local and state government that might complement or conflict with Federal ocean management efforts. Federal agencies have found some programs often obstructed by proposed state coastal management programs, and states have encountered resistance to coordination in coastal management. Local government units, as of 1978, remain largely unrecognized and uninvolved in ocean programs, while being affected by and affecting them.

The role of local and state government requires increased attention. International Law of the Sea negotiations are considering the concept of a 12-mile territorial sea and of a 200-mile national ocean economic zone. What responsibilities, interests, and authorities will or should coastal states and local governments have within this larger territorial sea? And what should be the authority and responsibility of states beyond the coastal zone; inland states may wish to benefit from offshore revenues and may, directly or indirectly, generate pollution or be responsible for other negative impact upon the ocean environment. Will inland states seeking Federal funds for solar energy development oppose federal support for offshore ocean energy systems in territorial waters?

Clarification of existing statutes is also needed. Are states prohibited from regulating the disposal of dredge spoil? If so, why? To what degree will state coastal management programs be able to control, or not control, this and other Federal programs, such as navigation? What is the intent and significance of Sections 2(e) and 3(d) of the Submerged Lands Act regarding "water power"; or "the use of water for the production of power"? Does this mean that state coastal management programs or other state management efforts will not be able to manage ocean energy systems such as Ocean Thermal Energy Conversion (OTEC).

Chapter Two of this report presented in some detail the difficult process, lasting at least 15 years, by which the United States established its first legislative articulation of the distribution of authority over the ocean and its resources. As was pointed out in that section, the focus of debate was upon oil and gas. Concepts of large scale ocean thermal energy conversion (OTEC), microwave harbor traffic control systems, massive supertanker oil spills, mariculture, weather modification, missile test ranges, marine sanctuaries, and floating nuclear power plants offshore were not foremost in the mind of those who resolved the issue of who should control what.

It is not clear now how authority and responsibility among Federal, state and local government should be allocated. Resolution of this issue requires, in part, a better understanding of how the ocean, as well as the adjacent land, will be used in the future, followed by a determination of the kinds of linkage or fit that will be needed between the two areas. This need for cooperation in this matter by all levels of government is relatively new. The Coastal Zone Management Act concept of a cooperative management effort based upon existing authorities may not work, but it is too soon to really know. Nonetheless, the present problems and pending decisions alluded to in this discussion suggest that it is both appropriate and necessary to specify the role of state and local government in much greater detail.

III. National Security and Ocean Management

A. Introduction

At least until the 1970's, United States ocean programs have been associated largely with national security, whether measured by annual expenditures or by sea power capabilities.[6] The U.S. Department of the Navy, Department of Defense, and associated intelligence organizations are virtually interested in worldwide ocean use for purposes of national defense and intelligence. This includes a major worldwide network of satellites, underwater detection systems, planes, vessels, weapons, communication networks, command systems, personnel, advanced research, strategies and policies. We would think that structures and activities taking place above, on, or beneath the ocean within several hundred miles of the United States coast are monitored, as part of a worldwide ocean information effort.

For many years such efforts have probably operated unhampered by competing domestic or international policies or programs and by the absence of competing activities. When coordination has been necessary with other nations, private industry, or various units of government, it

---

[6] Edward Wenk, *The Politics of the Ocean* (Seattle: University of Washington Press, 1972).

has been done informally, and most conflicts were quietly resolved through appropriate negotiations.

But times are rapidly changing. The seabed beneath the high seas may come under the management control of a formal international seabed regime. How ocean space and ocean resources are used, both in U.S. coastal waters and elsewhere, is being determined more and more through complex and formal national and international management programs. The ability to locate national security facilities or operations within the relative obscurity of ocean space is rapidly diminishing, and the ability to navigate at high speeds on or beneath the ocean's surface is becoming more difficult as ocean development increases. Further, those developments may become an additional defense burden, requiring physical protection and defense strategies.

At the present time there is a tacitly accepted policy that U.S. security interests will have priority over all other national ocean interests and programs. If this policy is to be maintained in the presence of growing numbers of state and Federal ocean management programs and policies, it will require complex and formal conflict resolution and siting procedures. The substantive context of "national security" interests may also be subjected to increasing scrutiny as other public and private interests are displaced in its name. The basic premise that national security interests should have priority over ocean space and resources may also be subject to increased challenges. Thus, it is important that this subject be included as an integral element of any discussion on ocean management.

B. Legislative Considerations for National Security Interests

The Department of the Navy was a strong advocate for Federal imposition of authority over offshore oil and gas resources during the 1930's, so that the Navy might obtain additional fuel supplies for its vessels. Measures introduced in Congress in 1938 and 1939 reflected this:

> . . . the conservation of petroleum deposits underlying submerged lands adjacent to and along the coast of the state of California, below lowwater mark and under the territorial waters of the United States of America is hereby declared to be essential for national defense, maintenance of the Navy, and regulation and protection of interstate and foreign commerce, and that in the exercise of the paramount and exclusive powers of the United States for these purposes, there are hereby reserved and set aside as a *naval petroleum reserve* any and all such deposits. (Emphasis added.)[7]

---

[7] Bartley, pp. 109-110.

Thus, the Navy attempted to gain control of all oil and gas in the beyond the territorial sea as a fuel reserve. At Senate hearings on this legislation, the Navy Judge Advocate General's Office went so far as to suggest that the President, using certain war powers,[8] could establish a *defense sea area* including all submerged oil fields and then issue regulations which would stop commercial drilling operations.[9]

Throughout the 1940's and 1950's, there was an ongoing dispute between the Department of the Interior and the Department of the Navy regarding national ocean management. The Navy supported the Department of State in opposing Interior's attempts to establish a 150-mile Federal ocean management regime continued to argue for Naval rather than commercial utilization of offshore oil deposits.

As related in Chapter Two, the Navy did briefly gain control of offshore oil from the Department of the Interior in 1953. Motivated by strong feelings about Federal versus State rights and perhaps by political animosity towards newly elected Dwight Eisenhower, President Truman issued Executive Order No. 10426 four days before leaving office. In this order, all submerged lands of the continental shelf, *including* those of the territorial sea, were declared to be administered by the Secretary of the Navy.[10]

1. Outer Continental Shelf Lands Act. When Congress enacted the OCS Lands Act of 1953, a special section was added to rescind Truman's action.

> Executive Order Number 10426, dated January 16, 1952, entitled 'Setting Aside Submerged Lands of the Continental Shelf as a Naval Petroleum Reserve' is hereby revoked.

But Congress recognized that important national security interests were associated with management of the outer continental shelf, and certain provisions were included in the OCS Lands Act to protect those interests:

> Section 12(a) The President has the authority to withdraw any unleased lands from the leasing process.
> Section 12(b) During time of war or when the President prescribes, the Federal Government has first claim at market prices to any minerals produced from the outer continental shelf.

---

[8] 40 Stat. 250, Section 8 (August 8, 1917).

[9] Bartley, p. 119.

[10] Nossaman, Waters, et al., *Study of Outer Continental Shelf Lands of the United States,* Volume II (Los Angeles: Public Land Law Review Commission, 1969), pp. 171-173.

> Section 12(c) During war or national emergency any leases can be suspended.
>
> Section 12(d) The United States reserves and retains the right to designate by and through the Secretary of Defense, with the approval of the President, as areas restricted from exploration and operation parts of the outer continental shelf needed for nation defense; and so long as such designation remains in effect, no exploration or operations may be conducted on any part of the surface of such area except with the concurrence of the Secretary of Defense. . . .
>
> Section 12(e) All uranium, thorium and other materials which are peculiarly essential to the production of fissionable material contained in the subsoil or seabed of the outer continental shelf are reserved for the use of the United States.
>
> Section 12(f) The United States reserves and retains ownership of and the right to extract all helium contained in gas obtained from the outer continental shelf.

These provisions allow the President and the Secretary of Defense to determine which areas of the outer continental shelf shall be available for commercial oil leasing, and which areas will be reserved for national defense activities and interests. It also assures Federal access to and control over all materials which might be useful for nuclear weapons and atomic power.

2. Engle Act. By 1958, Congress felt compelled to diminish the national security provisions of the Outer Continental Shelf Lands Act and enacted the Engle Act.[11] This law requires an act of Congress for the withdrawal of more than 5,000 acres in the aggregate for any one defense project or facility of the Department of Defense. The Act also requires that, in requesting approval for a withdrawal of more than 5,000 acres, the Department of Defense state the purpose or purposes for which the area is proposed to be withdrawn, reserved or restricted, or, if the purpose or purposes are classified for national security reasons, a statement that is an indication

> whether, and if so to what extent, the proposed use will affect continuing full operation of the public land laws and federal regulations relating to conservation, utilization, and development of mineral resources. . . . (Sec. 3(7))

a. Problems. The Department of Defense and other national security organizations have and do use the domestic and international oceans for a

---

[11] 72 Stat. 27 (1958), P.L. 85-337.

variety of purposes, some of which are highly classified and politically sensitive. It has been claimed by some that there is a need to provide evaluation of such activities and to have substantive review of the military uses. Yet the Engle formulation appears on its face to be unsatisfactory. If there is a highly sensitive national security interest, a public declaration to that effect will probably compromise it, even if the exact nature of the interest is not specified. So, it is not a workable system. Furthermore, in those instances when the Department of Defense has submitted legislative proposals for withdrawal, Congress has been reluctant to act upon them. As of 1969, none had been approved.[12]

b. Policy change. In 1965, the Senate Committee on Interior and Insular Affairs considered several bills submitted under the Engle Act and received a suggestion from Interior that the Secretary should have a greater consultative role in the withdrawal process. The Senate Committee requests that DOD confer with the non-military interests involved in the proposed area and attempt to work out an agreement that would be mutually satisfactory to the government and private industry. Subsequent to that directive DOD withdrew its legislative proposals and worked out an informal process with the Department of the Interior.[13]

c. Present situation. There is still no formal mechanism for sorting out DOD interests in the OCS leasing process, and the Engle Act is, more often than not, ignored with the knowledge of Congress. The process is informal, not subject to formal public scrutiny. Ad hoc negotiations between the Department of Defense and the Bureau of Land Management (BLM) can result in the withdrawal of hundred of thousands of acres from lease sales. The criteria used in such decisions are not visible, nor have they been developed through any kind of formal public policy process. Significant tradeoffs are involved, and BLM is placed in the position of evaluating national security claims and the national interests involved in acceding to or rejecting DOD requests.

3. The Coastal Zone Management Act. Virtually all major Federal ocean programs contain a provision which ensures a consideration of national security interests. While these provisions may normally be of little public interest or concern, they constitute a national policy of giving priority to national security interests over all others. The Coastal Zone Management Act is quite explicit on this point. Section 307(c)(3)(A) stipulates that Federal licenses or permits can be issued by a Federal agency, even if it would be inconsistent with a state's management pro-

---

[12] *Study of Outer Continental Shelf Lands,* p. 254.
[13] *Ibid.,* pp. 326-327.

gram, provided the Secretary of Commerce finds that the activity is "necessary in the interest of national security." Section 307(c)(3)(B) and Section 307(d) contain similar override provisions, allowing the Secretary of Commerce to bypass state coastal management programs for certain purposes, if it is determined to be "necessary in the interest of national security."

One of the potential issues associated with this type of provision is that "national security" is not clearly defined and could conceivably be applied to a variety of activities or proposals.

C. National Security Policy Formulation

National security involves more than strictly military interests. Depending upon how one defines "national security" it involves intelligence functions, military functions, and perhaps several more areas of national interest such as:

- Sufficient merchant marine capacity to ensure transport of goods into the United States and from the United States to allies;
- A secure supply of all materials upon which we are dependent, such as various minerals;
- A secure supply of fuel in the form of oil, coal, nuclear material, etc.,
- Anti-terrorist capabilities.

Much of the present structure of national security management is classified. In fact, one can assume that various procedures related to national security uses of the ocean are covered by classified executive orders or other means. But it is clear that this process is complex and not totally unified. There does appear to be conflict, overlap, and problems with communication and coordination. Even within the Department of Defense there occasionally appear interservice rivalries over the use of ocean space and other ocean-related matters. As a result when Interior is "informally" requested to withdraw lands for national security purposes, those purposes may be withheld from other members of the "national security" community. In theory the Department of Defense structure and the National Security Council, along with the newly reorganized intelligence network, can achieve a rational process for policy formation and program coordination, but it is not clear that this has yet been achieved. A structured ocean policy and program which identifies national security interests and then coordinates these with domestic programs would help achieve some degree of consistency and long-range cooperation.

D. Security Classification

A serious difficulty in evaluating or coordinating national ocean programs is the continued classification of both present and historic documents, policies, activities, and decisions procedures. Beyond that difficulty is a basic conflict between the need to restrict access to national security information and the need for public understanding of and participation in national programs affecting the ocean.

1. Ocean management information. United States military and intelligence agencies may have an extensive inventory of information on the ocean and its resources, and a multi-billion dollar system for the collection and evaluation of additional information. Domestic ocean management programs are now being established, such as the regulation of ocean dumping; control of commercial fishing activities; and vessel traffic control systems; new, expensive, and relatively sophisticated inventory, monitoring and communications systems, which will not begin to duplicate the systems which the nation may have already established for national security purposes. This situation gives rise to the following two problems.

a. Avoidance of duplication. It may be asked with growing frequency whether or not the information and equipment developed for national security purposes cannot be made available, at least partially, for domestic ocean management purposes. The Department of Defense will, of course, argue that its systems must remain classified and must be dedicated to military use at all times, if military missions are to be fulfilled. In many instances, the defense and intelligence agencies have provided compelling arguments for the necessity of separate domestic and national security systems. But if domestic ocean management efforts continue to expand, and the cost of necessary information and control systems increases, this issue may receive additional attention.

b. Protection of necessary security. Systems developed to discover submerged deposits of oil or minerals can also be used to locate submarines. Satellites used to monitor sea conditions and merchant vessel traffic would also be used for the identification of military targets and the gathering of intelligence information. Extensive biological, geological, and chemical information on coastal waters could be used by hostile forces. Detailed inventories of ocean activities could identify military or intelligence installations or activities.

The United States has often suppressed or delayed the utilization of advanced optics and sensors in its domestic remote sensing satellites as one means of dealing with this problem, and the sale of certain computers and oil exploration equipment to particular nations has likewise been discouraged. But the problem is likely to become increasingly difficult, especially in ocean management, as domestic control programs begin to require sophisticated information in order to achieve their goals.

2. National ocean policy and decision procedure. Security classification of Department of State and Department of Defense programs, policies, and activities makes it difficult to achieve coordination of national programs and objectives. Because so much of this type of information is classified, there is a possibility that much of the usual public decision process will be consistently bypassed. While many members of Congress and administrators within Federal agencies have security clearances, that by no means assures that they have access to classified information. It creates a situation in which the general public is asked to accept the good judgment of the National Security Council and other decision groups without having any means of fully understanding the decisions that are being made and the tradeoffs involved.

Once it may have been relatively easy to establish a clear distinction between domestic and national security interests. But as both public and private ocean activities increase, this distinction will be more and more difficult to sustain. Some method for allowing an interface of domestic and national security interests in ocean management programs will become increasingly important, and it may require something more workable than the Engle Act, and something more accessible than the National Security Council and associated decision groups. Such a mechanism will be necessary, not only to provide increased information and assistance to domestic ocean management programs, but also to ensure the continued protection of necessary national security secrecy.

E. Additional National Security Considerations

- Terrorism, vandalism and criminal extortion: As ocean development occurs, problems of this type will probably emerge. Who should have authority and responsibility to deal with them? Private ocean users? The Coast Guard? State police? The Navy? Some special force or group?
- Military capabilities: The Navy and other national security organizations have equipment, research results, technical skills,

management networks, and considerable experience in a wide variety of ocean-related areas. Is it possible to transfer some of this information to coastal states, private industry, other Federal agencies, or other nations? Can military equipment be used for non-military purposes? Can military personnel be used on U.S. soil for enforcement?

- Communications: As private and public use of oceans increases, important national security communication networks may be disrupted either electronically or physically. Dedication of special ocean-related frequencies may be important. DOD is investigating new communications technologies which will expose ocean systems and ocean users to new forms of electromagnetic radiation. What are the biological and political implications?

- Facilities: National security projects will increasingly face the same problem as oil companies, electric utilities, and others who wish to place large facilities within the coastal zone or the oceans beyond. The Coast Guard has experienced opposition to the placement of microwave towers in New York City as part of its New York Harbor vessel traffic control system. The Navy has experienced strong opposition in the Midwest to the construction of an extremely low frequency (ELF) antenna system. DOD must find locations to bring ashore connections to its underwater detection networks. Local governments and coastal states are in many instances questioning traditional national security uses of coastal lands and waters, as well as the authority of DOD to utilize special operation areas in ocean space. And yet in many instances the accommodation of facilities is vital to the operation of various national security programs.

- Military ocean dumping: In many parts of the ocean, there are unexploded shells, mines and bombs, radioactive wastes and probably other hazardous materials resulting from military activities. They represent a hazard and obstacle to increased use. Yet they are not accurately mapped or inventoried, and the cost of proper mapping or removal is unknown; it probably would cost millions of dollars. Aside from costs, removal may not be technically possible or environmentally acceptable. Given the wide variety of materials and systems with which the military has been involved at various times, it is not even clear just what has been dumped.

Given hazardous materials such as nerve gas and agent orange, as well as nuclear waste and biological weapons, there remains the issue of how to dispose of them. Special incinerating ships at sea may be one answer, but as ocean use and management increases, alternatives may be required.

F. Conflict Resolution

An issue which may require additional consideration is how to resolve conflicts between specific national security activities and other national interests in the utilization of ocean space and ocean resources. The Marine Protection, Research and Sanctuaries Act, the Deepwater Port Act, The Submerged Lands Act and The Coastal Zone Management Act each contain language regarding national security or defense considerations. Yet there is no clear conflict resolution mechanism should a major disagreement arise. One can assume that the President and/or National Security Council would intervene, but it is not clear that this should always be the process, nor is the criteria by which final decisions should be made.

G. The Establishment of a National Ocean Management Program

Since the 1930's the Navy has argued that it is counter to the national interest to have a national management program that extends beyond the territorial sea. This position is promoted by concern about departmental turf and by serious concerns that such programs might encourage other Nations to establish similar programs, thereby constraining U.S. national security operations. Is the Navy correct? If it is correct, then any new national ocean management effort must consider how various national ocean related interests can be met within the context of international constraints. This subject is discussed in later sections.

H. Conclusions

National security interests have played a key role in the formation of national ocean policies and programs, and national security ocean activities still represent the single largest national ocean-related expenditure. Yet these interests change dramatically over time. The national security structure has been reorganized, most recently the intelligence community. The future role of the Navy in national security is being debated, and the resolution of this debate could have profound effect upon the role of the Navy in national ocean management programs and policies.

Military and intelligence uses of ocean space and resources and their impacts on national ocean programs and policies are significant and may become more important in the future. It appears an appropriate time to evaluate fully present needs, conflicts, mechanisms, and opportunities involving the role of national security in national ocean management. This brief discussion has only touched upon some of the many important issues involved. Such an evaluation may, of necessity, have to take place beyond the context of ocean management, but any national ocean management formulation should include a national security component, somehow dealing with these and additional issues.

IV. Private Industry and Federal Ocean Control

During the 1930's and 1940's, The Department of the Navy argued that offshore deposits of oil should be held in reserve for naval use and not be made available for private commercial purposes. During the 1970's many commercial fishermen have expressed the view that the Federal Government should not be so extensively involved in the regulation of fishing, telling fishermen how often they can fish, what gear they can use, or what they can catch. There are two aspects to this issue: one is the degree to which government should attempt to control private use of the ocean, and the other is how private enterprise should be granted access to the public resources of the ocean as well as the extent of that access. An associated matter, although having less to do with control or management, is whether Federal assistance should be provided to private enterprise in its use of ocean space and resources, and if assistance is provided, who should pay for it.

A. Industry's View

When the Stratton Commission considered these questions as part of its study of national ocean programs and interests it determined from industrial sources that private industry desired certain types of government assistance, primarily in form of basic services, clarification of legal regimes, the provision of pre-investment reconnaissance surveys and support and financial support or development of basic technology.[14] The Commission went so far as to develop a list of the appropriate actions of the Federal Government relative to the ocean, from the private sector point of view:

- establish and enunciate national policies and objectives concerning U.S. marine interests;

---

[14] *Our Nation and the Sea*, p. 158.

- assist in planning for optimum use of limited public resources, including the resolution of conflicts among users of the sea which cannot otherwise be adjudicated;
- adopt regulatory policies which will not discourage private investment;
- provide special incentives to encourage certain embryonic marine industries, if it is in the national interest;
- undertake and improve the description and prediction of the marine environment and assess possibilities of modifying it beneficially;
- initiate, support, and encourage marine education and training programs;
- protect life and property at sea;
- sponsor programs to obtain basic information for industry's subsequent delineation and development of marine resources.[15]

Those proposals appear to be consistent with many of the interests or opinions of the ocean industry today, and they also reflect the content of many present Federal ocean programs.

1. Establishing management regimes. Large-scale development or major financial investment requires well thought out objectives, policies and regulatory framework within which investment decisions can be made. During the mid- and late-1970's, the ocean mining industry has argued that national ocean mining legislation is necessary, if the development of new technologies and mineral resources is to take place. There is a reluctance to invest money or equipment in the deep seabeds without some clear understanding of what rules and regulations will apply. This was the reason, in part, for the Deepwater Port Act and was, to a large extent, behind the passage of the Submerged Lands Act and the Outer Continental Shelf Lands Act in 1953. It was not until after the territorial sea and OCS lands jurisdictional dispute had been resolved that full-scale offshore oil development and other coastal activities could take place with any sense of investment security.

Industry at times appears to have supported government regulation in an effort to overcome resistance to private projects. At the present time, the oil industry is arguing that there is a national interest in both onshore and offshore energy development and that state coastal management programs should to some degree accommodate necessary energy-related facilities and activities.[16] (Also see the discussion of national

---

[15] *Ibid.*

[16] Interviews with staff of American Petroleum Institute, June 1978, plus API letter to William Harsch, Executive Office of the President, dated February 16, 1978.

interest in this chapter.) If private industry can get its interests equated with those of the nation, then formidable Federal or state governmental authorities can assist. However, while industry in some instances desires governmental regulation or assistance, there is also frequent opposition to government constraint of private activities or active government development of public resources.

2. Federal development of resources. Industry has often supported financial assistance for the development of new technology which would allow increased development of ocean resources. But private industry tends to oppose direct government development of those resources. At various times proposals have been made to have the Federal Government undertake either exploratory drilling for or actual production of offshore oil supplies. The petroleum industry has argued against this, declaring that, while the Federal government has a right to control how offshore oil and gas are developed through a leasing/regulatory process, the actual development of those resources should be left to the private sector. And that is the system which has prevailed, with government tending to supply support, protection, policy and regulation, and the private sector undertaking the actual development.

B. Information

A major problem relating to government/industry participation in ocean development is that for resources such as offshore oil and gas, private industry holds most of the available information as to resource supply and techniques for development. The problem develops when the Federal Government attempts to exert control over how these resources are developed. Although the situation has greatly improved, it would appear that the Federal Government still must rely to a very great extent upon private industry to know what areas are promising for oil development. Therefore, since the public does not know what resources it has, it cannot properly manage them or know what its best interests are. Furthermore, because this type of information is privately developed, it is often kept, quite understandably, by the private sector to protect patent rights and to maintain a competitive advantage. The problem is not dissimilar to that of classified information discussed previously.

In addition, if Federal ocean control programs increase in number and scope as they have during the last ten years, we can expect demands for more information and proposals to establish complex and expensive public ocean information systems. A question which warrants careful consideration relative to such systems is the degree to which the private sector could provide it, without the need for major public expenditures.

1. Who pays? The Federal Government maintains extensive and expensive ocean services, including vessel traffic control systems for major harbors, search and rescue, and dredging of navigational channels. There is Federally provided weather information, considerable financial and technical assistance, and other services to ocean users. Some of these programs are at least nominally self-supporting, such as some financial assistance program for the fishing industry. But there are many other services which clearly are not paid for by those members of the private sector who benefit directly from them. The rationale for public programs which are not paid for by a user group is usually that the benefits of the program are so widespread as to be considered to benefit the general public, and thus warrant public financial support. In other instances there is a cooperative agreement in which the Federal Government provides certain services but receives information from ocean users in return. This presently applies in some degree to national security, weather, charts, other information programs.

C. Financial Assistance

During the 1960's, there was a particularly strong push by industry for major Federal expenditures for new research and development. There was considerable discussion of a "wet NASA" approach to the ocean, with industry providing equipment and the Federal Government providing research and development money. However, it was argued then, and still is, that domestic industry, to be competitive with foreign industries, should do most of its own research and development and not rely on government.

Yet, other nations provide financial assistance, especially to the fishing industry and the opposing argument is that, unless the United States provides a similar level of financial support, U.S. industry will not be able to remain competitive. It remains a complex issue involving not only the appropriate relationship between the public and private sector, but also political and economic considerations related to the balance of trade.

D. A Merging of Public and Private Interests

For the fishing industry, the Federal Government provides a variety of financial and other types of assistance, including the funding of research, technical assistance and regulatory protection from the U.S. Fish and Wildlife Service and the National Marine Fisheries Service; vessel construction assistance; hatchery research and production; regulation of foreign vessels (thus creating a monopoly); marketing assistance from market surveys of customer preference to the development and testing of new seafood products; and operation of the Sea Grant marine advisory services.

These forms of assistance blur the distinction between private and public market economics and again raise the question as to the appropriate relationship between the public and private sector. Through several legislative statements of policy, Congress has declared that ocean fishing (and many other ocean activities) are in the national interest, as a material contribution to our economy, as an important source of employment, and as the source of essential materials.

One of the results of public assistance is sometimes a higher public cost for goods and services.

> . . . when government programs serve to enhance demand on *established* fish products, the programs have the effect . . . of typically increasing prices and profits. Thus, it is the consumer that pays, through taxes, for a program that raises consumer prices.[17]

But when it works properly, financial assistance can also assure a broader supply base leading to a stabilizing effect on prices; it can lead to a more secure supply, and may encourage greater efficiency and conservation leading perhaps to a lowering of prices. The interest and capabilities of individual ocean users may not match public needs or interests, and government assistance can be used as a form of management, as a method of public intervention in the private market to influence industry towards areas of public interest. It is estimated that at the present time the United States spends in excess of $2 billion per year on ocean programs. Whether those programs are in the form of assistance or prohibitive regulation, the question of where the money will come from to pay for these programs will continue to grow in importance.

E. Regulation and Delay

The time, expense, and complexity of Federal regulations are of growing concern to industry. As with most of the issues mentioned, these

---

[17] B.J. Rothchild, *A Policy Framework for Fishery Management* (unpublished manuscript. Department of Commerce, 1978), p. 131.

problems are not confined to ocean management programs. But coastal and ocean rules, procedures, standards, and regulations are expanding, and they are, in many instances, complex. Within the territorial sea, basic procedures or standards may radically differ from one state to the next. Federal programs are administered quite differently from region to region. Partially in response to state and Federal requirements, local government is also increasingly involved in various regulatory programs, adding further complexity.

As Federal control of ocean space, resources, and activities expands, it can be increasingly difficult to work through the control process. The permit process for obtaining government approval to construct a liquefied natural gas terminal at Cove Point, Maryland, extended over a period of 49 months. The details of this example can be seen in a report on liquefied natural gas by the Office of Technology Assessment and provide an interesting insight into the complexity of at least one marine development problem of the type mentioned here.[18] At issue in some instances is whether the public interest is really being served by imposing such long delays upon both public and private projects. However, as more controls are applied, as more public interests are identified, it is difficult to avoid this situation.

F. Conclusion

Both Federal and state governments are charged with a public trust to ensure that the ocean is managed in the public interest. This public trust would appear at times to come into conflict with private industry interests in using coastal or ocean resources for private purposes, even though the private activities are often aimed at satisfying a public demand. The number of controls imposed upon ocean users can be expected to increase. To the degree that the nation still desires to allow or encourage ocean development, it will probably be legally, economically, politically, and technically necessary to rely upon the private sector to undertake that development. If this is the case, then the Federal efforts to control and direct ocean space and activities in the public interest will have to somehow be reconciled with the needs, objectives, and capabilities of private industry.

The greatest immediate challenge seems to lie in the area of coastal accommodation of private projects such as power plants, refineries, and pipelines, and in other questions of access, such as limited entrance

---

[18] Office of Technology Assessment, *Transportation of Liquefied Natural Gas* (September 1977), Appendix A.

for all fishing interests including private fishermen. It will be interesting and valuable to follow these developments closely with respect to the question of industry/government interactions in longer term ocean management issues.

V. The National Interest

A. Background

Efforts by coastal states to gain approval for coastal management programs developed under the authority of the Coastal Zone Management Act of 1972 have revealed that there are certain basic difficulties in thinking about and defining the concept of "national interest." The CZMA requires that states give "adequate consideration of the national interest" involved in the planning for and siting of facilities. More broadly, states are charged with recognizing national interests in the process of coastal management programs formulation and with implementing coastal programs that reflect local, state, Federal, and private industry interests.

The problems that have arisen for the coastal management planning program as it attempts to deal with the question of national interest are similar to, although not always synonymous with, problems that have been encountered in attempting to undertake management efforts for ocean space and ocean resources beyond the territorial sea. The issue involves both procedural and substantive elements.

1. Defining the "National Interest." As a political concept, it appears that almost all interest groups equate their own concerns with those of the nation. If a group's interests can be enshrouded with "national" importance, there is a probability of higher priority, improved access, and increased funding. This makes the process of defining or attempting to accommodate and reconcile a variety of interests more difficult, since there may be no objective test of what is and what is not a "national" interest.

"National interest" suggests an amalgam of local, state, regional, and Federal interests, of both public and private concerns. There is not one national interest in the oceans, but rather several interests which in some instances may be contradictory or mutually exclusive. It is not clear that "multiple use" (the simultaneous accommodation of multiple interests within a particular time and place) is always possible or desirable. It would seem that national interests are often whatever the formal political and legal decision process can come up with; they are whatever Congress, the courts, or the President declare them to be. One particularly interesting comment was made by the Interagency Committee in 1963:

> There are, of course, many special groups within the nation that are concerned with (the oceans) in their own behalf, without explicity equating their interest to that of the nation as a whole. Fostering their healthy development, subject to normal political, social, and economic constraints, is almost a definition of the national interest. The fishing industry, the shipping industry, mining and oil industries, and in a sense, the scientific community are among the groups in our society for whom the oceans have a special significance. . . .
>
> . . . Nevertheless, the national goals are not merely the sum of the special interest goals. They are rather those goals like the preservation of peace, the extension of the rule of law and justice, the maintenance of a strong economy, and the safeguarding of health, property, and resources held in common which must be achieved to permit the full realization of the goals held by individuals and special groups which constitute our society. A centralized plan is therefore needed because of the size, complexity, and importance of the field and the fact that its growth (oceanography, being so sensitive to decisions made at the Federal level) introduces considerations of national interest.[19]

B. Some National Studies

As early as the 1940's, the United States was faced with a need to identify what its ocean interests might be, and, as described in Chapter Two, a major national study was undertaken in 1943 and 1944. Additional studies were undertaken in preparation for the 1958 Law of the Sea meetings.

By the late 1950's and early 1960's several domestic groups began to consider what the Nation's interest in the ocean were, and what, if any, ocean programs should be established. During that time, the usual conclusion was that the national interests in the ocean could best be served by establishing major new efforts in marine research and development. The Navy, in a study entitled, "Ten Years in Oceanography" (1959), and the National Academy of Sciences in "Oceanography 1960-1970" (1959) both came to the conclusion that the Federal Government needed to upgrade and coordinate oceanographic research.

1. Interagency Committee on Oceanography. One of the major studies of that period was undertaken by a committee of the Federal Council

---

[19] Interagency Committee on Oceanography, *Oceanography—The Ten Years Ahead* (Washington, 1963), pp. 4-5.

for Science and Technology which had been established in 1960. The Interagency Committee on Oceanography (ICO) in 1963 prepared a long-range national oceanographic plan for the years 1963-1972 ("Oceanography: The Ten Years Ahead"). According to this plan, the basic interests of the United States in the ocean and its resources should be:

> To comprehend the world ocean, its boundaries, its properties, and its processes, and to exploit this comprehension in the public interest, in enhancement of our society, our culture, international posture, and our economic growth.[20]

While this general statement of national interest was not very specific, ICO also suggested the need for federal programs to achieve the following five objectives:

- strengthen basic sciences,
- improve national defense,
- manage resources in the world ocean,
- manage resources in domestic waters, and
- protect life and property, ensuring the safety of operations at sea.[21]

2. Marine Resources and Engineering Development Act of 1966. The year 1966 was a particularly active period in the oceanic and environmental fields. The Coast Guard was placed within the new Department of Transportation (P.L. 89-670), an important estuarine pollution study was authorized (Clean Water Restoration Act, P.L. 89-753), the Water Resources Council was established and river basin commissions authorized (Water Resources Planning Act, P.L. 89-90), a 12-mile continuous fishery zone was declared (P.L. 89-958), the Sea Grant Program was established (P.L. 89-688), the Cabinet-level Marine Science Council was set up and a national ocean study was authorized by the Marine Resources and Engineering Development Act of 1966.

The Marine Resources and Engineering Development Act (MREDA) of 1966, as its name indicates, had moved beyond the oceanographic focus of the late 1950's and early 1960's and reflected a growing number of assertions that the nation should do something with ocean resources in additions to activities relating to petroleum and fisheries. While major emphasis was still given to the need for research, there was also a new emphasis placed on ocean utilization and expanded development, including both military and civilian areas. The policy statement of the

---

[20] *Ibid.*, p. 1.
[21] *Ibid.*, p. 15.

MREDA, which is reproduced below, was the first legislatively articulated statement of national ocean interests and expands in scope upon the interests and focus of the earlier policy statements on the territorial sea and outer continental shelf made in 1953.

> Section 2(a) It is hereby declared to be the policy of the United States to develop, encourage, and maintain a coordinated, comprehensive, and long-range national program in marine science for the benefit of mankind, to assist in protection of health and property, enhancement of commerce, transportation, and national security rehabilitation of our commercial fisheries, and increased utilization of these and other resources.
>
> (b) The marine science activities of the United States should be conducted so as to contribute to the following objectives:
>
> (1) The accelerated development of the resources of the marine environment;
> (2) The expansion of human knowledge of the marine environment;
> (3) The encouragement of private investment enterprise in exploration, technological development, marine commerce, and economic utilization of the resources of the marine environment;
> (4) The preservation of the role of the United States as a leader in marine science and resource development;
> (5) The advancement of education and training in marine sciences;
> (6) The development and improvement of the capabilities, performance, use, and efficiency of vehicles, equipment, and instruments for use in exploration, research, surveys, the recovery of resources, and transmission of energy in the marine environment;
> (7) The effective utilization of the scientific and engineering resources of the nation, with close cooperation among all interested agencies, public and private, in order to avoid unnecessary duplication of effort, facilities, and equipment or waste;
> (8) The cooperation by the United States with other nations and groups of nation and international organizations in marine science activities when such cooperation is in the national interest.

Even though this set of objectives seems closer to the generic issue of resource management, it still does not deal directly with the issues of conflict resolution and control of ocean resources and uses.

3. Our Nation and the Sea. The Marine Resources and Engineering Development Act provided for the establishment of a special commission to undertake a study of national ocean programs and interests. In 1967, President Johnson appointed Julius Stratton as Chairman, and in 1969 the so-called Stratton Commission published *Our Nation and the Sea,* which has served as a principal guide for many subsequent

Congressional and Presidential ocean-related actions. The report was wide-ranging and included a number of specific recommendations for new legislation, for international agreements, and for new institutional arrangements. Its concept of the national interest was basically the same as that contained in the MREDA, although the implications and complications of protecting those interests was considered in much greater detail.

One significant difference from prior discussions of the nation's interest in the ocean was the Stratton Commission's declaration as to just how important the ocean and its resources were and would become. *Our Nation and the Sea* frequently emphasized that there is a national interest in the ocean that goes beyond programs of research and development. The Commission concluded that essentially the ocean is linked to all of the Nation's interests and that advancing the Nation's ocean interests should become a major mission of government:

> How fully and wisely the United States uses the sea in the decades ahead will affect profoundly its security, its economy, its ability to meet increasing demands for food and raw materials, its position and influence in the world community and the quality of the environment in which its people live.[22]

And further,

> The advancement of this Nation's capability to use more effectively its marine environment deserves recognition as a major mission of government.[23]

The efforts described in this section were various attempts to understand the position of oceans as a subject of national value and concern. They did not in themselves form an implementing mechanism in which the national interest in the oceans had to be actually used in a management sense. The following section describes one formal programmatic effort that does have to cope with defining and using the national interest in management of coastal resources including the territorial sea.

C. The Coastal Zone Management Act

Some of the most recent considerations of national ocean interests have been associated with the Coastal Zone Management Act of 1972 and its 1976 amendments.

---

[22] *Our Nation and the Sea,* p. 1.
[23] *Ibid.,* p. 230.

1. **National interest as process.** In section 302 (a) of the Coast Zone Management Act, Congress declared that:

> There is a national interest in the effective management, beneficial use, protection, and development of the coastal zone.

Congress did make some substantive identification of national interests in the coastal zone, to be discussed below, but to a considerable extent, the precise nature of national interests was unspecified, and there was almost no indication of how these interests were to be accommodated or conflicting interests reconciled.

Emphasis was given instead to a *process* by which national interests could be identified for the coastal zone. All interested groups are to have access to the program formulation process, and a program is not to be approved unless broad participation can be demonstrated. From a multitude of interests, needs, and options the state is to establish a set of priorities and permissible uses for its portions of the territorial sea.

Specific topics or issues, such as energy facility siting and shore access are to be considered, as another effort to ensure that the national interests are protected. However, if these elements have been considered, no matter what the substantive results, in most instances the program will have met the requirements of the Act.

2. **Substantive issues.** Various provisions of the Coastal Zone Management Act indicate a congressional determination that there is a national interest in beaches and public access to the coastal zone; in energy facilities and their siting and impacts; in shoreline erosion; in adequate communication with local government; in increased coordination between state management of the territorial sea and shore and the Federal leasing of OCS lands.

From an ocean management viewpoint, Congress did not attempt to determine a national interest in developing a territorial sea policy, except to declare that coastal waters should be subject to improved public management. As a result, there are a number of Federal ocean policies and programs and many private interests affected by the lack of clear Federal intent in the territorial sea.

A marked contrast to this absence of substantive indication of national interests, especially in terms of how they might specifically be accommodated with the coastal zone, is contained in the provisions relating to national security. Section 307 of the CZMA provides for a by-pass of the state coastal management program by the Secretary of Commerce for purposes of national security. As will be seen, national security has been given priority over other national interests in many ocean programs and is an implied national policy.

3. The Integration of Previous National Interests. There are many Federal programs and policies on energy, increased OCS leasing, wetland and flood-plain protection, mitigation of environmental impact, protection of endangered species, and many others impinge to some degree on the coastal zone. It has been argued by some Federal agencies and by private interest groups, such as the American Petroleum Institute, that these Federal programs and policies must be included and accommodated by the state coastal programs. The thrust of this argument, which is still emerging, is that once Congress or the President, through proper exercise of Constitutional authorities, has established a policy or program, it becomes a national interest, and coastal states are bound to ensure that these interests are implemented and protected.

Thus, the petroleum industry has argued that since Congress and the White House have approved a program of accelerated offshore petroleum production to help meet the goal of energy independence that coastal states have an obligation not only to consider such programs and policies, but also to make sure that they are implemented. Following this line of argument, which could just as easily be applied to the protection of wetland or fish habitat, for example, one might conclude that the number of national considerations required could overwhelm the state's ability to assemble an effective coastal management program.

Caution is necessary when considering the imposition of mandatory provisions within state coastal management programs. This follows from two factors:

(a) The national interest is not synonymous with Federal interests. At a minimum it also includes state, local, and private interests, although that fact is sometimes obscured. The argument that Congress is the mechanism by which local, state, and Federal interests are formed into the national interest is true to a great extent. Neither the Constitution nor the courts have declared that if Congress articulates a national interest, and one or more states do not choose to accommodate that interest, the state will, in all instances, be forced to comply. There are Congressionally funded state and local programs which seek to encourage historic preservation, housing development, economic development, and environmental protection. A particular national program such as accelerated offshore oil and gas leasing may not always be compatible with these other "national interests," and it is at the local and state level where those incompatibilities become evident. Before mandatory requirements are dictated, it would be necessary to ensure that they could actually be accommodated without violating basic Constitutional protections or other equally important but conflicting national interests.

(b) Second, and of considerable importance, under present law, it is the states who own the submerged lands and resources of the territorial sea. These states are impressed with a public trust to manage those submerged lands and resources so as to protect the health, safety, and welfare of their citizens. While each state may be required or obligated to accommodate or attempt to accommodate the interest of Federal agencies and other states and regions, there is still a basic duty to the interests of the citizens of the state, and those interests may differ considerably from region to region. The premise of the Coastal Zone Management Act is that these interests are so different that no fair or workable set of standard provisions can be identified by Congress and the best approach is to allow full participation and comment, so that each state to works out its own version of what "wise use" constitutes.

D. Implementing or Using the National Interests

There are problems in attempting to identify or define what national interests are, and additional problems in reconciling conflicting interests. Even if and when those problems are resolved, there remains the issue of how national interests are to be actually accommodated or implemented in ocean management efforts.

In the coastal zone, it is not clear that a workable accommodation of a growing number of national ocean interests can be achieved through a series of ad hoc negotiations between the many individual Federal agencies and 30 coastal states. It is not clear that it is in the national interest to have a national territorial sea in which there may be as many as 30 separate definitions of what is permitted and what has priority. It seems possible that there are certain basic national interests, such as national security, navigation, food production, energy production, and recreation which might warrant a more uniform territorial sea policy.

E. Conclusions

For a variety of reasons, a growing number of interest groups are increasingly effective in asserting their interests in public and private decisions. It is a relatively new phenomenon, emerging during the last decade, and it has been stimulated, in part, by numerous Federal efforts to encourage and facilitate public participation.

The most important aspect of this phenomenon is a growing sensitivity and sophistication about the interconnection of issues, environmentally, economically, and politically. As a result, fishermen protest power plants as dangers to estuarine finfish and shellfish breeding grounds. Local communities protest Federal OCS lease sales out of concern for possible oil spill damage to beaches and the changes in the social fabric of the community which such leasing may induce.

This suggests at least two significant implications for national ocean management:

(1) The oceans may be the only place in which activities or facilities can be located, the only place in which the costs of displacement are not so high as to be unacceptable. Yet, at the same time, much of ocean space is already allocated: to fishing, navigation, national security, recreation, atmospheric maintenance, and sustenance of a vast web of interconnected life forms and geological processes. They are not a last frontier in the sense of unused land, nor are they free of jurisdictional and policy constraint.

(2) Greater pressure to use the oceans can already be seen, but its full force is probably some years away. It is also probable that not all of this demand can be accommodated, although national philosophy and political inclinations may be reluctant to respond to this limitation.

If more interests are to be accommodated within ocean space, certain changes in Federal ocean programs can be expected:

- More structure in the allocative decision process will probably be required to ensure that new activities fit within the growing web of national ocean interests. The shore and the ocean will require increasing "management" or control, if only to prevent a growing number of activities from getting in each others' way.
- A process will not lessen the need to resolve basic conflicts of interest, the finite nature of ocean space, or the sensitivities and limited carrying capacity of the ocean. Bringing every interest group into the decision process in and of itself will not ensure that the national interest is met, or that it will be defined.
- Decisions will take longer, if a serious attempt is made to reconcile all of the interests involved in major ocean decisions.
- Neither government nor private industry will be able to initiate actions or place facilities with the freedom they have enjoyed in the past. Federal projects will not be able to easily assert a "national" interest unless local and state governments are allowed a meaningful role in the planning and decision process.
- Rather than a narrow or single purpose decision, such as, which

sections of OCS land to lease or how many yellowtail flounder should be caught, decisions will expand into systems evaluation, seeking out impact networks, long-range cumulative implications. This means greater cost, more time, and more skill will be needed in reaching decisions.

This kind of change can already be seen. In a recent Georges Bank leasing decision, the Department of the Interior considered the following wide variety of factors in selecting tracts for final sale:

1. Industry nominations;
2. Geological and geophysical data, including Geological Survey opinion on oil and gas potential of tracts based on this information;
3. Oil and gas resource estimates;
4. Geological hazards (based on bottom sediments, faulting, earthquake potential, etc.);
5. Current technology;
6. General climatology and seasonal weather patterns (visibility, temperature, winds, storms, precipitation);
7. Physical hazards (ocean dumping areas, military activities, sites of unexploded ammunition, undersea cables, navigation lanes, shipwrecks, harbor areas);
8. Physical oceanography (sea temperatures, surface circulation including waves, swells, and tides);
9. Potential oil spill trajectories and time to shore;
10. Commercial and sport fisheries;
11. Marine and intertidal biological communities;
12. Onshore biological communities;
13. Rare and endangered species;
14. Archeologic and historic sites;
15. Onshore and offshore recreation;
16. Existing infrastructure relating to the petroleum industry in the region (refining, pipelines, oil terminals);
17. Transportation network; and
18. Water quality.[24]

Amendments to the Outer Continental Shelf Land Act, changes in the leasing process made by the Department of the Interior, and 1976 amendments to the Coastal Zone Management Act would indicate that even more factors will be considered in future leasing decisions, such

---

[24] Department of the Interior, *Final Environmental Statement, OCS Sale No. 42* (1977), Volume 1, p. 21.

as the objectives and provisions of the state coastal management programs and the land use plans and public service infrastructure of local communities.

The "national interest" in the ocean would appear to be a collection of interests that is growing, it includes local, state, and Federal concerns, it involves virtually all sectors of the economy and it changes over time. Because of the change, because of the diversity, there is probably a need to rely to some degree upon the various decision processes to determine what the national interest is for a particular proposal at a particular time and place.

But there would also appear to be a need to make some hard choices between basic conflicting national interests. Long-range viability of the marine environment and assured access to ocean space and resources to meet vital national interests cannot be assured if the national interest is articulated solely on a case-by-case basis.

Whether or not it was a wise or necessary action, the Federal Government has taken upon itself, especially since 1970, the control of how the ocean is used. The physical and chemical properties of ocean water, or the number and type of fish found in that water historically have been a function of natural dynamics and human activities. These properties and characteristics have become influenced by expressions of national interest with all of the burdens and complexities which attach to the national interest. If the United States continues to attempt to exert more control over ocean activities and ocean conditions, the task of defining the national interest will become increasingly cumbersome.

CHAPTER FIVE

SOME MANAGEMENT ASPECTS OF OCEAN CONTROL

Introduction

Previous chapters have shown that since the 1930's there has been a change in the level and type of government involvement in ocean-related programs and policies. In broad terms the Federal Government has, over a period of some forty years, established a major presence in the ocean if not an accompanying framework of policy. Prior to that time, there had been some regulation of navigation, some revenue collection, and most noticeably, military activities, but it was at the state level of government where authority and responsibility were assumed to exist for fishery management, mineral leasing, or other ocean resource controls. Further, there was only a limited perception that *any* government involvement was needed in ocean affairs.

Starting from an interest in developing offshore oil, defense, and intelligence requirements, the efforts to transfer control of primary ocean resources from the state to the Federal level, and an interest in asserting national jurisdiction over ocean fisheries beyond the three mile limit, the nation by 1953 had established a series of regimes for the management of the territorial sea, the regulation of fishing, the leasing of outer continental shelf lands and support for science. During the 1970's increasing ocean use and a growing concern for environmental protection led to the establishment of yet another type and kind of ocean program with the United States assuming through legislation some form of responsibility for a sizeable portion of ocean space and resources. We now find that determining the number and type of whales that swim in the sea as well as their management have become not only a topic of public debate, but also a matter of national policy. And four times a year, the number of yellowtail flounder that can be harvested by New England fishermen is set by the U.S. Government. In theory, what can take place and cannot take place within the territorial sea, and which activities will have priority, is supposed to be carefully explicated in a series of coastal management programs which attempt to coordinate all local, state, Federal and private actions taking place within these "management zones."

The following diagram shows the general permitting process for ocean dredging projects in California. As presently structured, it requires at least 18 months to obtain a permit, and it can take 2 to 3 years. As this diagram illustrates, the amount of governmental control over ocean activities has become extensive; the decision process is increasingly complex. The cost to both the private sector and the public is increasing.

These control efforts have been constructed without any formal framework of national ocean management. The absence of such a framework reflects a policy choice evolved in the 1940's, and it is a choice which, at this point, might warrant additional evaluation.

Since the early 1960's, proposals have been advanced to establish a central Federal ocean department or agency and to develop additional ocean control or management programs. As interest in the direct use of the ocean for the production of energy, weather modification, mariculture, offshore siting of facilities, and new international ocean regimes, continues to grow, proposals for new Federal ocean management efforts can be expected. However, with few, if any, exceptions, these proposals focus upon some institutional arrangement. The Interagency Committee on Oceanography, The Stratton Commission, and to a lesser degree the General Accounting Office and the National Ocean Policy Study of the U.S. Senate have all advocated the formation of new policies or organizational arrangements.

Before workable decisions can be made as to how ocean programs should be structured or which department or agency should be given authority over them, it seems appropriate to identify more clearly what it is that the Federal Government is actually attempting to manage, why it must be managed, what problems or conflicts require additional Federal action, and what would constitute a solution to them. It is also important that we improve our ability to assess objectively existing and proposed ocean control or management efforts. Telling a "good" management program from a "bad" one is very difficult given our present measures of effectiveness.

As an aid to that process, this chapter examines in greater detail the basic concept of Federal ocean control or management and some of the components and options of ocean control systems.

I. Character, Nature, and Degree of Control

Perhaps one of the most basic issues or questions to be considered is how much control the Federal Government wishes or needs to exert over

MARINE PROJECT PERMIT PROCESS
DETAILED FLOW CHART

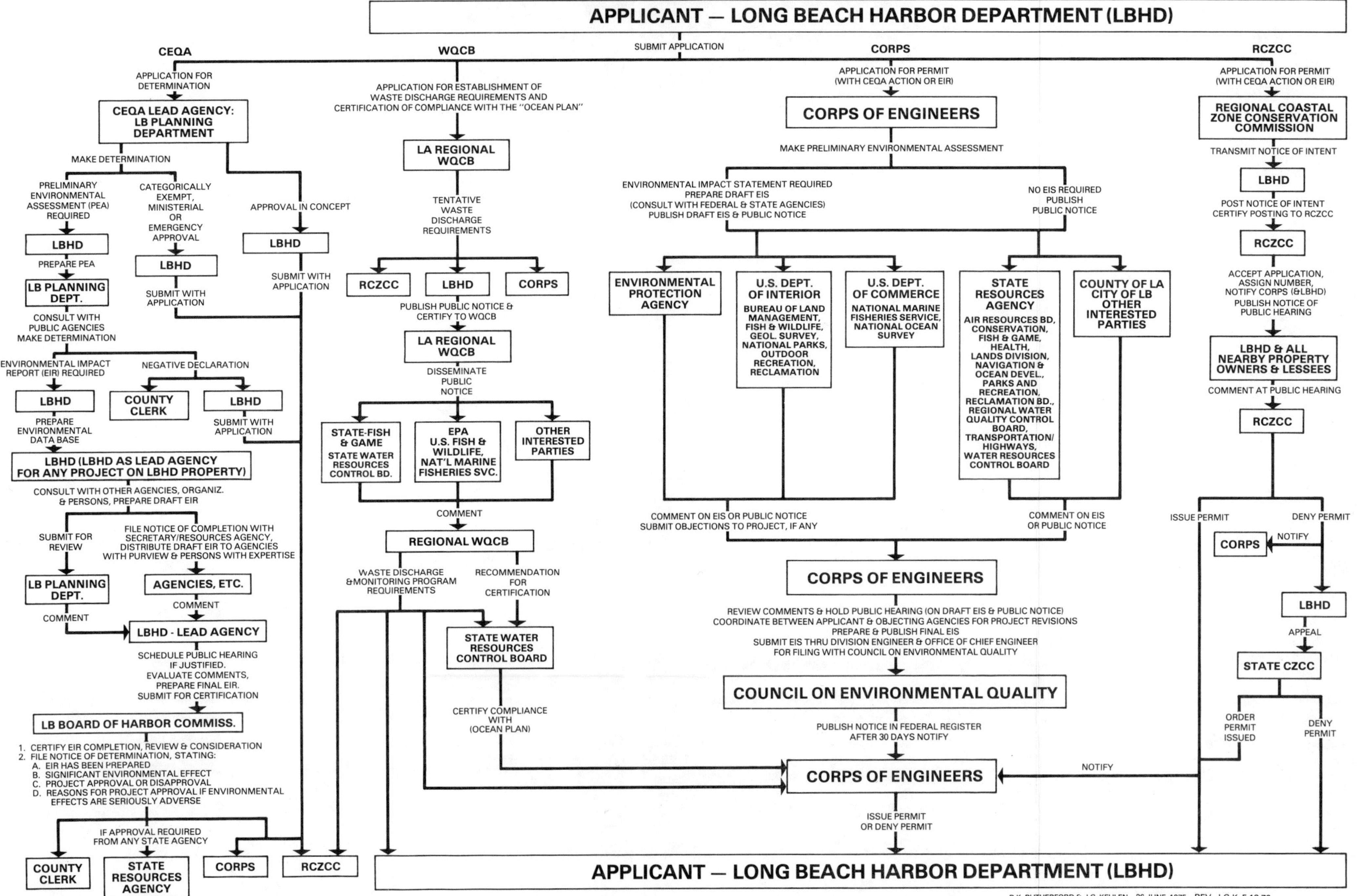

the ocean, and this includes a need to identify what is to be controlled: ocean space, ocean resources, ocean activities, ocean-related governmental programs.

As suggested in Chapter One, there is a spectrum of control which can be exerted by the Federal Government. During the 1940's and 1950's, the United States adopted an approach to ocean management that was constrained by global ocean policy considerations. Since that approach was adopted, as described in Chapter Two, Federal ocean control efforts have been legislatively designed so as to avoid the appearance of exerting control over the ocean itself or more accurately, have been designed to deal with specific problems. Thus the Deepwater Port Act is presented, not as a control of the ocean, but of deepwater ports. The Fisheries Conservation and Management Act involves controls over fishing, not the ocean. There are other programs which control oil spills, tanker safety, navigational patterns, pollution, pipelines, outer continental shelf mineral leasing, or marine mammals. In each instance the point is made by Congress that these are not controls of the ocean, but instead, of activities, special issues, or resources. However, in its control of deepwater ports the United States is dedicating a portion of ocean space to a single use and in that process controlling ocean space, ocean activities, and to some degree, ocean resources. The leasing of outer continental shelf lands is but one small part of an entire collection of ocean and coastal uses entailed in offshore petroleum production and requires decisions on air quality, navigation patterns, use of the water column, ports, the territorial sea, and shorelands. If the nation truly wishes to manage fish populations, there may be a need to control estuaries, surface runoff and discharge, air quality, weather modification, ocean energy production, and a variety of other related activities and conditions.

It is one thing to minimize assertions of national jurisdiction for foreign policy purposes. It is an altogether different thing to understand the scope and degree of control that will be required to meet a particular national ocean objective. In particular the United States has attempted to avoid the appearance of controlling ocean waters, including both surface waters and the water column. In an effort to maintain the "high seas" status of oceans throughout the world, the United States has refrained from the type of assertions of authority advocated by Ickes and others and has instead asserted control over activities or conditions. Yet control of any major ocean activity would seem to involve control of ocean space; and the United States is presently committed in legislation to a considerable degree of ocean management. Consider, for example, the Coastal Zone Management Act, which, if taken at face value, implies an extension of control over the territorial sea portion of the ocean. It is somewhat analogous to comprehensive planning and zoning for a major urban area, but it is similar to some of our western public lands programs in the space it applies to.

However, it does appear that the magnitude of control implicit in present Federal ocean management related programs has not been fully appreciated. It is not clear that in all instances the Federal Government needs to exert so much control; that it is capable of achieving control of this scope and type; or that the nation can afford such control efforts. And it seems prudent, if not necessary, to give further consideration to the complexities and implications of attempting to control the ocean before major new institutional arrangements are formulated or new ocean management efforts attempted.

When, and if, a determination is made as to what more should be managed, beyond our current efforts, the problem of evaluating a management approach to achieve that new control still must be faced. Assume we can measure a "gross ocean product" in total dollars. If it is X dollars under our present "ocean management" system, will it be more or less than X under new ocean management arrangements that could be implemented?

Even if we were to decide that "gross ocean product" is a proper decision variable, it is doubtful that we could quantify it to the degree necessary to make program choices.

II. Tools for Ocean Management

There are a variety of means by which the United States can effect its goals, principles, or interests in ocean space and ocean resources. The means must, of course, be suited to the task and the situation. Choice will be different if one is attempting to influence the taking of marine mammals by Japanese fishermen in Japanese waters or if one is attempting to regulate how many yellowtail flounder fishermen from Gloucester catch.

It is also important to remember that *national ocean management* would involve at least three separate but related types of tasks:

- managing various natural ocean systems;
- managing human ocean-related activities; and
- managing government ocean programs and policies.

When discussing tools for ocean management, it is sometimes useful, although difficult, to differentiate conceptually among these tasks. Ocean management tools are considered below.

A. Economic Sanctions

Canada has for several years followed a policy of subsidizing fishermen and processors for fish they export to the United States, allowing Canadians to charge lower prices than American fishermen. According to a recent Department of Labor finding:

> Many American fish distributors and wholesalers use the imports of Canadian groundfish, flatfish, and scallops as leverage in bidding down the prices paid to domestic fishermen for the same species of groundfish, flatfish and scallops.[1]

In June of 1978, forty Congressmen wrote to Secretary of the Treasury Blumenthal requesting that a countervailing import duty be imposed upon Canadian fish imported into the United States. The Treasury Department turned down the request, but this exemplifies the motivation and method of using economic sanctions as a fish management tool.

Perhaps the strongest example of the use of economic sanctions as a fish management tool is contained in Section 205 of the Fishery Conservation and Management Act. That section provides that if:

1. the United States cannot gain an agreement with other nations to allow American fishermen desired amounts of access to that nation's fishing grounds; or
2. a nation prevents American fishermen from engaging in fishing for highly migratory species; or
3. if a foreign nation seizes an American fishing vessel or otherwise subjects American fishermen to undue harrassment;

then the Secretary of the Treasury is authorized to implement various economic sanctions against that country until such time as the dispute is resolved, including specifically the prohibition of importation into the United States of fish or fish products from that nation.

Similar legislation has been proposed which imposes economic sanctions on countries which fail to abide by whale catch quotas established by the International Whaling Commission.

Economic sanctions have been referred to as "the ultimate weapon in the arsenal of fishery managers."[2] However, economic sanctions are a limited tool that in many instances are not usable or are ineffective. At times all such sanctions accomplish is to let other nations know the degree of our displeasure. At worst, such actions can generate anger

---

[1] Paul Kemprecos, *The Cape Codder,* June 23, 1978.
[2] Lester Brown, et al., "Living Resources of the Sea," in *Progress as if Survival Mattered,* (San Francisco: Friends of the Earth, 1977), p. 135.

and resentment with severe long-range impacts upon United States interests. Economic sanctions must be evaluated within the broad context of national interests, international relationships, and military affairs.

It is true that economic sanctions are a tool that can be used to further our ocean related interests. And within the generic category of "economic sanctions" falls a diverse group of covert and overt actions which can and have been used by many nations. But the use of economic sanctions as a tool of ocean management is a prime example of the importance of evaluating the connections between ocean affairs and other areas of national interest.

The world has become a complex, intractable, and interconnected place and to assert one's national interest in it, by whatever means, requires careful analysis, considerable skill, and a certain amount of luck.

Example: Brazil and Mexico

Brazil and Mexico have recently indicated an intention of excluding U.S. shrimp fishermen from their two-hundred mile national fishing zones. This will probably result in increased competition and fishing pressure upon United States shrimp fisheries in the Gulf of Mexico and the South Atlantic as some three hundred large U.S. shrimping vessels currently fishing in Mexican or Brazilian waters are displaced.

In response to this situation, U.S. fishermen have suggested that economic sanctions should be used as leverage to ensure continued access of U.S. boats to the waters of Brazil and Mexico.

The response of the deputy director of the National Marine Fisheries Service Southeast Region was:

> . . . let's face it, there's [sic] many other things involved in all of these negotiations. Trade of the United States with Mexico and Brazil does not involve just fisheries products.[3]

Brazil, Mexico and other nations which might be subjected to economic sanctions are part of a changing world in which we seek friendships. We face major ocean-related decisions in the years ahead regarding the South Atlantic and the entire Pacific Basin. A new era with changed resource utilization, military alliances, and economic networks is emerging. It is within this context that any ocean-related economic sanctions must be evaluated. No management tool is free of cost, and the trade-offs involved in imposing sanctions upon a foreign nation over ocean man-

---

[3] M. Gene Mearns, "Shrimpers Upset Over Superport and Shrinking Gulf Fishing Areas," *National Fisherman,* May 1978, p. 3.

agement issues are often subtle and long-lasting. At a minimum the evaluation of the trade-offs should take into account Defense Department concerns and be based on a comprehensive understanding of all our ocean-related interests, and the effects the application of such sanctions will have on them. The ability to undertake such an assessment is presently difficult, given the lack of a coordinated program or coherent set of national ocean policies and mechanisms for the formation and modification of such policies over time. Without careful evaluation, the use of any significant management tool has as much potential for mischief as it does for furthering our ocean-related national interests.

B. Coordination of Shore Access and Offshore Ocean Use

Since access to the shore is needed for ocean egress or ingress or for the siting of support facilities for ocean activities, control of the shore can have significant impact upon how the ocean is used. Similar management of ocean uses could support and enhance desired landside policies and objectives. However, at the present time this land/water coordination is more a matter of contention than an effective management tool. During 1977 several coastal communities intervened in Federal courts to slow, modify, or block Federal leasing of Baltimore Canyon OCS lands. They were successful in gaining initial court recognition of the ability of local communities and states to prevent or severely limit OCS developments by denying access for pipelines and ancillary facilities. The American Petroleum Institute (API) has initiated a series of suits against coastal states whose coastal management programs do not provide sufficient guarantee of access for energy-related facilities to meet API's interests.

Although land/water coordination was not fully spelled out or conceptually developed at the time of its passage, one of the principal objectives of the Coastal Zone Management Act is to bring about such coordination within the territorial sea. To date that effort does not seem to have been properly conceived or implemented and in most instances has not led to such coordination.

Example 1: California's Land/Water Coordination for Commercial Fisheries Management

To maintain a strong commercial fishery, several conditions must be met, including regulation of fishing pressure to maintain a "sustained" yield of commercial fisheries stocks, the maintenance of certain quality standards for the marine environment, and the provision of adequate shoreside facilities. This last condition is becoming a serious problem in many parts of the country, and the Fisheries Management and Conservation Act of 1976 will ultimately fail if the necessary fish processing plants, equipment storage sites, and adequate harbor space are not provided.

In recognition of the link between ocean fishing and shoreside land use policies, the State of California has adopted as a coastal management principle that shoreside facilities for commercial fishing should be protected and improved, along with management efforts to ensure the sustained biological productivity of coastal waters. This water land coordination is contained in the California Coastal Act (SB 1277) of 1976.

a. Water Policy Relative to Commercial Fishing

Uses of the marine environment shall be carried out in a manner that will sustain the biological productivity of coastal waters and that will maintain healthy populations of all species or marine organisms adequate for long-term commercial, recreational, scientific, and education purposes. (Sec. 3230)

b. Land Policy Relative to Commercial Fishing

Facilities serving the commercial fishing and recreational boating industries shall be protected and, where feasible, upgraded. Existing commercial fishing and recreational boating harbor space shall not be reduced unless the demand for those facilities no longer exists or adequate substitute space has been provided. Proposed recreational boating facilities shall, where feasible, be designed and located in such a fashion as not to interfere with the needs of the commercial fishing industry. (Sec. 30234)

Example 2: Coastal Zone Management Act

With reference to this problem, and the potential use of shore access management as a tool to support ocean management objectives, a provision of the 1976 amendments to the Coastal Zone Management Act is of particular interest. Section 305 (b)(7) requires that approved state coastal management programs contain:

A definition of the term 'beach' and a planning process for the protection of, and access to, public beaches and other public coastal areas of environmental, recreational, historical, aesthetic, ecological, or culture value.

While these provisions are rather limited in scope, reflecting legislation that had been introduced for several years to establish a national beach access planning program, the concept of a coastal access planning process and/or management program could be expanded to coordinating national ocean management with state and local shoreland management.

If beach access planning were expanded to include shore access planning, and if environmental, recreational, historical, esthetic, ecological, and cultural values were expanded to include economic and national security values, an effective land/water coordinating mechanism might be achieved. The potential of this tool is great, if cooperation among local, state and Federal Government can be achieved. It may be that, with existing state control of the land and Federal control of the water, effective coordination may, in most instances, not be possible and that coastal access management will never be available as a general ocean management tool. However, if coastal policy cannot be used as a positive ocean management tool (or ocean management as a positive shoreland management tool), at least there must be some increased degree of coordination and cooperation.

C. Impact Analysis as an Ocean Management Tool

Section 102(2)(c) of the National Environmental Policy Act requires that each Federal agency

> . . . include in every recommendation or report on proposals for . . . major federal actions significantly affecting the quality of the human environment a detailed statement by the responsible official on—
> (i) the environmental impact of the proposed action,
> (ii) any adverse environmental effects which cannot be avoided should the proposal be implemented,
> (iii) alternatives to the proposed action,
> (iv) the relationship between local short-term uses of man's environment and the maintenance and enhancement of long-term productivity, and
> (v) any irreversible and irretrievable commitments of resources which would be involved in the proposed action should it be implemented.

The purpose of this provision, which has recently been expanded through administrative ruling of CEQ to require a justification of major adverse impact, is to provide a tool for achieving compliance with declared national policy of minimizing adverse environmental impacts. However, this same impact assessment device could be used as a tool to enforce or monitor compliance with *any* policy or principle, including those which might be included in national ocean management programs.

Consider, for example, the impact statement required by the Engle Act for OCS lands that are proposed for withdrawal from minerals leasing for national security purposes. An application to Congress for withdrawal of public OCS lands for national security purposes must include a statement of:

> Whether, and if so, to what extent, the proposed use will affect continuing full operation of the public land laws and Federal regulations relating to conservation, utilization, and development of mineral resources. . . . (Sec. 3(7))

The Fish and Wildlife Coordination Act is another example of the use of the impact assessment device, requiring that every major Federal water project be reviewed for its possible impacts upon fish or wildlife values. Any one of these programs could be modified to provide a review of the potential impacts of a proposed policy, program, or activity upon a nation ocean management program.

On March 27, 1978, in a Message to Congress on a National Urban Policy, President Carter outlined a new program which could be adopted for use in ocean management.

> Each agency submitting a major domestic initiative must include its own urban and community impact analysis. DPS (Domestic Policy Staff) and OMB (Office of Management and Budget) will review these submissions and will ensure that any anti-urban impacts of proposed Federal policies will be brought to my attention.[4]

One of the particular attractions of this tool is that it can be utilized separately from other management functions or programs. Thus, CEQ and the Environmental Protection Agency can monitor Section 102 environmental impact statements (EIS's) without having to have legislative authority over activities which will create those impacts.

A separate function could be established, which does not now fully exist, to specifically evaluate the impact of proposed policies and activities upon national ocean programs, policies, principles, and interests. While ultimately it would make no sense to collect such information, except as an academic exercise, unless it were to be used, the very act of assessing impacts, both short-range and cumulative/long-range could have significant influence upon how future ocean-related activities and programs were designed, as the National Environmental Policy Act demonstrated.

---

[4] *Weekly Compilation of Presidential Documents,* April 3, 1978.

If a certain set of standards or policies were adopted, a mandatory impact assessment, such as is incorporated in the National Urban Policy Program or the Engle Act, could be used to assure consistency with those standards or policies. This, in fact, is the approach which Texas has chosen to use in the management of its coastal zone, having rejected the idea of a comprehensive planning approach and focusing on permitted impacts rather than upon permitted uses.[5]

1. NEPA and the oceans. The National Environmental Policy Act (NEPA) already requires an *environmental* impact statement for any significant Federal action. It is not clear how far outward in the ocean NEPA might apply, but Section 102 EIS's have been prepared on EPA's ocean dumping regulations and the designation of a site for the incineration of chemical wastes. There have been ocean-related EIS's carried out for such activities as LOS, deep seabed mining, INDFC, fishery negotiations with Japan, the tuna/porpoise issue.

What constitutes an "adequate" environmental impact statement for any ocean-related activity? How many of the vast number of possible parameters should be considered? How will cumulative impacts be calculated? If information is not available, it is the responsibility of the activity sponsor to develop that information, or is that a Federal Governmental function? What constitutes a "significant impact" in the oceans? Which changes should be avoided, and which are permissible? Are *rates* of change important? What about seasonal shifts in ocean system sensitivities?

There is considerable potential in the National Environmental Policy Act with reference to living resources management and ocean management per se, but there remain many questions which need to be answered.

2. Marine Protection, Research, and Sanctuaries Act. One of the potentially most important provisions of Federal ocean-related legislation is Section 202 of the Marine Protection, Research, and Sanctuaries Act of 1972.

> The Secretary of Commerce, in consultation with other appropriate Federal departments, agencies, and instrumentalities shall . . . initiate a comprehensive and continuing program of research with respect to the possible long-range *effects* of pollution, over fishing, and man-induced changes of ocean ecosystems. In carrying out such research, the Secretary of Commerce shall take into account such factors as existing and

---

[5] Office of Coastal Zone Management, Department of Commerce, *Texas Coastal Zone Management Program Environmental Impact Statement,* 1978.

proposed international policies affecting oceanic problems, economic considerations involved in both the protection and the use of the oceans, possible alternatives to existing programs, and *ways in which* the health of the oceans may best be preserved for the benefit of succeeding generations of mankind. (Emphasis added.)

It is not clear that Congress intended the kind of research effort which this Section appears to call for. There is a danger of reading into these provisions more than was intended. However, aside from the important issue of the intent of this provision, the needs are real. If it is in the national interest to protect the oceans, what constraints must be placed upon human activities to achieve that protection? And, if the promotion or enhancement of certain activities is in the national interest, what protection must be afforded those activities? What are permissible uses? What should have priority? Certainly the exact type and scope of information called for in this legislation would provide many of these answers.

The amount of time, money, and effort involved in deriving such answers is not easily calculated, but it can be estimated to cost considerably more than is currently being expended, and perhaps more than the United States is willing or able to expend. But this program and the idea of impact analysis as an ocean management tool warrant further consideration.

If the nation's ability to undertake ocean impact analysis (OIA) were improved, the cost of securing permits, litigation, or clearing up after mistakes, might be reduced. Ultimately, it should expand our ability to use the oceans, by giving us the means of designing facilities and activities so that they fit within the complex patterns of ocean dynamics and human ocean uses rather than conflict with them.

Perhaps the most important question now is: when are the costs resulting from our ignorance of the cumulative impacts of ocean-related policies, programs, and activities greater than the costs involved in attempting to establish a workable OIA capability? While it is not clear that we have reached this threshold for all issues or all parts of the ocean, it would appear that some system may be needed now for heavily used areas such as Georges Bank and the New York Bight.

D. Ocean Zoning

At the present time the United States makes extensive use of zoning in its ocean programs.

- There are *management or jurisdictional* zones or regimes representing how government is structured. Thus, there is the coastal

zone, the OCS lands zone, the fishery conservation and management zone, the contiguous zone.
- There are *activity zones,* either to protect a particular activity or sort out several activities. Thus, there are military activity zones, navigational fairway zones, ocean dumping zones, oil rig safety zones, deepwater port safety zones.
- There are also *resource or "ocean zones"* directed at protecting the resource itself. Several states have established some type of ocean sanctuary system, protecting breeding grounds, unique geologic formations, or sensitive estuaries. The Federal Marine Sanctuary Program is also based on this concept.

There are also natural zones created by tide, current, nutrient cycles, migratory routes, thermal patterns, and geologic structures, and there are informal patterns or zones of human activity, often reflecting the natural patterns and cycles.

1. Existing zones. Existing zones of resource concentration, ocean dynamics, and human activities represent a series of constraints upon and opportunities for future ocean actions. By identifying these patterns or zones, it may be possible to "fit" new activities into existing patterns with minimal disruption; to avoid "inappropriate" locations for a particular type of activity; to enhance an activity by placing it within a set of uses and dynamics which are compatible and supportive of it.

This kind of work for ocean management is not really being done at the present time. There is a great expenditure of both public and private money to do "inventory" work, especially as part of the Federal EIS process and state coastal program development. But often this inventory work has no focus, no clear purpose, no directed sense of what information might be of use and in what form it should be collected and stored. Focusing upon the patterns and the dynamics of change could lead to the establishment of a reactive inventory of information useful for a wide variety of purposes.

In the siting of any new activity there is a choice, although not always explicit, of whether or not to disrupt existing patterns of the natural world and of human activity. It is no longer possible to look at the ocean as empty space, and this choice is becoming increasingly explicit, formal, contentious, and difficult. It is our belief that the point will soon be reached when it will not only be useful but also essential to develop a clear understanding of the present ocean patterns or zones and the changing dynamics with which they interact. It is only when these natural and human zones are clearly denoted and described that decisions on new uses can be thoughtfully and reasonably made. These decisions cannot be undertaken without a spatial and temporal identification of zones and patterns and dynamics. To ignore these zones is to risk fish kills, ship collisions, storm damage, pollution, financial loss, and the inadvertent loss of opportunities.

2. Establishing new zones. "Ocean management," as described in this report, includes many elements and has changed in both purpose and scope since the 1930's when the Federal Government first considered the idea. But one aspect of ocean management is an attempt to establish, enhance, or protect a specific activity or mixture of activities in time and space within some portion of the ocean. The activity (or activities) could be whale breeding, oil extraction, ship transit, weapons testing, or trawl fishing. Quite often in attempting this, a "zone" is established, if only conceptually within the mind of those involved in the management task.

In establishing any zone, there are some basic questions to be asked. These include where the zone should be; whether it involves the air, the surface waters, the water column, the seabed, the subsoil, shoreland; how large it should be; whether it should be fixed in space; whether it should change its characteristics over time; what type of control and enforcement should take place within this zone; how much needs to be known about this zone; what activities should be allowed, encouraged, prohibited, controlled.

There are several existing, formal processes used by the Federal Government to answer these questions although those processes are not always considered as, or thought of, in terms of establishing zones. Establishing dredge spoil disposal sites; selling **OCS** oil leases; and constructing an intake pipe for power plant cooling water are all examples of setting up a zone within which a special degree of control is exerted over ocean activities to enhance a primary value or within which a particular activity is specially controlled and regulated.

An example is the criteria used by EPA in evaluating permit applications for ocean dumping:

1. The need for the proposed dumping;
2. The effect of such dumping on human health and welfare, including economic, esthetic and recreational values;
3. The effect of such dumping on fisheries resources, plankton, fish, shellfish, wildlife, shorelines and beaches;
4. The effect of such dumping on marine ecosystems particularly with respect to: (a) the transfer, concentration and dispersion of such

material and its by-products through biological, physical, and chemical processes; and (b) potential changes in marine ecosystem diversity, productivity, and stability;

5. The persistence and permanence of the effects of the dumping;
6. The effect of dumping particular volumes and concentrations of such materials;
7. Appropriate locations and methods of disposal or recycling, including land-based alternatives and the probable impact of requiring use of such alternative locations or methods upon considerations affecting the public interest;
8. The effect of alternative uses of oceans, such as scientific study, fishing and other living resource exploitation, and non-living resource exploitation, and
9. In designating recommended sites, the Administrator shall utilize, wherever feasible, locations beyond the edge of the continental shelf.[6]

3. Enforcement of zones. To establish an ocean zone is to create rules, standards, objectives, and an enforcement burden which depends upon the purpose, location, and degree of public acceptance of the zone. Obviously, a coral reef at the bottom of the ocean or an ocean dump site that consists of no more than designations of longitude and latitude requires a different degree of enforcement, perhaps even a different concept of enforcement, than would land-based zones, which are more visible, more accessible, more precisely defined, and which are not as fluid in time or space as ocean zones.

a. Legal complexity. Consider for example that regulations establish a marine sanctuary through which no U.S. oil tankers will be allowed to transit, or a deepwater port safety zone in which no commercial fishing vessels will be allowed. Suppose that contrary to these regulations, a prohibited vessel enters and then leaves the restricted area. Does the enforcing agency have the authority to pursue and detain the vessel even though it is no longer within the restricted area?

In "The Legal Background to North Sea Oil and Gas Development," Patricia W. Birnie discusses this problem as it relates to United Kingdom oil rig safety zones in the North Sea and suggests that violations of special ocean zones may be difficult to enforce beyond the territorial sea. This involves an extension of national ocean authority that may not

---

[6] Environmental Protection Agency, "Ocean Dumping Final Revision of Regulations and Criteria," *Federal Register,* January 11, 1977, Section 227.

presently be recognized by international law. There are, of course, some existing principles of international law and practice that relate to this issue, for example, Article 23 Convention on the High Seas, and Article 111 of the Informal Composite Negotiating Text (LOS Conference).

> Enforcement of coastal state laws for foreign vessels on the high seas outside the safety zones (of oil rigs) for breaches of the safety zones is, in view of the increasing frequency of such offenses, now needing consideration. Such enforcement would depend on whether the right to Hot Pursuit, i.e., the right to pursue and arrest a vessel on the high seas for offenses committed within territorial waters, also extends to offenses committed in zones of limited coastal state jurisdiction. The area of safety zones was fixed in 1958 before the advent of super-tankers, and may need review. Problems also arise where zones overlap around complexes of installations, and foreign shipping is prohibited from entering large areas of the high seas. Arrest of offenders against the safety of the installations, and against other laws and regulations, once the offender is outside the safety zone also presents problems in international law.
>
> This is clearly . . . an area in which harmonization of laws is necessary . . . because there may be attempts to enforce these laws against foreign nations and vessels on the high seas.[7]

The marine sanctuaries provisions of the MPRSA include a very clear statement that any restrictions associated with a marine sanctuary will apply only to citizens of the United States, and not to foreign vessels. This provision was included for the very reasons alluded to by Birnie. And the Deepwater Port Act appears to contain the same type of declaration by stating that the Department of State will work out any necessary restrictions upon foreign vessels with those nations through principles of international law.

At this writing, the Department of State has concluded Deepwater Port Agreements with Norway, Denmark, and Sweden. The agreements state that vessels registered in, or flying the flag of signatories and the personnel aboard such vessels, are subject to concurrent jurisdiction by the U.S. while in the safety zone of U.S. deepwater ports. Such agreements have been sought with other nations as well.

This suggests three points. First, that the establishment of any zone within ocean space requires a rather complex networking of public and private, national and international interests, and may even require multinational or international agreements, especially if it is essential that all regulations be fully complied with. Second, the authority to zone, if

---

[7] Patricia W. Birnie, "The Legal Background to North Sea Oil and Gas," *Political Implications of the North Sea Oil and Gas* (Universitetisforlaget and IPC Science and Technology Press, Ltd., 1975), p. 28.

"zoning" includes the authority to enforce that zone, is not clear. If the UNCLOS negotiations are ever successful in establishing new international ocean management regimes and regulations, this authority, especially within a two-hundred mile economic zone, may be clarified. Third, if an ocean zone applies only to United States citizens and to United States vessels, it may not be worth establishing. There is extensive merchant vessel traffic in ocean space adjacent to the United States, and even if foreign fishing within two hundred miles is severely restricted or eliminated, tanker and cargo traffic will continue if not increase.

b. Political complexity. In July of 1977, new International Regulations for Preventing Collisions at Sea (COLREGS) went into effect for U.S. vessels. These regulations were formulated by the Inter-Governmental Maritime Consultative Organization (IMCO) and contain, as Rule 10, the provision that:

> A vessel engaged in fishing shall not impede the passage of any vessel following a traffic lane and that vessel shall so far as practicable avoid anchoring in a traffic separation scheme or in areas near its termination.
> . . . a vessel engaged in fishing shall not impede the passage of any vessel following a traffic lane.

The Traffic Separation Scheme (TSS) established for the New York Bight area includes six sea lanes, three separation lanes, two free lanes, and a precautionary zone (see Figure 7). This vessel traffic management system has been established to coordinate a very large amount of commercial vessel traffic using the New York-New Jersey port area. In addition to this commercial traffic, it is estimated that there are between 75,000 and 100,000 private boats, 100 party boats (fishing), and between 300 and 400 charter boats that fish the waters of the New York Bight.[8]

The six traffic lanes incorporate several popular fishing areas, and there have been increasing conflicts between fishermen and merchant vessels, including at least one near collision. In response to requests to take action on this situation, the Coast Guard ruled in February of 1978, that Rule 10 of the COLREGS meant that no fishing would be allowed within the traffic lanes.

However, to commercial and recreational fishing interests this was an unacceptable restriction on their multimillion dollar industry. Congressional assistance was utilized in obtaining a Coast Guard review of

---

[8] *Ibid.*

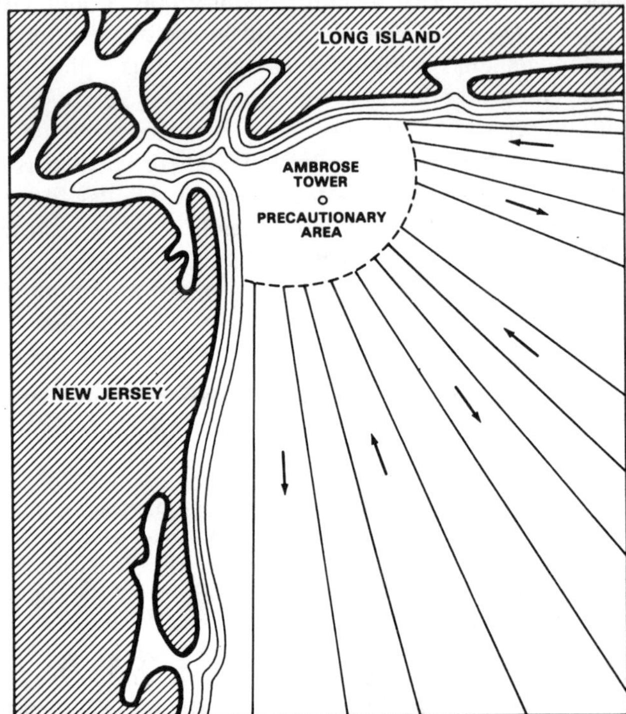

Figure 7:

New York bight traffic separation scheme (TSS).

its ruling, and in March of 1978 a determination was made that fishing would be allowed, but that anchoring would be prohibited and that fishing vessels must follow the same rules and directions of travel as merchant vessels.

The degree to which any ocean management conceptual approach or tool can be successfully applied is constrained by factors such as which interest groups would be displaced or negatively impacted. (Ocean management is a political process and any new management scheme must be acceptable within that process.) It is not clear what types and levels of control are at this time politically acceptable.

The establishment of exclusive use areas, or areas where certain activities have priority, may be the best way of achieving some management objectives for certain locations. But if the area involved is susceptible to use for other purposes, the optimum may not be possible. Just as the Coast Guard is unable to exclude fishing boats from vessel traffic lanes, the Secretary of Commerce may be unable to exclude oil rigs from marine sanctuaries. These constraints, be they political, economic, or technical, help to define what ocean management is and can be.

4. Ocean zones and foreign policy. Additional complexities arise in the use of ocean management tools such as zoning when they apply to foreign nationals or to foreign vessels. The type of problem that could evolve is indicated in initial enforcement efforts under the Fishery Conservation and Management Act, with reference to compliance by foreign fishing vessels with the 200 mile management system that Act established.

The decision to act or not to act on a violation of the restrictions within this zone by a foreign vessel has been made by the Department of State. And State correctly perceives that how we treat the vessels of foreign nations might have an impact far beyond how they, in turn, treat our fishing vessels within their waters.

While there have been few problems with violations of the zone by foreign vessels, American fishermen have taken exception to instances in which foreign policy considerations have taken precedence over the punishment of clear violations of fishery regulations. The same dynamics can be expected to exist in other types of zones, such as a "marine sanctuary."

5. Communicating the existence of ocean zones. The present means by which the growing number of ocean zones are made known to ocean users is through the distribution of nautical charts and the issuance of various bulletins, such as *Notice to Mariners*. But the growing number of regulations associated with ocean management in general suggests the need for additional efforts, devices, and concepts.

Charts and maps may need to be redesigned, on an international uniform basis, to clearly communicate the broad and growing spectrum of regulations, policies, and activities located within ocean space. It is probable that the United States is the leading nation in the world regarding ocean management, and the problem of intelligently communicating a broad variety of ocean management details so that they are understood and followed is a challenge and a burden which may be uniquely ours at the present time. As more precision is required of those who use the oceans, it may not be sufficient to place the burden of compliance upon ocean users. It is probably impossible for anyone to know all of the rules, policies, and activities taking place within some heavily "managed" ocean space. Those who wish to design and control how ocean space and ocean resources will be used have the task of figuring out how to let the great variety and number of ocean users know what the control system is.

This problem of communicating regulations, especially as they apply to special areas or "zones," is of particular importance for the state coastal zone management programs, and is an issue that has not received sufficient attention. Within the coastal zone, many users are unaccustomed to the *Notice to Mariners,* the publications of the Defense Mapping Institute, or, in many instances, even basic "rules of the road." The Coastal Zone Management Act calls for the establishment of priorities of use, permitted use designations, areas of particular concern, management systems, etc. There is a very real question of how those affected by this evolving web of restrictions and principles are supposed to know about it.

This is a general problem that our society faces as more and more regulations are created, but it seems especially difficult in the coastal zone or the oceans beyond for those who are accustomed to treating the shoreline and the oceans as a free good, available to all people for all purposes. The majority of recreational fishermen, boat owners, and shoreland property owners are not accustomed to ocean regulations—a fishing license is usually not required for recreational finfishing in the oceans, and a driver's license is not required in order to operate a private boat.

For some management purposes the shoreline can be literally marked with signs. Navigational zones are marked with buoys, flashing lights, and often printed signs, as well as being designated on charts. But for those rules, regulations, and ocean areas where this is not possible or practical, how are the rules to be made clear? This is particularly difficult because historically there have been few, if any, rules here.

6. Who should establish zones? The Deepwater Port Act contains a detailed process for the designation of a special ocean zone, and as discussed previously, this process appears to be adequate. By the procedure contained in the Act, the Secretary of Transportation establishes a Deepwater Port Zone, after having communicated with numerous interest groups. Any regulations affecting foreign vessels must be worked out with the Department of State, thus ensuring the inclusion of foreign policy considerations. Thus, it is an administrative decision.

Defense area withdrawals from OCS leasing, as specified in the Outer Continental Shelf Lands Act of 1953, can be approved by the Secretary of the Interior or by the President and both have done so. In the late 1950's, Congress asserted authority over such withdrawals through the passage of the Engle Act which, in effect, requires Congressional approval of any withdrawals or restrictions for military purposes, since it applied to areas 5,000 acres or larger and the leasing unit used by the Bureau of Land Management was 5,700 acres. However, as described elsewhere in this report, Congress has encouraged the Department of Defense to work these arrangements out informally with the oil industry and Interior, thus turning these into administrative decisions.

The Marine Sanctuaries program requires the approval of the President. However, amendments proposed in 1978 would require Congressional approval, by both the House and the Senate, for the designation of a marine sanctuary of more than 1,000 nautical square miles, and the Senate committee report of this legislation contains a strong declaration of Congressional interest in any designation.

The Outer Continental Shelf, as a "national management zone," was first established by Presidential declaration, as was the concept of a fishery conservation zone. Both declarations were made by President Truman. Presidential authority was also used by Theodore Roosevelt to establish the Northwestern Hawaiian Island Wildlife Preserve, in the early 1900's, and by Franklin D. Roosevelt to establish a 200-mile national ocean defense zone in 1939.

There are a variety of ocean zones and a variety of procedures, criteria and authorities for their establishment. The Coastal Management Act and the 1977 Presidential directive to give increased consideration to the establishment of marine sanctuaries indicate that this situation will continue to grow more complex, and a review seems to be needed. The Congress has involved the U.S. in some ocean zoning decisions and removed it from others. When does the Government participate and by what method should it do so? When should the President be involved? Should the National Security Council be explicitly included? Should all ocean zoning be done under a uniform set of procedures and criteria which follows from a careful inquiry to assure that a zone is needed and that, as proposed, it will achieve its stated objectives while minimizing administrative, environmental, or functional problems? It also seems appropriate to reexamine some of the previously established processes and see if they might not be coordinated and improved. Within the territorial sea, should designations of "areas of particular concern" require a special approved process separate from the coastal program approval? What should be the approval process for estuarine sanctuaries? What should be the decision process and criteria for establishment of OCS navigational fairways, and of port vessel traffic safety schemes? There seems to be an identifiable and important set of issues associated with the establishment of some portion of ocean space for special management attention. These "zones" are management tools and are currently being used by many independent functional programs in separate ocean management regimes. As a result of the Coastal Zone Management Act there could be as many as thirty separate zoning procedures and sets of criteria for the territorial sea, and there may be nearly as many as that at the Federal level for the ocean space beyond.

Determining the questions that have to be asked prior to establishing an ocean zone and identifying which interest groups, policies, and agencies should be included in an ocean zone decision would seem to deserve further attention.

III. Principles for Ocean Management

Guidelines or principles are tools which can provide criteria for assigning priorities, determining public expenditures, and resolving conflicts.

A. Multiple Use

Congress has provided a definition of multiple use in the *Multiple Use and Sustained Yield Act of 1960* (Forest Service) and the *Classification and Multiple Use Act of 1964* (Bureau of Land Management). Both acts define multiple use as:

> The management of all the various renewable surface resources of the national forests so that they are utilized in the combination that will best meet the needs of the American people; making the most judicious use of land for some or all of these resources or related services over areas large enough to provide sufficient latitude for periodic adjustments in use to conform to changing needs and conditions; that some land will be used for less than all of the resources; and harmonious and coordinated management of the various resources, each with each other, without impairment of the productivity of the land, with consideration being given to the relative values of the various resources, and not necessarily the combination of uses that will give the greatest dollar return or the greatest unit output.

These acts then go on to specify various products or services for which the lands are to be administered or managed, including things such as outdoor recreation, timber production, watershed protection, fish and wildlife, wilderness or mineral production.[9]

---

[9] Public Land Law Review Commission, *Federal Public Land Laws and Policies Relating to Multiple Use of Public Lands,* (Washington, D.C., 1970).

Multiple use can be seen as the opposite of exclusive, single-purpose use (such as special defense areas in the oceans). Primary-use areas, e.g., the way marine sanctuaries are currently defined, in which a primary use is designated for an area and other uses are allowed so long as they do not clash with that primary use, represent a middle ground between the other two approaches.

Multiple use of the oceans is presently a definition of the status quo as much as a management principle, and in most instances, it is exceedingly difficult to gain political acceptance for its opposite: exclusive use. If this principle is formally applied to ocean control, it has certain limitations as an effective management tool.

First, multiple use assumes, implies, or requires that there are no clearcut priorities among national interests, and allocative decisions must be made by those attempting to implement the principle. The principle itself provides little real guidance as to how conflicts should be resolved or priorities assigned. Second, it requires a very large resource base so that conflicting uses may be accommodated by allowing each activity to have its own area when uses are not compatible. As this principle was applied to national forest lands and other public lands during the 1960's, Congress determined a specific set of key interests that would somehow be accommodated and then left it up to the administrators of the program to implement the idea.

But perhaps the most important limitation of the concept is that it was formulated and incorporated into American natural resources policies prior to the emergence of a national awareness of and concern about environmental impacts and ecological protection. Multiple use and its companion principle to be discussed next, that of sustained yield, are not necessarily invalid, but they do not necessarily reflect all of the present national interests in natural resources management. Certain areas may have inherent carrying capabilities or be interconnected in bio-geo-chemical cycles or energy flows. Thus, multiple use tends to ignore both the nature of the pie being sliced and the nature of the activities seeking accommodation. Not all activities have the same impact. Not all activities have equal need for coastal or ocean access, and not all activities have an equal footing in the national interest.

B. Sustained Yield and Optimum Yield

As defined in the legislation cited above, sustained yield means

> . . . the achievement and maintenance in perpetuity of a high level annual or regular periodic output of the various renewable resources of the national forest without impairment of the productivity of the land.

In 1976, Congress modified this concept to include social as well as biological factors, referring in the Fishery Conservation and Management Act to *optimum* yield.

> Fishery resources are finite but renewable. If placed under sound management before overfishing has caused irreversible effects, the fisheries can be conserved and maintained so as to provide optimum yields on a continuing basis. (Sec. 2(a)(5))

As defined in the Act, optimum yield is a somewhat curious and imprecise principle upon which to base a national ocean fishing resources management program.

> The term 'optimum' with respect to the yield from a fishery, means the amount of fish—
> (a) which will provide the greatest overall benefit to the nation, with particular reference to food production and recreational opportunities; and
> (b) which is prescribed as such on the basis of the maximum substainable yield from such fishery, as modified by any *relevant economic, social, or ecological factor*. (Emphasis added.) (Sec. 3(18))

As might be expected, both the National Marine Fisheries Service and the regional fishery management councils have had problems defining what "optimum yield" is for various commercial and recreational fisheries. One danger with virtually all resource management principles is that they often become meaningless, providing no specific guidance, allowing any pattern of use. As a result of the inclusion of modifiers in subsection b, any allocative scheme produced by the administrators of the Act could be justified.

It is not unusual for regional council members to be reminded by fishermen that fishing represents a way of life for entire communities and that to limit catches would have a severe social impact. These are, under the Act's definition of optimum yield, legitimate and important factors that should influence the catch levels allowed. And if, in some instances, the fishermen can be suspected of being disingenous, there are very real social and economic impacts associated with fish catch allocations. But somehow fisheries management is not the same as zoning a community, and the consequences of granting a variance from the regulations, which is what the optimum yield principle amounts to, may not work for living resources.

Another basic problem with either sustained yield or optimum yield, as discussed in the Chapter Three section on fisheries management, is that these principles tend to focus upon individual populations of finfish and shellfish, as if these populations were totally independent of each other and of other biological and chemical parameters. Yet, if the proposed Antarctic Living Resources Management Regime establishes a quota for the commercial harvesting of Antarctic krill, on a sustained yield or optimum yield basis, given present krill population levels, it is also a decision that populations of certain whales, seals, and perhaps other living resources will be smaller in the future because of the interconnection through complex and not fully understood food chains.

Ultimately, sustained yield and multiple use provide little useful guidance for resource management, and may even fail to reflect fully the various national interests which have emerged since these concepts were first articulated. In recognition of the limitations of these principles, Congress has mandated the formulation of new principles for the management of public lands, in the *Federal Land Policy and Management Act of 1976* (P.L. 94-579). The formulation is now taking place and should be coordinated with national considerations of ocean management.

C. Dependency

Many states have attempted some degree of planning and management for their shorelands and the adjacent territorial sea, either as a result of the Coastal Zone Management Act of 1972 or on their own initiative. As a result of this effort, they have been faced with the need to develop principles for the allocation of ocean space and ocean resources, i.e., some method of sorting out conflicting and growing numbers of claims and demands.

An often-discussed principle for coastal planning is that of dependency. As with sustained yield, optimum yield, or multiple use, dependency is ultimately a somewhat elusive principle which has been suggested as an objective method by which allocation decisions can be made.

As generally used, states establish as policy which activities or facilities will have priority of access to coastal resources and coastal space on the basis of how "dependent" those activities or facilities are upon a coastal zone location. If something does not have to be in the coastal zone, it will either be precluded or assigned a lower priority. While this has some merit, there are also certain problems:

1. There are different kinds of dependency, such as economic or financial dependency. A factory may not have an inherent need to be on, in or near the water, but may take advantage of a coastal location to reduce shipping costs. And while it is difficult with today's shoreland prices to fully appreciate the fact, it was often the case in the past that

a coastal location was the least expensive site that could be obtained, even though proximity to the shore or water was otherwise of no importance. Without further clarification as to what kind of dependency is meant, the principle is of limited use in making choices through some objective standard.

2. Not all uses may be "dependent" upon a coastal or ocean location, but most would benefit from it, if only to provide amenities for the people associated with it, e.g., a nice view. While the merits of their demands may be less compelling than activities which cannot take place without a coastal or ocean setting, these non-dependent uses nonetheless are those of the public for whom the oceans are supposed to be managed. There is no dependency involved, yet residential and recreational housing remains one of the most popular uses of the coast, as evidenced by the many coastal developments in areas highly vulnerable to hurricane and storm damage. Given that situation, dependency may not be a politically acceptable criterion.

3. To allocate ocean resources on the basis of dependency is to reward and enshroud with legitimacy those activities which in the past have presumed to utilize ocean space and ocean resources. It does not, in fact, follow that just because an activity cannot take place if it is denied access to the oceans that access should be granted. As a part of a coastal zone management effort, the dependency concept could be viewed by some as arbitrary and capricious.

4. Dependency as a management principle tends to ignore the whole question of social choices and changing public priorities. Dependency might be most effective in the absence of public programs and priorities.

5. Dependency, unless combined with other management principles, tends to exclude consideration of the capacity of the oceans to accommodate activities. It either downplays or ignores susceptibility to damage and concepts such as suitability. It tends to favor the demand side of resources management at the expense of the resource base.

D. Suitability/Capability

A modification or expansion of the concept of sustained yield is the principle of allocating ocean space and ocean resources on the basis of "fit" between the proposed activity and the existing web of natural systems and human activities.

To use this principle for ocean management, it is first necessary to accept a basic premise that there may be limits to the capacity of various ocean systems to support or withstand the impacts of human activities, and that it is reasonable to allocate ocean space and ocean resources on the basis of the degree to which a given activity or facility "fits" with or is compatible with these natural limitations. To some degree this principle is similar to *sustained yield*. However, suitability/capability places more emphasis upon finite resources than renewable resources and upon resource protection rather than resource production. The focus is upon taking any user demands and seeing where and if they can be accommodated without diminishing the existing ocean system. This could be expanded to include determining the sensitivities of various human activities that are to be encouraged and protected and then using these sensitivities as further criteria to decide what should go where. It is a more general form of key value management described previously. An example is given below.

New Hampshire

As part of its coastal zone management effort, the state of New Hampshire developed a methodology of Coastal Zone Water Use Capability Analysis (1976) which represents an interesting, but not completely proven, use of this management principle. One of the important observations made in the report which describes this methodology is that a full development of this methodology would require "years of effort" and a great deal of money.

An initial inventory was taken of coastal ecosystems, marine and estuarine species, offshore bottom sediments, and existing and estimated demands for ocean use. Several maps were then prepared, using an overlay system similar to several evaluatory systems used in land use planning. The maps included:

1. Spawning areas for major ocean species,
2. Offshore fishing areas of importance to the state,
3. Clamming and oystering areas,
4. Existing offshore activity areas, and
5. Offshore sand and gravel deposits.

The analysis determined several activities likely to experience significant increase as well as others that might take place.

At that point in the process, several concepts or definitions of suitability and of capability were considered, and a seven-parameter system chosen, with emphasis on existing uses and natural systems sensitivities as a measure of future suitability. The overlay maps were then used in combination with these parameters and new maps were created that showed a four-area system indicating a good-to-bad continuum of use capability. Class I areas can support nearly all water uses that are currently technically feasible, and Class IV areas can only support a limited set of activities such as aquaculture, commercial fishing and lobstering, recreational fishing and boating, research and education, swimming, and esthetic enjoyment. It is interesting to note that New Hampshire determined that there were no Class I waters within its coastal zone, the first locations for high-impact activities being fourteen miles from shore.[10]

Texas has also chosen a version of suitability/capability for the management of its coastal zone. In general, it appears to be an important approach to ocean decisions, and it is generally what is implied in the environmental review process mandated by the Environmental Protection Agency. However, the limitations of the natural world have rarely been seen as the standard by which man should conduct his affairs, and wide-spread use of this principle would perhaps require significant changes in our political, economic, and even legal principles which now tend to recognize human rights and interests more than the capacity of natural systems as a measure of suitability. Also, a proper job of capability analysis requires the expenditure of enormous amounts of time and money. However, increasingly, the necessary research for such analysis is being done and is mandated in Title II of the Marine Protection, Research, and Sanctuaries Act.

A more basic limitation of this principle is that natural "capability" is to some extent a subjective measure, based upon a judgment as to when induced rates, degrees, or types of change are unacceptable. Moving from such assessments to a determination of suitability requires another major subjective judgment. While the principle can be used to good effect, there is a certain questionable underlying assumption within it that there is an inherent "best" pattern of use which can be revealed through this process. Unfortunately, the national interest is not so easily defined or accommodated.

E. Conclusions

The reliance upon broad principles, such as "multiple use," tends to avoid most of the important questions involved in ocean management and might result in a less-structured and less-viable determination by program administrators as to how the ocean will actually be allocated. These principles have the sound and appearance of substance yet a sufficient degree of ambiguity to accommodate virtually all activities.

---

[10] Armstrong and Ryner, pp. 216-222.

The most popular principles for ocean management would be to ensure access for all human activities, maximize human enjoyment, and ensure the continued viability and richness of natural ocean systems. However, experience indicates that, while such principles might be quite successful politically, they would fail to secure either long-range protection of ocean systems or of human interests. As we are learning in our coastal zone, natural systems cannot be all things to all people.

The issuance of national principles for ocean use can be a form of management, by which the Federal Government attempts to influence ocean activities. But since most, if not all, principles suffer from the limitations of ambiguity and subjectivity, the nation in some instance, may need to make specific choices as to what should or should not occur. Such choices would also imply an increased degree of control to enforce those choices. When there are clear priorities or needs, then policies and plans may be required.

IV. Types of Ocean Management

The tools that could be used for ocean management, or the principles that might be appropriate, depend, in part, upon the type of control being attempted. In using governmental authority and power to control the ocean and its resources, there is a range of objectives and types of control that could be used. Chapter Three described two programs, the Fishery Conservation and Management Act and the Deepwater Port Act, which focus upon particular types of control effort, including "traffic control," management of special values or interest, area management, and "comprehensive" management.

A. Traffic Control

One of the activities which the Federal Government currently undertakes is literally to direct vessel traffic in crowded sea lanes, such as the New York Bight Vessel Traffic Control System. As more activities take place within ocean space, the need for keeping activities out of each others' way will become increasingly important, and increasingly difficult.

Attempting to maintain order and safety implies ocean space management, perhaps with the establishment of zones and rules of usage. The costs, legal complexities and political difficulties in such activity are probably significant. One of the questions which arises when considering such programs is which level of government should be responsible. The U.S. Coast Guard has been given most of the enforcement or police functions related to Federal ocean programs. But considering the amount of control that may be needed to maintain safety and order in future, more crowded ocean systems, thought might be given to restructuring such programs. It is not clear that a single agency could accomplish these traffic control functions, nor is it clear that this should be fully a Federal responsibility. Many state and local governments have harbor patrols, marine sheriff departments, and marine safety teams. Marine traffic control could be accomplished at the state level through coastal management programs with local and state enforcement working in partnership with the Coast Guard and other Federal agencies.

As more Federal ocean programs exert control over ocean space, some degree of coordination of traffic control may be necessary, and thus this type of management need not be confined to the control of private ocean users, such as oil companies or marine vessel operators. Establishing vessel traffic control sea lanes, marine sanctuaries, dredge disposal sites, deepwater port sites, OCS lands leasing sites, floating nuclear power plants, and national security project areas may require increased governmental effort, and the assignment of a coordinating authority or responsibility to some unit of government. An evaluation of space and atmospheric management programs might provide useful concepts, techniques, and lessons. In terms of international traffic implications, it may be useful to consider the role of IMCO because of its function as an existing international body that acts as an information exchange forum (including standards) where concepts of ocean traffic control can be discussed.

B. Ocean Management of Special Values

Chapter Four includes a discussion of national interests and suggests that there may be some national ocean values or uses which warrant special Federal attention, such as national security, protection of specific marine species, or the maintenance of navigational capacity. Federal ocean management would involve the identification of certain key values or activities that it wants to protect or enhance. "Management" might then consist of regulating ocean activities to secure consistency with these preferred activities and values, and/or efforts to encourage or promote certain types of ocean use that might not otherwise occur. Thus the Federal Government might not wish to take on control of all activities and all ocean dynamics, but it might wish to control a limited number of specified national interests.

1. Military testing sites. At the present time, the Department of Defense operates two major national missile test ranges, one in the Gulf of Mexico and one in the Channel Island area of the Pacific Ocean off the coast of California. With expansion of offshore oil and gas leasing, as well as the development of deepwater ports, marine sanctuaries, floating power plants, pipelines, and other ocean activities, there may be problems in keeping these ranges open. In order to protect these ranges the Department of Defense has, in the past, found it necessary to intervene in the OCS leasing process and to attempt to guide other Federal decisions so as not to allow development of these ranges. There are additional military or intelligence ocean space needs, but these exemplify the problem.

A basic space allocation question arises here; is it necessary and desirable that these facilities remain available for the testing of missiles and other military systems? If it is, then what must be done to protect these areas? As has been suggested earlier in this report, the present process for resolving such conflict is imperfect and is not always based upon a clear national use of policy decision made by Congress and/or the Office of the President.

The Bureau of Land Management appears to have attempted to accommodate national security interests, although there are several problems with the process by which that accommodation is attempted, as previously discussed. The Outer Continental Shelf Lands Act states that OCS lands can be removed from the leasing process for purposes of national security and recognizes the authority of the President to do so. It would seem clear that the protection of fairways necessary for the safe firing of missiles falls within the intent of the Outer Continental Shelf Lands Act. But it is not assured that these particular corridors, falling within unknown or suspected deposits of hydrocarbons, will be protected under the present system. There is strong political and economic pressure for the development of all offshore hydrocarbon deposits, and arguments may arise that the need for energy supplies is more important than the maintenance of a large ocean corridor for the exclusive use of the military.

To protect these ranges, if it is determined to be in the national interest to do so, the Federal Government might have to establish a permanent military test zone, perhaps by Presidential Executive Order. If such a zone were structured along the line of the marine sanctuaries program or the deepwater port program, then other activities would not automatically be excluded, but would be controlled in time and space so as to be consistent with the primary use of that ocean and air corridor for missile testing purposes.

2. Navigational fairways. The ability of the ocean to support navigation has long been a recognized national interest, and a variety of management programs have been developed to protect that interest. The Traffic Separation Schemes (TSS) for major harbor and port areas such as the New York Bight, and more comprehensive and complicated vessel traffic services (VTS) being completed for Puget Sound and the Strait of Juan de Fuca illustrate this type of management.

But as ocean space beyond traditional port areas becomes more crowded with activities and structures, formal navigational fairways may be needed extending far from shore, perhaps as far as the outer edge of the continental shelf. The U.S. Army Corps of Engineers currently has authority to establish such systems under provisions of the Outer Continental Shelf Lands Act (which raises questions as to the linkages between Coast Guard and Corps of Engineers' navigational management programs). Vessel transit lanes may have to be established as permanent ocean zones, similar to missile test ranges, to insure the continued safety of navigation and yet allow expanded development of ocean resources and use of ocean space.

Other national ocean values that might suggest the need for some type of Federal ocean control include:

- National security interests other than weapons testing,
- Food production (biological productivity of the ocean),
- Marine species protection, and
- Recreation

For each of these values, the thrust of "management" would not be to attempt to exert control over ocean activities and ocean space per se but to ensure that a limited number of specific values or interests are protected as the ocean is used.

C. Management of Special Areas

Closely associated with the concept of management of special values is the concept of management of special areas. This approach emphasizes the spatial dimension of national interests and focuses upon geographic areas of particular concern. There are at least four categories of special interest ocean areas that might warrant Federal management attention.

1. Areas of resource concentration. This might include deposits of sand, gravel, manganese nodules or oil and gas; fish concentration areas such as Georges Bank or Bristol Bay; ocean energy concentration areas such as the Gulf Stream, estuaries or deepwater ports.

2. Areas of ocean sensitivity. There may be areas of the ocean which are particularly susceptible to damage or disruption which require special monitoring, siting and control to minimize or prevent damage. This might include estuaries, migratory routes, breeding grounds. In terms of sensitivity, the *temporal* aspects of ocean dynamics becomes critical. At certain limited times of the year, the surface waters of the ocean become especially sensitive to disruption, as shellfish and finfish larvae are held in suspension at the surface. If an oil spill were to occur, or other disruptive event were to take place at this time, a whole year class of sea clams, lobsters, or other finfish or shellfish species might be decimated or possibly destroyed. Thus controls might be applied to such areas only under certain conditions or at specific times of the year.

3. Ocean hazard areas. There are areas where natural or manmade hazards represent threats to human safety or the natural environment which might require special monitoring and control. This might include strong tide and current areas, storm pathways, areas of tectonic activity, weapons testing and ammunition disposal sites, shipwrecks, barrels of radioactive material, cables, pipelines, etc. There may also be moving hazards. A special floating hazard zone is established by the Coast Guard around each liquefied natural gas tanker as it moves into Boston Harbor, and the hazard zone moves with the tanker in time and space.

4. High activity areas. Major ports and harbors, such as Boston and New York, Chesapeake Bay, Puget Sound, the St. Mary's River in the Great Lakes, the St. Lawrence Seaway, and the Houston Ship Channel may require special management, not only to avoid physical collision but also to resolve policy conflicts and administrative difficulties. As fishing, vessel transit, national security interests, and offshore hydrocarbon production interact in time and space, other offshore areas, such as Georges Bank, the Straits of Florida, and the Gulf of Mexico may also require control, setting of priorities, conflict resolution, monitoring, and other forms of management activity.

D. Comprehensive Ocean Management

The last conceptual construct considered here is that of "comprehensive" ocean management. Under this approach, the entire collection of resources, ocean dynamics, and human activities within a given amount of ocean space would be the focus of attention. It can be seen as an expansion of special areas management, suggesting that the ocean or some significant portion thereof is a "special area" requiring attention.

The United States has opted for this approach within its territorial seas, or at least moved in that direction, through the passage of the Coastal Zone Management Act of 1972. The Act encourages states to establish broad priorities of use as well as designations as to what will and will not be permitted within this ocean area. Areas of particular concern are to be designated and detailed management strategies within this regime are to be coordinated and made consistent with this set of priorities and use principles to the degree practicable. While this kind of management has roots in national forest planning, public lands planning, and river basin planning, it is really an evolutionary extension of those earlier multiple use natural resource programs.

"Comprehensive" ocean management is a concept which suggests the extension and adoption of this kind of approach to a broader portion of ocean space. This does not automatically imply an extension of the coastal zone seaward, although obviously that is one interesting conceptual option. However, it is also possible to dissolve the "coastal" zone and create a new "ocean" zone with an entirely different institutional structure than that contained in the Coastal Zone Management Act. For that matter, OCS management could be upward and shoreward and be redefined to include more than minerals leasing, as we shall see.

If the comprehensive model were applied to submerged lands and waters of both the territorial sea and the outer continental shelf, it would imply an immense undertaking. If one takes the Coastal Zone Management Act at face value and translates the concepts of comprehensive zone management it contains to this larger area of ocean space and ocean resources, a national identification of "wise use" of this space and the resources would be needed. Then a monitoring and enforcement network would be required to ensure compliance with that definition of wise use.

In one sense, this concept is not alien to our present ocean-related programs and policies. There are at least four areas (national security, fisheries management, OCS leasing, and navigation) where the approach is increasingly comprehensive, yet still single purpose. What is really different about this approach is the focus upon some portion of the oceans, and all uses of it as a single system, rather than dividing it up into multiple management programs. Rather than having an outer continental shelf lands leasing program, there would be an ocean minerals leasing program, undertaken as part of ocean energy management and extractive uses management; and these would be seen as being interrelated to decisions regarding living resources management, navigation, recreation, and national security.

This "comprehensive" approach was suggested as early as the 1930's for an area of ocean space and ocean resources extending to the outer edge of the continental shelf (as discussed in Chapter Two). That proposal was rejected on the basis of foreign policy constraints and the absence of a compelling need. Recent suggestions for such an approach have been met with very strong and quite appropriate skepticism as to what such an approach would accomplish, how much it would cost, and whether or not there is any actual need. As the Coastal Zone Management Act comes up for review prior to its expiration, there have also been challenges as to whether the comprehensive concept contained in the Act has worked or is needed.

It is probable that this concept will continue to be evoked and will require serious consideration. It is an approach that has been attempted for land-based public resource areas, from forests to national parks and water basins; and aside from the important issue of whether this approach has worked or whether other approaches make as much or more sense, it is a way of structuring management efforts that frequently appears to be advocated for Federal management efforts.

E. Constraints to Adopting a More Comprehensive Concept of Ocean Management

Initial difficulties with the Marine Sanctuaries Program and the Coastal Zone Management Program indicates that there are many problems in attempting to establish some form of comprehensive understanding of and control over a portion of ocean space and related ocean resources. Considering the case of the New York Bight where the perception that improved ocean space management and coordination of public and private actions were needed, several questions are raised which may act as constraints upon adopting new approaches. In addition to those issues already discussed, two additional points are presented as indications of the kind of thinking required before undertaking new ocean management efforts.

1. Who will pay. In the New York Bight ensuring that boats do not run into each other; that the water is not polluted; that national security interests are protected; that finfish and shellfish are harvested so as to maintain an "optimum" yield, these and additional actions represent a potentially expensive program. For land highway systems, there are provisions for special funding, through gasoline tax, license and registration fees, and highway tolls. Although there have been major debates over the Highway Trust Fund and the national transportation system, a system does exist which to some degree is supported by users.

The various vessel traffic control efforts undertaken by the U.S. Coast Guard cost millions of dollars to establish and considerable sums to maintain. It may be in the national interest or even a national security issue of great importance that we have safe and efficient marine transit networks. But do the vessel owners who benefit from this coordinated system support its establishment and maintenance? Should they? In a similar vein, commercial fishing is a private industry. Yet, it is supported with millions of public dollars per year on the assumption that without federal intervention, finfish and shellfish stocks would be depleted by overfishing. It is likewise assumed that wetlands and estuaries need to be protected, new gear developed, treaties with other nations established and maintained, and additional services and research undertaken. Who should pay for all of this Federal fisheries-related activity?

This issue has recently received considerable attention in connection with our inland waterway system since that system is maintained at public expense without significant user fees or other private enterprise contributions. This not only represents a demand on public revenues but also can constitute a public subsidy which provides marine cargo carriers a price advantage over other forms of transportation not receiving the same amount of public assistance.

Perhaps a cargo import or export fee, a tonnage transported fee, a percentage of revenues landed fee, licensing fees, or similar methods should be used. However, there are also problems in that many ocean activities may not be able to afford significant financial contributions towards these costly governmental systems. The costs of not undertaking government ocean management in areas such as the New York Bight are not known, but they may be in their own way as significant as the costs of attempting such programs. The tradeoffs involved and the actual interests at stake need to be more fully understood before a more comprehensive management scheme is either rejected or attempted.

2. The complexities of "comprehensive" management; information requirement. Recently, a Russian satellite crashed into northern Canada and brought to the public attention the existence of a United States comprehensive information system which maintains real-time monitoring of every artificial satellite in space. This is only one part of a global monitoring system including underwater, surface, and space monitoring systems, the full capabilities of which are highly classified.

If the nation really wants to control ocean-use situations, such as those developing in Georges Bank or the New York Bight, increasingly complex information systems similar to those used by the Defense Department may be needed to keep track of what is happening in time and space, involving not only vessel traffic patterns but also chemical and biological patterns. These are already emerging, especially for navigation in major waterways

The establishment of ocean management information systems requires and deserves a study in and of itself and involves considerations of cost, content, technical problems, legal issues, complexities of interagency coordination, and the role of private enterprise in paying for, providing information to, or gaining access to such systems. It also involves national security interests which may represent constraints upon the design, operation, or even the establishment of such information control systems.

The point to be made here is that for "comprehensive" control of even a small portion of ocean space, an enormous amount of data and a complex information system would be needed.

3. Security aspects. It is likely that we have an extensive ocean information effort in place. The Department of Defense and the National Security Council conduct this for national security purposes. This effort, combined with the activities of various security agencies, probably provides our nation with information of the utmost military and intelligence importance. The capabilities of this system are perhaps understandably seen by the Department of Defense as being unavailable for utilization by the general public. Therefore, it is likely that a new, costly system will have to be built for domestic purposes if a more intensive level of management is attempted, and the technology may have to be redeveloped if the military determines not to transfer advanced information system technology to the domestic sector.

The other major security-related problem with developing ocean management information systems is that if such systems were to provide good information on what is occurring in time and space, they, by definition, would contain information which could reveal military actions or systems, or facilitate the disruption of U.S. domestic ocean activities and facilities by pinpointing their location and status. As a result, it can be assumed that national security agencies would argue that the United States either does not need a comprehensive ocean information system or that it would be counter to the national security interests to have such a system. One solution would be to build into such systems a capability of turning them off, for national security purposes.

One of the most obvious problems with that type of arrangement is that over time several critical domestic ocean management programs might become dependent upon advanced information and control systems, just as the military has. To suddenly shut those systems down is to invite a loss of control that might be avoided if some less drastic measures could be taken. As patterns of ocean use become more complex and as the need to make real-time decisions becomes more important, this will require further consideration and resolution.

V. Regimes

In Chapter Two a description is provided of how and why various ocean management "regimes" (as were defined in Chapter One) were established. Figures 3, 4, and 5 indicate the evolution of the present ocean management structure wherein the territorial sea, ocean waters, and outer continental shelf lands are treated as three separate entities.

As a way of seeking further insight into the nature of ocean management, let us assume that the only reasons those regimes were established as they were was because of (a) debate over Federal and state authority, and (b) an effort to minimize constraints upon American interests in foreign waters. Let us further assume, for the moment, that a new international agreement was reached by which the foreign policy aspects become moot. Let us assume that it was agreed that every nation could and would establish national sovereignty out to 200 miles from its shores and that the United States no longer perceived a significant linkage between the forms of authority imposed over its 200 mile band and its interests in foreign waters.

Given those assumptions, how should "U.S. ocean space" be structured for management purposes? Should the present system be retained? Should it change? If so, in what way? For example, would we want to keep the territorial sea the way it is, either in size or character? Would the states want or seek new definitions of the territorial sea? The intent of this discussion is not to answer these questions, which would require a major study. The intent is to evoke a variety of issues which help to indicate the degree to which ocean management is presently influenced by the system of regimes under which it operates, and to suggest some of the issues which lie ahead for states, the Federal Government and private industry. Using a graphic format introduced in Chapter Two for the discussion of regimes, this section provides an initial discussion of some alternative regime structures.

A. The Coastal Zone Management Act: Designing Regimes

In 1972 the territorial sea regime that had been established by the Submerged Lands Act of 1953 was modified conceptually by the enactment of the Coastal Zone Management Act. The "coastal zone" envisioned in the Act includes not only submerged lands and resources, but also, quite explicitly, the waters of the territorial sea, which had been undefined in the earlier state-controlled regime. This "coastal zone" also includes a portion of the shore adjacent to the ocean, rather than stopping at the water's edge, and although not clearly defined, appears to also include some portion of the atmosphere above the water. See Figure 8.

But the unique feature of the Coastal Zone Management Act is that it can be characterized as a process for the formation of special ocean management regimes on a state-by-state basis. There may be up to 30 separate regimes, each with different shore components, each with different Federal-state relationships.

It is also conceivable that two or more coastal states might form joint uniform regimes with consistent priorities and objectives, developing a regional regimes that could possibly extend along an entire seaboard, although there has been no evidence that such patterns will emerge in the near future.

B. Expanding the Territorial Sea or the Coastal Zone

During the 1930's and 1940's both Roosevelt and Ickes thought of moving the territorial sea outward as a method of obtaining national control over ocean resources such as fisheries and petroleum. The present UNCLOS negotiations include the concept of an internationally accepted 12-mile territorial sea. If this extension takes place, as shown in Figure 9, will it carry with it the coastal zone structure created in 1972? Would the states be recognized as owning the submerged lands and resources of this expanded territorial sea? If 3-mile coastal zones established under the present system were not automatically extended to the outer boundaries of the new territorial sea, what would be the management structure, the distribution of authority between state and Federal Government in the nine miles of space beyond present coastal zones? Would state coastal management still be voluntary? Would land-locked states obtain some portion of revenues derived from this new territorial sea? How would this affect the 200-mile Fishery Conservation Zone established in 1976? How would it affect the Outer Continental Shelf regime? Could state control be extended over the submerged lands and resources, but not over the waters of this enlarged zone?

C. Combining Coastal Waters and Ocean Waters

If the United States were no longer constrained by foreign policy considerations from establishing a formal management regime for ocean

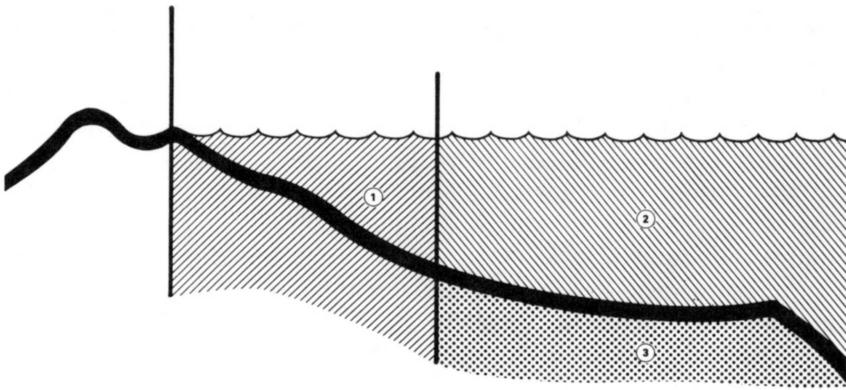

Figure 8: THE PRESENT SYSTEM OF REGIMES

There is an outer continental shelf regime (3), a deliberate absence of a regime for the ocean waters above the continental shelf (2), and a territorial sea that can through an elaborate process be turned into a specially designed coastal zone regime (1).

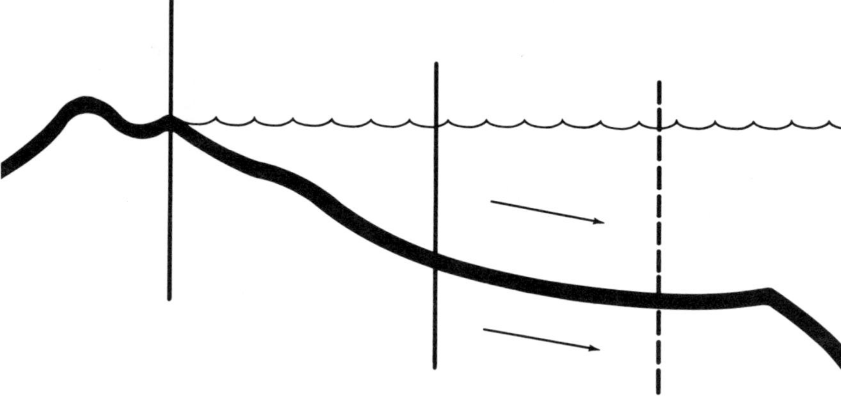

Figure 9: EXTENDING THE TERRITORIAL SEA

If the territorial sea was extended from 3 to 12 miles, how would it affect State and Federal ocean programs?

waters, should such a regime be established? Ocean waters could be treated as a unit, similar in some ways to treating the outer continental shelf as a management unit. If this were done, as shown in Figure 10, coordination of programs such as marine sanctuaries, fisheries conservation, water quality, and navigation might be improved, and problems of ocean space management might be more easily resolved.

Under the Submerged Lands Act, states are not recognized as "owning" the waters of the territorial sea, and many management responsibilities and authorities are reserved for the Federal Government. These two separate water areas could be combined into a single ocean waters or coastal waters management regime.

The management of this could either be a Federal task, or a joint Federal-state venture, perhaps under some new institutional mechanism suggestive of the Regional Fisheries Council. If such an approach were taken, it would avoid the complex and contentious issue of ownership of the submerged lands.

D. Expanding the Outer Continental Shelf "Regime" or Expanding the Coastal Zone

Through the Truman Proclamation of 1945, the submerged lands and resources of the outer continental shelf were established as public lands of the United States. As described in Chapter Two, for two years preceding the Truman Proclamation there was a sustained and intense debate as to whether or not the waters above the continental shelf should be included with the continental shelf as a single unit of national jurisdiction and management. If one momentarily accepts the assumptions articulated at the beginning of this section, that foreign policy concerns of the 1940's may no longer be as relevant today as they were then, the question arises as to whether or not the outer continental shelf and the waters above it could or should be combined in a single "management" unit. The "economic zone" concept which is evolving at the UNCLOS negotiations appear to incorporate portions of this idea, of a 200-mile area where the resources of the zone would be under control of the coastal state.

As an additional consideration, the Federal Government has already asserted control over many water-related activities, from navigation to water quality, even within the territorial sea, which is otherwise largely a state domain. The waters of the territorial sea could in the future be combined with the waters over the outer continental shelf into a "domestic ocean management regime." Such a regime could be Federally controlled. See Figure 11. But it also could be a partnership of Federal and state control, reflecting the linkages between offshore activities and shoreland access. This approach could lead to the very thing that our foreign policy and security agencies would like to avoid, e.g., the carving of ocean space into a series of "national lakes" with attendant difficulties in security and policy.

The inverse of this idea represents another option where the submerged lands and waters of the territorial sea, or the larger coastal zone (including shorelands), would be combined with the waters of the ocean for some distance beyond 200 miles. This would retain Federal "ownership" of the outer continental shelf and combine shorelands, the territorial sea, and ocean waters into a single unit under joint state/Federal authority, as in Figure 12. This would appear to be in keeping with the increased recognition of state interests in ocean management decisions discussed in Chapter Four.

E. Combining Federal and State Interests

Until the late 1930's, there was little United States management beyond the three mile limit, and none related to natural resources. When consideration was first given to extending national control beyond three miles, the proposal was made to combine the territorial sea with outer continental shelf lands and overlying waters into a single national unit. If one now momentarily assumes that the historic foreign policy constraints (including national security interests) are dissolved, would such a structure make sense?

How would state interests be dealt with? Could this be a joint Federal-state zone? If it were, would land-locked states be somehow included? What would be the relationship between such a regime and the atmospheric and land-based public management programs that exist at both the Federal and state level? What would be the impact of such an approach upon private industry? Would coastal zone regimes have to be dissolved? Would such a regime be constitutionally valid? Would states have to give up some of their present authority? If such a regime were established, how would it affect existing ocean management programs? What would be the extent or range of control which the public would need or be able to apply upon such a zone? How would it interfere with an international seabed regime? Could this type of coordination be achieved without having to change regimes?

F. Conclusion

As the objectives and complexities of management change, the boundaries of management regimes may also need adjustment. The pattern of regimes currently used for ocean management was established after serious and prolonged study and debate. The debaters could not foresee the diversity and level of control that is now being attempted. The United States has had more than twenty years experience with ocean programs

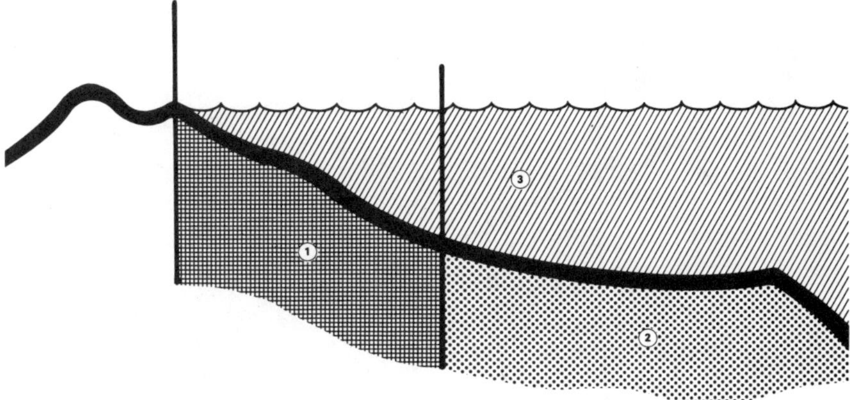

Figure 10: COMBINING COASTAL AND OCEAN WATERS

Submerged lands have traditionally been treated separately from the waters above them. The waters of the territorial sea could be managed in unison with the waters overlaying the continental shelf as a single ocean water management regime.

and the present regimes. As new programs are considered and different institutional arrangements evaluated, it should be remembered why those regimes were established, the degree to which the structure of regimes can determine how well programs work, and that regimes can be changed.

VI. Concepts of Special Interest

Three major topics warrant brief, but special, mention in this study of ocean management. They are: (1) conflict and resolution of conflict; (2) coordination of ocean activities, programs, and policies; and (3) recognition of, assessment of, and management capabilities to deal with long-term cumulative effects associated with ocean resource uses.

A. Coordination

The United States has historically viewed the ocean space adjacent to its shores as having several management regimes. Within those regimes, a growing number of policies and programs have been established on a single purpose functional basis. One result of this is an immediate need for coordination between each single purpose or narrow focus area of management.

One part of a general "ocean management" concept might be the idea of somehow linking each of these regimes, programs, and policies

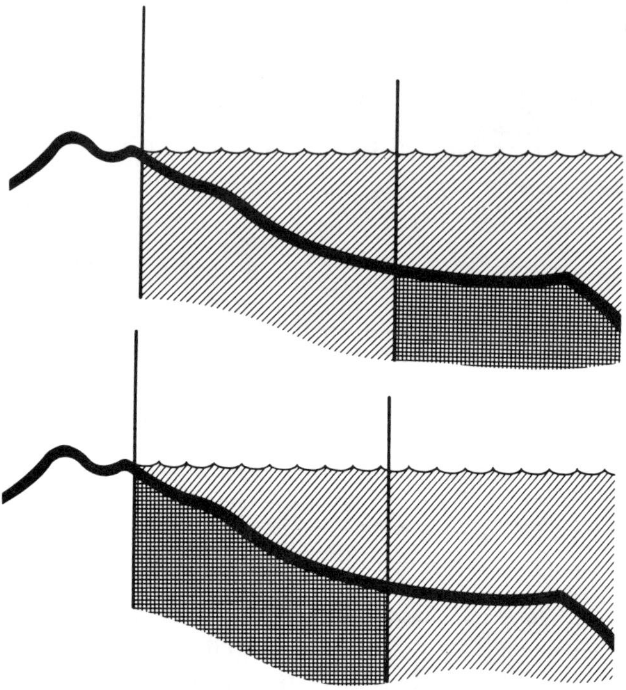

**Figure 11: EXPANSION OF THE COASTAL ZONE OR
THE OUTER CONTINENTAL SHELF**

The Coastal Zone could be expanded to include water beyond the territorial sea increasing the jurisdiction of the states as shown above, or, as shown below, the Outer Continental Shelf regime could be expanded to include superjacent waters of the territorial sea, increasing the jurisdiction of the Federal Government.

into a directed cohesive whole, a system based on "ocean" space and "ocean" resources, as opposed to say, managing uses. This method of achieving or improving coordination is considered in the preceding section of this chapter. But coordination might also be achieved without a major restructuring.

There are a number of institutional or administrative arrangements by which coordination could be accomplished. These specific arrangements are not in the scope of this study although they are important. There are a number of existing mechanisms that could be examined to learn more about the mechanics of coordination, e.g., P.L. 95-273, the National Ocean Pollution Research and Development and Monitoring Act. This Act requires rather extensive coordination of ocean pollution research and monitoring and calls for an assessment and ranking of national needs and problems related to ocean pollution. The specific coordinating mechanism of this Act could serve as one possible source of insight for a more general ocean coordinating function. There are many other examples, such as the CZMA, regional planning organization, and concepts in the National Urban Policy Program and others.

A detailed review and analysis of existing coordinating mechanisms for ocean-related activities and programs could be undertaken. There are probably hundreds of memoranda of understanding, less formal inter-program letters and agreements, ad hoc coordination committees, regional variations of the Federal-state review process, and other devices that themselves need to be coordinated, but which may provide a sufficient level of coordination in some instances.

But one of the easiest ways of starting to improve coordination is through the process of information flow. Aside from the military, very few companies, individuals, or agencies have a clear idea of who is

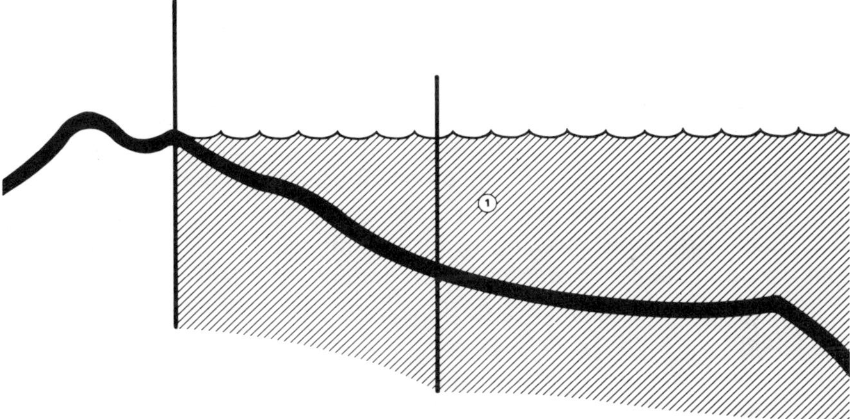

Figure 12: JOINT FEDERAL/STATE AUTHORITY

In terms of natural resources management and coordination of government policy and effort, this approach has a great deal of merit. It has been suggested, but rejected because of concerns over international repercussions, although several nations have adopted this strategy themselves. This may never come to pass in terms of institutional structure or explicit policy, for a wide variety of reasons alluded to in the report. However, if there is not a structural shift in this direction, a unit incorporating both the lands and waters of the oceans, and the air above to some degree will still be necessary in terms of program review, evaluation of long-range impacts, and identification of national interests. How this can be accomplished without the creation of a total oceans approach to national ocean-related programs and policies requires considerable study and skill. It is possible that it cannot be done, and that the United States will not realize the full benefits of or be able to afford full protection on the oceans.

doing what within the oceans, and it is this basic information which is often sufficient to achieve coordination or the beginnings of it.

The continued debate as to what information states should be provided regarding outer continental shelf oil and gas activities reflects the importance of obtaining information, the degree to which good communication/information does not exist, and the extent to which communication and coordination are interconnected.

If the Government were totally restructured and a new Department of the Oceans created, there would still be a need for basic information flow and a requirement, at some point, that programs and agencies cooperate. And ultimately, coordination implies an outside authority with the ability to make a final decision, resolving conflicts and making a choice among competing interests. No one currently has that authority for either the coastal zone or the oceans beyond. Perhaps regional Federal/state ocean coordination councils or an interagency structure within the Executive Office of the President might be able to achieve coordination without the need for broader reorganization.

It is very difficult to determine for any portion of ocean space what policies, regulations, programs, or long-range plans might apply. The Bureau of Land Management is perhaps unique in its publication of long-range lease schedules that allow lead time of up to two or three years. It is striking how little communication between and among agencies and programs takes place, either on a regional or a national level. The creation of some mechanism for communication of what is being done could significantly improve coordination, the lack of which may as often result from ignorance of other programs and activities as from indifference or willful isolation.

1. Regional ocean atlas and ocean program bulletin concepts. If informational atlases were to be prepared for ocean space on a regional basis, perhaps reflecting the regional divisions of the Fishery Conservation and Management Act, it would provide each agency, program, and interest group with a common set of information not only as to natural conditions, but also about existing patterns of human activity. These atlases could also contain clear indications of laws, regulations, and programs that apply to portions of that region or to activities or resources within that region.

If on an annual basis, some publication which, for purposes of discussion, will be called an ocean program bulletin were issued on a regional basis, it could significantly improve communication and coordination. If each state coastal program were assigned the task of mapping activities of its local and state units of government, and if some similar

Federal responsibility were assigned for Federal programs and activities that were to take place within the next twelve to thirty-six months, then there would be an opportunity to interact, to coordinate, to resolve conflicts, avoid inadvertent duplication, and to join in mutually supportive efforts. It would not be an easy task, but it is difficult to see how the need for some such device can be avoided in the future.

At the state level, a coastal activity bulletin might be published more frequently, perhaps through the Sea Grant Programs, which would use input from university researchers, fishermen, ship operators, property owners, Federal agencies, and state agencies. This bulletin would review and summarize pending decisions, applicable EIS's, future public hearings, new hazards, new publications and reports, etc. Such an information flow and use could provide the basis for a more effective linking of programs and policy objectives. It could be done without a major administrative change in the current agency structure, and if done correctly, it could lead to a better "fitting" of programs and activities in the oceans.

Any major activity, program, or policy must consider several elements if it is to "fit" within the ocean "system." Without attempting to develop a complete list, the following items are some of the elements which can determine the degree to which a new ocean activity (including programs or policies) causes disruption, has no noticeable effect, or augments the existing system:

- foreign policy;
- national security;
- navigation;
- atmosphere (pollution, climate, weather);
- state coastal management programs;
- regional fishery management programs;
- OCS leasing programs;
- water quality;
- marine quality;
- marine mammals;
- endangered species;
- recreation;
- marine sanctuaries;
- regulations, programs, plans of any other Federal, state or local agency;
- interests, intentions, activities of private industry;
- ocean dynamics, including waves, currents and thermal gradients as well as hazards, such as hurricanes and high winds;

- physical characteristics of site: location and nature of materials dumped, pipelines, cables, wellheads, oil rigs, deepwater ports, floating power plants, etc.

These types of elements would be included in any "ocean activity/use atlas" and would make up the information input and character of the dynamic atlas system.

B. Conflict Resolution

Conflict resolution is an often mentioned subject when one discusses the topic of "ocean management." Throughout this report, the topic of conflict and conflict resolution has emerged either by name or by implication. Many times when viewed closely, it is seen to have many features similar to that elusive topic of national interest. It means many things to many people. Everyone thinks it is needed, few people completely agree on what it is and no one can describe a consistent set of criteria by which we can judge one particular conflict resolution approach against another.

What is conflict? What are the conflicts in the ocean? There are conflicts among uses, among users, among institutions, among agencies, among states, among regions, between many uses and the natural system of the ocean, and indeed among systems set up to resolve conflicts.

What is resolution? When is an ocean conflict resolved? Is there a certain level of mutual compromise that indicates that an issue is now resolved, e.g., has the relative role of states versus Federal Government been resolved? If so, what level is it?

In recent years, there has been a growing number of conflicts in ocean resource use. States have had conflicts with the Federal Government over resource ownership, over the right to regulate, over the ability to set and enforce standards and other related issues. They have had conflicts with industry over facility siting, establishment of guidelines for operating facilities, and other issues. They have had conflicts with local units of government over the right to control coastal development, the establishment of procedures to determine impacts, and different segments of the public have had conflict over what the national interest in the oceans should be, most particularly on the issue of ocean protection versus resource use.

One could go on to list literally hundreds of ocean and coastal conflicts that have been, are, or will be, subject to resolution procedures. However, the basic idea here is to illustrate that conflict resolution is a problem of many facets and dimensions.

It also is a concept that is not new in the oceans. In Chapter Two it was shown that ocean resource conflict resolution was accomplished on a number of basic issues during 1940's and 1950's. This resolution was accomplished by the mechanisms that were established to resolve conflict by the founders of our country: the legislative body and the courts. While conflict resolution can occur at a number of levels or to a variety of "degrees," the ultimate conflict resolution mechanisms are the courts and the Congress.

If we think of the problem of conflict resolution in the same way as the "spectrum" of management, the complexity of the concept can be seen. Passing from one end of the spectrum called complete agreement (and really nonconflict) we would envision passing through several intermediate stages, where through various external mechanisms we have achieved compromise or partial satisfaction, to the opposite end of the spectrum where full agreement is needed.

The mechanisms that provide the mid-range components of the conflict resolution mechanism are many and varied in character. The consistency provision of the CZMA is one of many examples of a mandated conflict resolution mechanism.

The conclusion one reaches is that it is extremely difficult, if not impossible, to spell out a single, comprehensive conflict resolution process for ocean management. Some of the conflicts that exist in ocean affairs are derived from the basic structure of the American government and economic system and may be unresolvable in the context of ocean management, however conceived. There are many existing and permanent approaches already in place for conflict resolution that cannot be ignored.

However, there are ways to assist these existing processes of conflict resolution. One is to provide information as discussed under the heading of Coordination. The other element which is particularly needed in ocean management is a means of assessing development or activity impacts. The United States does not have an effective mechanism by which ocean resource development alternatives can be adequately assessed across the full range of effects and implications associated with them.

C. Long-Range Cumulative Impacts

If management and control of the ocean is attempted, its success will depend upon a number of variables. One of the most of these is the achievement of increased knowledge and understanding of ocean uses, ocean resources, and the effects of one upon the other. The ability to control a system successfully depends to a significant degree upon a clear understanding of how that system is affected by external forces and the impacts which that system imparts upon its surrounding environment.

A considerable amount of effort has gone into the development of assessing and predicting the impacts of various ocean activities and events, such as oil spills, changes in fishing strategies, the mining of seabed minerals, ocean disposal of waste, the use of ocean thermal gradients for the production of power, and several other activities.

Most of these assessments, whether actual impact calculations or general predictions, have focused attention upon how individual activities and natural systems would interact in time and space. One element of ocean management for which there does not presently appear to be an assignment of responsibility or authority is to identify, evaluate, and propose actions based upon the long-range cumulative impacts of the individual decisions being made by private industry, local and state government, and the Federal Government.

Impact assessment which treats each project as an isolated incident in time and space is valuable for insuring that a given activity "fits" within the existing web of other activities and dynamics of natural ocean systems and national ocean policies. But long-range, cumulative impacts of multiple activities lead to an entirely different level and type of decision and control.

As individual OCS leasing decisions, deepwater port license permits, marine sanctuary designations, and associated activities take place, the cumulative impact may be to preclude the use of some portion of ocean space for missile testing; to preclude the existence of some species of ocean life; to prevent extraction of a desirable resource; to prevent the utilization of some portion or dynamic of the ocean for the production of power. In a similar fashion, the cumulative long-range impact of filling in more wetlands and estuaries may be the reduction of the biological carrying capacity of the ocean, as well as increased erosion and flooding problems on shore.

The government does not have to identify these impacts, as demonstrated by the fact that little effort is presently devoted to that type of activity. And in many instances, it might be exceedingly difficult, and expensive, to accomplish such analysis. Once a trend is identified, once alternative futures can be predicted, it creates a need to make additional difficult public choices which can be both unpopular and impossible to resolve successfully.

Perhaps the strongest argument against attempting long-range cumulative impact assessment as part of ocean management is that if long-range impacts can be determined, if the consequences of decisions made for a variety of activities and locations can be traced to subsequent conditions and options, it leads to the concept of attempting to manipulate all of the individual goals, programs, policies, and decisions for some long-range purpose that depends upon the control of several otherwise uncoordinated activities. Considering the difficulties of controlling individual activities for immediate purposes, the task of attempting to manipulate several activities for a, perhaps difficult to perceive, long-range purpose would be immense.

However, over time individual actions establish the future. If some aspects of that future are of sufficient national importance, then it becomes necessary to know what factors can be and must be controlled. Thus, it was suggested in Chapter Four that if the national objectives were to be long-range increases in the quality and quantity of finfish and shellfish, these factors will need control, including water pollution, facility siting, weather modification, air pollution, and others which may have little or nothing to do with the direct problem of overfishing.

If it is actually in the national interest to control some aspects of the ocean, then it is important to know where impacts come from, what represents a threat, what is not important. And it will be increasingly important to understand the impacts of ocean management upon the atmosphere and the land. What land-based options are being preempted by ocean management decisions? What are the cumulative long-range impacts upon the shorelands of the United States of the development of offshore oil, or the prohibition of ocean dumping?

The United States has moved into a complex web of ocean management programs, especially since the early 1970's, without having identified the long-range implications of these control efforts, the cumulative impacts upon national budgets, size of government, cost of ocean use, or the other factors alluded to above. Several other nations are now engaged in or contemplating a similar degree of "management," and it would seem not only appropriate, but also vitally important, that these long-range and collective impacts receive greater attention.

CHAPTER SIX

THINKING OF THE FUTURE

I. Introduction

Ocean management is a complex matter and will require consideration beyond this initial examination. However, a number of opinions and reactions that the authors have developed may be of interest to those involved in further consideration of this important issue. The New York Bight situation is used as an example since it is increasingly typical of the type of arena in which we must begin to view the concept of "ocean management."

In the New York Bight area, there are estimated to be more than four hundred local, state, and Federal agencies.[1] These governmental entities are involved in the operation of port authorities; increasing employment and economic development; the disposal of surface runoff, solid waste and sewage sludge; the provision of recreation; and the management of coastal zones.

Even if fishing and navigation were the only two principal activities in the Bight area, there would still be serious ocean management problems. But the Bight has also been used for more than fifty years for the dumping of municipal sewage sludge; it is now also part of a 200-mile wide fishery conservation and management zone. Its submerged lands are crisscrossed with cables and pipelines; its subsoil contains several tunnels; and there is a vast accumulation of solid waste and sediment which is a pollution hazard and a costly obstruction to trawl fishing.

Because of the levels of vessel traffic, the Coast Guard not only has a six-lane Traffic Separation Scheme (TSS), but also is attempting to complete a radar-assisted vessel traffic control network for the New York area, similar to air traffic control systems at major airports. The city of New York has resisted this system, voicing fears that the microwave

---

[1] Paul Marr, *Jurisdictional Zones and Governmental Responsibilities,* New York Sea Grant Institute, New York Bight Monograph 22 (in press 1979).

171

towers proposed as part of the communications/identification network may represent a health hazard to city residents.

However, there are even more important considerations. The Bight sits on the edge of the Baltimore Canyon area, now being leased by the Department of the Interior for offshore hydrocarbon exploration and development. The Coast Guard's TSS system transects some of the lease sites, and further complicates the allocation of space among activities. Also, two floating nuclear power plants have been suggested for the north coast of New Jersey, at the edge of the Bight area, raising further concerns, requiring more inputs into siting decisions, and increasing the likelihood of conflict.

There are no policies for viewing or controlling the New York Bight as an ocean "space" or system. There are policies for navigation, for fishing, for ocean dumping, for recreation, for wetland protection, for dredge and fill, for air quality, for surface water runoff, for coastal management, and for offshore oil and gas development. The effects of these policies come together in time and space within the New York Bight, and as each program attempts to enforce its regulations and advance its interests, ocean space becomes more crowded and conflicts increase. When disputes are settled, it is most often on an ad hoc basis, as often as not the result of small-scale political battles, and not on the basis of any overall plan or goal. Is this the only or best way to manage? Does the Bight represent a microcosm of future U.S. "ocean management" problems?

Because the conceptual approach of our present ocean-related programs is that of functional "separatism," the Federal Government has neither the authority nor the responsibility to make sure that all of the programs fit with each other and with the sensitivities of the natural ocean system, so that important values are not destroyed. As Elliot Richardson observed about our national ocean-related programs:

> . . . it is not the lack of policies that is the issue; rather, the problem is the lack of a comprehensive approach to setting ocean policies. Certainly the policies we adopt for the use of the coastal zone should be consistent with those we adopt for fisheries management and for the development of our OCS oil and gas resources. Policies with regard to OCS resources should, in turn, be consistent with those for the control of ocean pollution. And policies with regard to our merchant marine or deep seabed interests should be consistent with our security and international economic and political interests.[2]

---

[2] National Ocean Policy Hearing Before the House Subcommittee on Oceanography, June 15, 1976.

"Consistency," as used by Mr. Richardson, is a somewhat abstract concept and to some degree it is not clear that consistency in and of itself is inherently necessary. The New York Bight represents a very clear picture as to what can and is happening under our present conceptual approach, an approach which had much of its origin in the rejection of the idea of a unified comprehensive approach and one which tends to prevent or impede coordination and consistency.

At this time not all of ocean space needs a comprehensive space and resource allocation system with clear priorities of use, detailed monitoring, and major enforcement and conflict resolution mechanisms. But something like that may be needed for the New York Bight, for Georges Bank, for some portions of the Gulf of Mexico, and other areas of heavy use and multiple management programs.

But what exactly is needed? Proposals continue to emerge for an ocean agency, for "comprehensive" ocean management, for additional expenditures, more research, more management. There needs to be a better understanding of what the actual problems are, what existing management programs really work, and why, what the role of various levels of government and private industry should or could be. There is much that could be done, that perhaps must be done, before major changes or additions are made in present ocean programs. The following areas of concern are not presumed to be exhaustive but hopefully include some of the important actions that could be taken now and that may serve to elicit additional suggestions by others.

II. Important Areas of Work: Recommendations

A. Program Review

In most instances there is no concise, central description of existing individual ocean-related programs which details the legislative/political process by which they are established, the complete legislative mandate, administrative actions taken to implement the program (including a sequential listing of memorandums of understanding and administrative directives and an indication of present status), Presidential orders relating to the program, publication, and research undertaken, and the relationships between individual programs with respect to national ocean management objectives. Few agencies are presently in a position to give a full, articulate, analytic identification of what the long- or medium-range needs of their program will be, or how it interacts with other ocean-related programs. It would seem to be in the interest of each program and of a national understanding of ocean management to have the administrator of each program prepare such a description, as some agencies are now beginning to do. In addition to this general need, some specific ocean-related programs would benefit from review at this time, perhaps by Congress, perhaps by some specially created review team, or by NACOA or other advisory group. For example:

1. Coastal zone management. If successfully implemented as currently written, the Coastal Zone Management Act will result in up to thirty definitions of what activities should have priority within the territorial sea of the United States. There could be thirty versions of how territorial sea decisions should be made, what criteria should be used in the siting of facilities, what activities should and should not be allowed access. If nothing else, there is a need to undertake a unified compilation of these programs so that there is a single source of information on and a clear national understanding of what the nation's territorial sea management program is, with all of its variations as derived from state coastal management efforts. However, there appears to be a need for additional review and analysis.

a. Each Federal ocean-related program should be traced across the various state coastal programs to see how those program elements and objectives have been incorporated, implemented, or accounted for within each of the state coastal programs. If there are major differences which lead to management inconsistency in one portion of the territorial sea compared to others and a major national interest is involved, then some special resolution should be undertaken now, rather than when such problems are revealed during implementation. Congress established an ad hoc negotiation process by which each state and each Federal program would attempt to work out some consensus on how segmented portions of the territorial sea should be managed. It is time to review what has come of those individual negotiations and see if they meet the needs of the nation and if they constitute a sufficient and workable management structure for the nation's territorial sea.

b. As suggested elsewhere in this report, authority over the water of the coastal zone is not clear. Federal navigational servitude, commerce, defense, and energy production powers come close to constituting ownership of territorial waters, and the Supreme Court has ruled that the Federal Government has paramount rights and authority. Congress has granted ownership and jurisdiction to the states over the submerged lands beneath these waters and to the living and non-living resources in these waters through the Submerged Lands Act and asserted that wise use of the territorial sea can best result from state administration and exercise of "full authority," which is incomplete and ambiguous. More precise distribution of both authority and responsibility is needed, not only for the three-mile territorial sea but for the oceans beyond, especially in anticipation of possible extensions of the territorial sea from three to twelve miles.

c. The entire concept of a "coastal zone" should, at this point, be reexamined, particularly the idea of meeting the national interests that may exist within this zone through a voluntary program administered by individual states largely at their own discretion as to content and direction. By now it should be obvious that, if the waters and submerged lands of the outer continental shelf region are to be developed and utilized, there must be not only physical but also policy and administrative linkages with the shore and the intervening territorial sea. Perhaps the coastal zone is too narrow a construct for some purposes and needs to be more sensitive conceptually and administratively to seaward needs and opportunities.

d. Our nation has an interest in, and a need for, policies and programs focusing upon economic utilization/development of natural resources. The Coastal Zone Management Act, with the exception of certain references, seems to give less than sufficient attention to the reality and importance of economic activity. While some coastal programs have attempted to address this aspect of ocean use, they remain the exception; such attention is not clearly required or encouraged in the Coastal Zone Management Act. It is unfortunate that this particular weakness of both the Act and subsequent program formulation and implementation has and will lead to efforts to undercut important protection and conservation provisions. Hopefully a positive effort could be made to supplement, rather than subvert, these coastal programs so that they incorporate the full range of territorial sea and coastal activities. There are basic value conflicts that will not be quickly or easily resolved, but emerging state programs provide a starting point which previously has not existed and which could serve as the basis for national discussions on how our territorial sea should and should not be used, and how best to achieve those desired results.

2. State ocean-related programs and policies. As described in Chapter Two, the coastal states were the traditional, if sometimes unknowing, administrators of the territorial sea until challenged by the Federal Government in the 1930's. Long before the Coastal Zone Management Act, many coastal states had initiated ocean-related management efforts, on wetland preservation, dredge and fill control, the siting of major facilities, port and harbor planning, and fisheries management. The concepts, mechanisms, successes, and failures of these state efforts should be reviewed in detail and utilized when appropriate in future local, state, and national ocean planning efforts.

3. Navigation. As pointed out in previous sections, ocean space management is a key concept in looking toward the future. Within this concept is the problem of surface management. Is navigation a key national ocean value? Is the present navigation management program sufficient? What about the present division of responsibility between the U.S. Army Corps of Engineers and the U.S. Coast Guard? Is it inefficient? Should this task be coordinated or unified into a single responsibility? Should navigation lanes be exclusive use zones free from fishing? What should be the navigational fairway designation process? Who should participate, what criteria should be used, and what should be the formal linkage between navigation concerns and all of the other programs and activities? To what degree should or can we regulate ships of other nations? How can coastal zone management be incorporated into or coordinated with Federal navigational management?

4. UNCLOS. Emerging from the present Law of the Sea negotiations is a new world ocean management regime and new principles and mechanisms for ocean-related decision making. The nation has not really formulated a national policy on the oceans, from which negotiations can proceed at the UNCLOS meetings. What often seems to happen is "formulation" of national ocean policy for UNCLOS purposes. The U.S. seems, at times, to accept new elements and new principles which run counter to those previously claimed to be in the national interest. The Department of State as lead agency at UNCLOS has not worked alone; and a significant, perhaps unique, effort has been undertaken by DOS to gain some input among national groups, from universities, industry, Congress, the military, and domestic agencies regarding our national ocean interests.

Because of the protracted negotiations at UNCLOS, it would seem prudent to review the implications of prior agreements and negotiations which might impinge on our future ocean use. If such a review waits until Congress and the nation are asked to ratify agreements already made, the whole process of gaining some degree of international consensus may be indefinitely delayed.

5. Atmospheric linkages. Since at least the 1960's, weather modification has been proposed as being another method of providing water for agriculture, hydroelectric power, and municipal water supplies. In the mid-1970's, the Federal Government moved toward the establishment of a national weather modification program, and by mid-1973, the new National Weather Modification Board was talking of precipitation augmentation by the early 1980's. Texts of once secret Congressional hearings indicate that the military had been extensively involved in both experimental and tactical use of weather modification and that Project Stormfury was started, in part, to gain the ability to modify severe storms which were causing property damage to homes built too close to the open sea.

In 1969 the Stratton Commission concluded that ocean management must be linked to atmospheric management and proposed a single Federal agency to coordinate and supervise both activities (National Oceanographic and Atmospheric Administration). Weather modification is no longer in the domain of science fiction, but it is a growing national program and significant private industry. Major weather modification could require manipulation of the ocean, or might affect the oceans as a secondary impact. Hurricanes which destroy coastal homes also distribute heat from the equator to northern regions; their currents are a primary mechanism of global thermal transfer. Changes in the surface temperature of the oceans which can shift jet streams and precipitation patterns can also affect the distribution of plankton, fish, mammals, migratory bird routes, and the cost of shipping.

The national weather modification program that is emerging needs to be coordinated with coastal and ocean management. The most appropriate time to achieve such coordination is now, as these programs are being designed, decision processes and criteria formulated, and long-range objectives established.

B. Regional Studies

If the nation is to undertake a broad assessment of its present and future ocean interests and ocean management options, it would seem necessary to do so not only in the abstract, but also in the various ocean regions adjacent to our shores, such as the Gulf of Mexico, the North Atlantic, and the Gulf of Alaska. "Regional studies" could take years and cost hundreds of millions of dollars. However, regional studies of an overview nature could also take two years or less, require relatively small amounts of new funds, and provide much useful information. By using available mapping and display techniques, the reviews could be structured in some uniform fashion from region to region and come up with visual documentation of present conditions and future options. Such studies might include:

- Survey and listing of all public resource programs which apply to that region;
- Identification of type and location of major ocean activities;
- Mapping of major ocean dynamics of the region;
- Seabed hazards inventory;
- Adjacent land planning/programs;
- International programs/interests associated with the region;
- Available information indication and evaluation;
- Air quality/loading;
- Water quality;
- Key value inventory (status of navigation, national security, fisheries, recreation, etc.);
- Major problems identification;
- Major opportunities identification; and
- Recommendations.

Such studies could also include a consideration of the specific policy/ issue topics listed below for a discussion of how they apply to the specific region. Such regional studies also address the issue as to whether or not it is necessary, desirable, or appropriate to undertake national ocean management programs on a regional basis, and if the answer is yes, what boundaries should be and why. If the answer is no, consideration could be given to how a national program could allow for regional differences and how present regional administration of national programs could be better coordinated. The studies might also spell out conditions, not yet in existence, that would be the threshold point for future regional or national management system development.

C. Policy/Issue Reviews

Throughout this report several issues associated with the scope, purpose, and design of national ocean management efforts have been identified. Those and others not included here could, and we feel should, be subjected to a detailed review by both Congress and the Executive Branch.

1. Role of private enterprise. What should be the role of private enterprise? To what degree should the Federal Government help private enterprise gain the access it needs at shore or offshore locations? Should private enterprise absorb more of the costs of various services they receive, such as ice breaking, weather forecasts, search and rescue? Should private enterprise be given financial assistance, more freedom from regulations, more restrictions?

2. Role of foreign and/or international interests in national ocean management. In the past the United States has given major consideration to various foreign policy considerations in the way it has conducted and organized its national ocean programs and policies. How should the still important linkages between these two spheres be coordinated?

3. National security interests in the oceans. What are the long-range opportunities and hazards of ocean utilization for national security operations? How should these be linked with other national interests in our national ocean management program? How can informed communication among and between interest groups as well as public knowledge of and supervision of national ocean activities be carried out without compromising security interests?

At the present time, we have two ocean management programs at the national level. One is a "civilian" program that is split into unconnected ocean regimes and undertaken on a narrowly defined, uncoordinated "functional basis." Its contents result from public debate and political compromise, and it clearly has many problems. The second system is much less visible, often because of security constraints. There is very little formal decision process for this second ocean management system, except within the National Security Council and its UNCLOS committee meetings. Congress may not have the same access to this system as it has to the domestic element, nor perhaps have individual elements of the national security community for which it exists. There are limited indications that it is also a fragmented approach and may not treat the ocean system as a total public resource.

4. Energy. What priority should be given to use of the oceans for energy production? How should ocean energy management be structured? How does the Department of Energy fit into ocean management? What is the role of private enterprise in ocean energy systems? What is the responsibility of the states to accommodate energy facilities within their coastal zone?

5. Living resource management. Is the continued biological productivity of the oceans a top national priority? How far do we have to go to assure such continuance? Are national patterns of land use, transportation, energy production, and waste disposal polluting the oceans? Should "ocean management" be able to establish air and water quality discharge standards for the ocean? What happens if ocean systems continue to be degraded? Can damaged systems be rehabilitated, or artificial ones created?

6. Ocean space management. How should we use ocean space? Should nuclear power plants be restricted to land? Are offshore facilities more vulnerable to accident or attack? Which activities should have priority in the use of ocean space? Should there be uniform national criteria and decision procedures for making such determinations? How can foreign vessels and citizens be regulated within our ocean space?

7. Boundaries. What should be the boundaries of ocean management? How far seaward? Should all of the subsoil beneath the seabed be included? What about the atmosphere (air quality, communications, air rights, weather modification)? Should shoreland be included? If so, how? If not, why not, and how will linkages be established?

8. Linkages. Associated with the boundary issue is one of linkages with things that are excluded from "ocean management," but which affect or are affected by the oceans.

- **National water policy.** Why isn't ocean management part of national water policy? Should ocean management be able to determine the characteristics of river discharges into the oceans? Should ocean management be able to control how weather modification that uses the ocean occurs, even though the target is inland? Should the current inland waterway study include a consideration of ocean management; is it not all part of a national water transportation management effort? Should it be? Why?
- **Agriculture/food management.** What should be the linkages between land food management and ocean food management? Should more national emphasis be placed upon ocean food production? Or will this be too restrictive upon other ocean uses and so food production should remain on the land? What about price support policies? Will land-based aquaculture be treated differently than ocean-based mariculture?
- **Urban planning.** The oceans provide both opportunity and problems for our coastal cities. Hazards from flooding, hurricanes, and erosion are serious and some urban development patterns are annually increasing the likelihood of major tragedy, e.g., occurrence of hurricanes in areas that were not developed with hurricane effects in mind. The water also can represent a unique urban asset, providing recreation, education, and jobs for urban residents, giving character to the community, enhancing the quality of life. How can urban planning and ocean management be

more effectively linked? The recent movement in urban water-front redevelopment may play an important role here.

D. Articulation of a National Ocean Philosophy

Perhaps subsequent to some or all of the studies and reviews suggested above, the President and/or Congress might prepare a new national statement of how and why the oceans are important to the United States and some broad general principles which we intend to follow. Such a statement was made by Truman in 1945 and by Congress in 1966. A new national ocean statement might include discussion of:

- Role of private enterprise;
- Role of local communities and state government;
- Role of the public;
- Role and importance of national security (military and intelligence findings);
- Attitude of United States regarding access of foreign nations to our waters and need for international ocean cooperation;
- How oceans relate to land-based interests and programs;
- Conflict resolution;
- Improving information and coordination; and
- Degree to which oceans serve as legitimate focal point for national concern.

These areas listed above are recommended as items that should be carried forward to support national and more informed decisions about which direction our nation might proceed.

III. Freedom of the Seas or "Creeping Jurisdiction"

> . . . as the oceanbeds are increasingly opened up at ever-greater depth to exploration and exploitation by various national and corporate interests, the limitations of the traditional freedoms of the sea become both more numerous and more disturbing. Exclusive national claims to exploit the resources of steadily widening areas of the oceanbed inevitably lead to political assertions designed to buttress such claims. And as drilling rigs, floating islands, stationary platforms, submersibles and artificial structures above and below the surface of the sea multiply, the traditional freedoms of fishing and shipping, however strongly they may be affirmed theoretically, must be qualified, restricted, and ultimately excluded.[3]

---

[3] Wolfgang Friedman, *The Future of the Ocean* (New York: George Braziller, Inc., 1971) p. 3.

A. Introduction

Within the United States and internationally, there are some individuals and groups who believe that our national ocean-related programs, such as the Fishery Conservation and Management Act of 1976, the proposed establishment of an international seabed authority, and other programs relating to resource management represent an undesirable intrusion upon traditional "freedom of the sea." This is often referred to as "creeping jurisdiction," indicating perhaps an assumed sinister nature of this trend. This issue is of particular importance because it has had a direct and major impact upon the scope and form of our own national ocean management efforts for more than 40 years, as described in Chapter Two.

However, at issue are not so much "freedoms" as are a set of traditional ocean activities which in a changing world can no longer expect consistent priority of access to ocean space. This issue includes several elements:

- There are concerns that the oceans should be used as the "common heritage of mankind" for the benefit of all peoples, rather than to serve the interests of individual nation states.
- There is concern over the growth of restrictions in general, i.e., the degree to which each activity is regulated by policy, international agreement, and management authority.
- But perhaps most important, there is concern that maritime nations will exclude ships of other nations from nearshore ocean waters; or that the passage of planes, surface ships or submarines will be regulated or prevented in or above larger and larger amounts of ocean space; or that submarine detection systems and other devices associated with national security may be restricted from increasingly larger portions of the ocean.

Thus, the discussion of "freedom of the seas" is somewhat misleading. Few seriously advocate leaving the oceans without any regulation, and this is especially true of the waters and submerged lands adjacent to our own coast.

B. Beginnings

Under Roman law the oceans were considered as being incapable of appropriation and ownership (**res nullius**). The oceans were held to be open to all people (**res communis**).[4] This should be considered, however, within the context of a political and military empire which exerted either control or influence over much of the known world.

After the dissolution of the Roman Empire and the onset of the Middle Ages, there emerged several major maritime powers, including England, France, Denmark, Sweden, Venice, Genoa, Spain, Portugal, and Holland, and each asserted claims or jurisdiction over some portion of the ocean. Perhaps the most dramatic example was the Treaty of Tordesillas (1494) whereby Spain and Portugal carved up the oceans and lands of the New World between themselves; Spain claiming total dominion over, and exclusive rights to navigate the Pacific, the Gulf of Mexico, and the Western Atlantic, and Portugal making similar claim over the Indian Ocean and the South Atlantic. By the 1600's, Venice claimed the Adriatic; Genoa, the Ligurian Sea; Denmark and Sweden claimed major rights in the Baltic; and both France and England asserted territorial zones adjacent to their own coasts.

With the defeat of the Spanish Armada in 1588 and the capture of a major Spanish treasure flect by the Dutchman, Piet Heyn, in 1628, the Spanish and Portuguese claims to ocean ownership were effectively silenced. The Dutch, through the works of Grotius, advocated a return to the Roman concept of freedom of the seas (**res communis**) and argued that the assertion of national jurisdiction was valid only for that part of the ocean to which a nation could physically control access. Selden advanced a somewhat different concept, of national dominion in some instances and freedom in others (dependent upon English interests).

By 1700 the more extravagant claims began to die and in their place emerged the concept that a nation could claim control over the oceans adjacent to its shores to the distance that a cannon shot could reach from shore; that is, to the degree that access could be prevented from shore positions. Bynkershoek first advanced this concisely in 1702[5] and Galinai, an Italian jurist, is one of those who proposed a fixed range of three miles.[6] While this concept of national jurisdiction over a zone extending three nautical miles from shore began to receive acceptance in international law, the degree of control that would be exercised within that zone remained in question.

---

4 Thomas Fern Percy, "Justice and Freedom of the Seas," *Journal of International Law,* 1928.

5 Bartley, p. 9.

6 M. W. Mouton, *The Continental Shelf* (The Hague: M. Nijhoff, 1952), pp. 193-200.

Up until 1945, the major maritime powers have, except in times of war, been supporters of a concept of "freedom of the seas" in which each nation was perceived as being free to transit any portion of the ocean space and to fish where it pleased. These maritime powers viewed the doctrine of freedom of the seas as essential to their interests since the oceans served as communication and trade links to their overseas colonies, were significant elements in their military programs, and were the source of fish often taken in distant waters. They used their naval power to enforce this doctrine. They also advocated a narrow territorial sea of three miles. Other nations with less maritime access, such as the Soviet Union, have consistently claimed wider territorial waters of 12 miles, which has been adopted by many countries and is generally accepted at UNCLOS.

But by the 1930's, the importance of the oceans had changed for most nations, due in large part to the emerging ability to extract hydrocarbons from submerged lands and the development of new military weapons and tactics. Some have suggested that the Truman Proclamations of 1945 regarding fisheries and outer continental shelf lands were the cause of subsequent claims to extensive areas of the seabed and ocean waters by several nations. While those actions by the United States have been used sometimes as a support for such claims by other nations, it seems clear that the real causes of such claims were new nationalistic assertions and shifts in technological capability, economic interests, and military strategies. Prior to 1945 both the United States and many other nations had given serious consideration to far more extensive claims than emerged from the Truman Proclamation.

As described earlier, there has been a consistent concern on the part of the Department of State and, increasingly, the Department of Defense about the extension of United States management controls over ocean space, fearing that such actions on our part would compel or support curtailment of our activities in international or foreign waters. They have strongly recommended narrow focus, functional approaches and looked critically upon attempts by our nation or others to extend the scope or boundaries of management efforts as intrusions upon "freedom of the seas." This report has already discussed the importance of including national security and foreign policy considerations in national ocean management programs, but the issue here is the validity and importance of the concept of "freedom of the seas." Relative to the concerns of Defense and State, it seems more appropriate to focus upon the specific activities they wish to protect rather than upon a nebulous concept of general "freedoms." If our national interests in unrestricted commercial exploitation and transit through ocean space could be linked to some inherent global concept of free access, it might be useful. But it seems unrealistic, and perhaps unproductive, in present circumstances to push the concept very far. There are more than 150 nations whose interests in the oceans must be accommodated, and the "frontier" attitude of former decades is untenable in an increasingly crowded world with multiple interests which cannot be accommodated without some degree of control, some formal, peaceful means of conflict resolution.

The real problem is not that of shortsighted national interests intruding upon some intrinsic "free" high seas regime. The real problem is that many new nation-states have emerged since World War II, several of which, learning in large part from developed maritime nations, have come to understand the degree to which the oceans are or can be linked with a variety of national interests. Aside from the growing number of players which makes any ocean-wide rule more difficult to enforce, there is the growing number of possible uses of the oceans which, as Friedman observes in the passage starting this section, intrude upon traditional ocean activities such as vessel transit and fishing. To suggest that the problem lies with national efforts to exert control and establish more comprehensive management programs is to miss the point.

C. Common Heritage

Another aspect of the concern over freedom of the seas has been the doctrine that the resources of the oceans should be put to the use of mankind, rather than of individual nations. The position taken by Borgese and Pardo exemplifies this point of view. However, in the last year or two, that concern has been translated, at least within the United Nations' Law of the Sea negotiations, into an interest in establishing a new economic and political world order. Initiated by a group of developing nations referred to as the Group of 77, but now extending beyond any particular faction, a shift in the Law of the Sea negotiations has occurred because of a realization that control of the oceans could have profound effect upon military, economic, and political systems throughout the world. Just as the United States and the U.S.S.R. perceive the freedom of transit through or above international straits is of considerable importance to their national security, so other nations perceive that preventing such passage may be of importance to their national security. And just as the United States has evidenced an interest in deep sea mining, some nations with land-based mining industries perceive it to be in their interest to prevent such mining:

> . . . there is a deepening and more sophisticated perception among both developed and developing countries that the issue of seabeds repre-

sents interests more fundamental than the immediate economic benefits envisioned. Thus, as the negotiations have progressed, the stakes in the process of 'Who gets what, when, and how' have been considerably enlarged and elevated. The issues are no longer confined to pragmatic questions of state practice and jurisdiction but encompass more issues of states' principles; the mandate is no longer the technical design or a regime for deep seabed mining but the architectronic [sic] construction of the contours of a future international, legal, economic, and political order; the struggle is no longer for the codification of international law but a competition for the control of future global institutions.[7]

D. United States Ocean Management

As described in Chapters Two and Three, concern over possible military, economic, and political repercussions of unilateral United States extension of authority or management programs into ocean space has had strong influence on the scope and structure of the present national ocean-related programs. Reminiscent of Selden's *Mar Clausum* (1635) we appear to have developed a curious mix of ocean programs and policies. On the one hand we claim a regime for resources in the submerged lands, exercise total control over access to our fisheries in a water zone extending 200 miles from shore, maintain certain pollution control capabilities in that zone, and have argued for and participated in the establishment of several multinational and international ocean management regimes to control ocean dumping, tanker construction, the killing of whales and other species of ocean life, the placement of certain weapon systems on or beneath the seabed, and the establishment of international navigational rules and controls. On the other hand, we argue in our foreign policy positions for minimal extensions of national jurisdiction and the maintenance of "freedom of the seas" especially regarding distant-water fisheries and transit through international straits.

Friedman is correct in his assessment of growing potential for exclusion or serious diminution of important ocean activities such as fishing and vessel transit. The continuance of these and other ocean uses requires the maintenance of certain physical, biological, and chemical qualities in the oceans, as well as control over and some degree of uniformity in how activities are distributed in both time and space. This, in turn, implies increased jurisdiction and control, rather than an absence of it. While some interest groups have argued for a minimal extension of

---

[7] Patsy Mink, *San Diego Law Review*, Vol. 15, No. 3, p. 363.

United States ocean-related management programs, there has emerged a concept of a world seabed authority to regulate and to some degree undertake exploitation of seabed resources beyond the continental shelf.

Because many factors lead us to look further at the need for an increased understanding of control, we now better understand the degree to which the world oceans are a key part of world and regional weather and climate patterns; the oceans are a vital source of human protein; the oceans support a vast and complexly interconnected population of life forms susceptible to diminution and extinction; the oceans represent a great potential for energy, minerals, and other essential or valuable resources; the oceans provide the major means of global transportation of goods people. All of these factors indicate that there must be some degree and form of control. The interests and issues involved are in many instances too important to leave to a laissez faire system of allocation, and many of the interests, opportunities and problems require positive programs beyond the capabilities of individual citizens, companies, and even single nations to implement successfully.

The oceans, indeed, are a common heritage of mankind; increasingly, the whole of mankind demands and must be included in decisions regarding how this heritage shall be used. The significance of the oceans is such that conflicts among activities or user groups have the potential for national or global economic, environmental, or military disruption. As the potential for such conflicts increases and as more users and large-scale activities seek access to the oceans, some mechanism(s) must exist to allow for a pragmatic and peaceful resolution of conflicts. But increasingly, efforts must also be made to settle a more basic conflict between the seemingly endless inventive efforts of mankind to utilize the oceans and the oceans' finite capacity to absorb change without degradation of its resource potential. Furthermore, positive efforts are needed to head off conflicts before they occur, rather than deal with them once they become dangerous or disruptive.

It would seem that United States ocean interests can no longer be ensured by resisting the formation of domestic, foreign, or international ocean management regimes. It is logical that the regimes which emerge will recognize and allow the continuance of important ocean uses. It is also important to appreciate that while images of "creeping jurisdiction" may still have some restraining or limiting effect upon the scope and form of United States ocean-related programs, such images may have decreasing relevance to the concerns and intentions of many maritime nations who are, both unilaterally and in concert, discussing various new types of ocean management "regimes" either formally or informally.

E. Summary and Conclusions

From the growing interest in ocean management, the phrase "creeping jurisdiction" has emerged. It represents a claim that national extensions of authority over various aspects of ocean space and ocean activities constitute an intrusion upon the "high seas." This concept implies that the high seas are not available for national appropriation or management and that there is supposed to be a vacuum of noncontrol in that part of the ocean known as the high seas.

That concept of "freedom of the seas" with respect to living and non-renewable resources is increasingly untenable for the very reasons cited by Friedman. Today, and perhaps in fact for several hundred years, the issue has not been if there should be rules regarding how ocean space will be used, but rather whose rules will apply; the degree to which these rules should be formalized and/or enforced; and what process is appropriate for the development of such rules.

There are too many national and international ocean interests to accept a total vacuum in which no controls would exist over resources, and too many public interests to allow a laissez faire distribution in a market sense. Nations can no longer make up their own ocean rules with respect to resources, which may have been interpreted in the past as "freedom of the seas." Then we must seek and are seeking formal rules and means by which our interests can be considered. There is, of course, a fairly well established legal framework made up of agreements and customary law that governs "freedom of the seas" concepts. The interpretation of this framework into "domestic ocean management" on a potentially expanded scale is not yet clear.

In conclusion, it is perhaps unrealistic to use terms such as "creeping jurisdiction" as a criticism of proposed national and international ocean management concepts. It is increasingly important for the United States to account for both national and international interests and their implications in any ocean-related management activity. It is true that there are very good reasons for extending management within ocean space and ocean affairs only when needed and then with caution. But if there are to be freedoms in the future, they will probably result from even more deliberate resource management efforts to insure those freedoms. It should be clear by now that national reticence to extend jurisdictional control over some aspect of ocean use or ocean space will not always be an effective method of instilling a similar reticence into other maritime nations. It has already become evident that traditional ocean uses or "freedoms" such as vessel transit and fishing will bequire multinational coordination. An awareness is needed on the part of all ocean users, both traditional and emerging, that the oceans can accommodate multiple uses and multiple interests only through a spirit of cooperation and that all users must exercise some constraint to accommodate other users and to preserve and protect the oceans themselves.

The United States seems to face a major turning point; it has reached a new juncture in history regarding organization of its ocean-related programs and interests. It is a unique time in history, for it would appear that some 150 other nations have also begun to realize the global importance of the oceans, for the future of the world, and for the future of individual nations. Since the 1940's the United States has led, although not always controlled, international ocean policy and foreign ocean management efforts. Our present complex of ocean programs and policies seem to exceed that of any other nation.

The choices we make regarding the ocean will be of importance not only to the United States but also, increasingly, to the world. And increasingly we must consider the world's needs and interests in shaping our programs and policies. It is time, certainly, to take action, but it must be action stemming from informed deliberation and the resolution of basic issues. If we initiate such deliberations now, we can look forward to the development of sound and effective means for ocean management. If it will, the United States can lead; if it will not, we can be confident that others will act without us.

APPENDIX

Ocean Management: Seeking a New Perspective

Submerged Lands Act

AN ACT

To confirm and establish the titles of the States to lands beneath navigable waters within State boundaries and to the natural resources within such lands and waters, to provide for the use and control of said lands and resources, and to confirm the jurisdiction and control of the United States over the natural resources of the seabed of the Continental Shelf seaward of State boundaries.

Be it enacted by the Senate and House of Representatives of the United States of America in Congress assembled, That this Act may be cited as the "Submerged Lands Act".

TITLE I

Definitions

Sec. 2. When used in this Act—(a) The term "lands beneath navigable waters" means—

(1) all lands within the boundaries of each of the respective States which are covered by nontidal waters that were navigable under the laws of the United States at the time such State became a member of the Union, or acquired sovereignty over such lands and waters there-

191

after, up to the ordinary high water mark as heretofore or hereafter modified by accretion, erosion, and reliction;

(2) all lands permanently or periodically covered by tidal waters up to but not above the line of mean high tide and seaward to a line three geographical miles distant from the coast line of each such State and to the boundary line of each such State where in any case such boundary as it existed at the time such State became a member of the Union, or as heretofore approved by Congress, extends seaward (or into the Gulf of Mexico) beyond three geographical miles, and

(3) all filled in, made, or reclaimed lands which formerly were lands beneath navigable waters, as hereinabove defined;

(b) The term "boundaries" includes the seaward boundaries of a State or its boundaries in the Gulf of Mexico or any of the Great Lakes as they existed at the time such State became a member of the Union, or as heretofore approved by the Congress, or as extended or confirmed pursuant to section 4 hereof but in no event shall the term "boundaries" or the term "lands beneath navigable waters" be interpreted as extending from the coast line more than three geographical miles into the Atlantic Ocean or the Pacific Ocean, or more than three marine leagues into the Gulf of Mexico;

"Boundaries"

(c) The term "coast line" means the line of ordinary low water along that portion of the coast which is in direct contact with the open sea and the line marking the seaward limit of inland waters;

"Coast line"

(d) The terms "grantees" and "lessees" include (without limiting the generality thereof) all political subdivisions, municipalities, public and private corporations, and other persons holding grants or leases from a State, or from its predecessor sovereign if legally validated, to lands beneath navigable waters if such grants or leases were issued in accordance with the constitution, statutes, and decisions of the courts of the State in which

"Grantees" and "lessees."

such lands are situated, or of its predecessor sovereign; *Provided, however,* That nothing herein shall be construed as conferring upon said grantees or lessees any greater rights or interests other than are described herein and in their respective grants from the State, or its predecessor sovereign;

(e) The term "natural resources" includes, without limiting the generality thereof, oil, gas, and all other minerals, and fish, shrimp, oysters, clams, crabs, lobsters, sponges, kelp, and other marine animal and plant life but does not include water power, or the use of water for the production of power;

(f) The term "lands beneath navigable waters" does not include the beds of streams in lands now or heretofore constituting a part of the public lands of the United States if such streams were not meandered in connection with the public survey of such lands under the laws of the United States and if the title to the beds of such streams was lawfully patented or conveyed by the United States or any States to any person;

(g) The term "State" means any State of the Union;

(h) The term "person" includes in addition to a natural person, an association, a State, a political subdivision of a State, or a private, public, or municipal corporation.

TITLE II

Lands Beneath Navigable Waters Within State Boundaries

Sec. 3. Rights of The States.—(a) It is hereby determined and declared to be in the public interest that (1) title to and ownership of the lands beneath navigable waters within the boundaries of the respective States, and the natural resources within such lands and waters, and (2) the right and power to manage, administer, lease, develop and use the said lands and natural resources all in accordance with applicable State law be, and they are hereby, subject to the provisions hereof, recognized, confirmed, established, and vested in and assigned to the respective States or the persons who were on June 5, 1950, entitled thereto under the law of the respective States in which the land is located, and the respective grantees, lessees, or successors in interest thereof;

(b)(1) The United States hereby releases and relinquishes unto said States and persons aforesaid, except as otherwise reserved herein, all right, title, and interest of the United States, if any it has, in and to all said lands, improvement, and natural resources; (2) the United States hereby releases and relinquishes all claims of the United States, if any it has, for money or damages arising out of any operations of said States or persons pursuant to State authority upon or within said lands and navigable waters; and (3) the Secretary of the Interior or the Secretary of the Navy or the Treasurer of the United States shall pay to the respective States or their grantees issuing leases covering such lands or natural resources all moneys paid thereunder to the Secretary of the Interior or to the Secretary of the Navy or to the Treasurer of the United States and subject to the control of any of them or to the control of the United States on the effective date of this Act, except that portion of such moneys which (1) is required to be returned to a lessee; or (2) is deductible as provided by stipulation or agreement between the United States and any of said States;

Claims of U.S.

(c) The rights, powers, and titles hereby recognized, confirmed, established, and vested in and assigned to the respective States and their grantees are subject to each lease executed by a State, or its grantee, which was in force and effect on June 5, 1950, in accordance with its terms and provisions and the laws of the State issuing, or whose grantee issued, such lease, and such rights, pow-

Leases in effect on June 5, 1950.

ers, and titles are further subject to the rights herein now granted to any person holding any such lease to continue to maintain the lease, and to conduct operations thereunder, in accordance with its provisions, for the full term thereof, and any extensions, renewals, or replacements authorized therein, or heretofore authorized by the laws of the States issuing, or whose grantee issued such lease: *Provided, however,* That, if oil or gas was not being produced from such lease on and before December 11, 1950, or if the primary term of such lease has expired since December 11, 1950, then for a term from the effective date hereof equal to the term remaining unexpired on December 11, 1950, under the provisions of such lease or any extensions, renewals, or replacements authorized therein, or heretofore authorized by the laws of thc State issuing, or whose grantee issued, such lease: *Provided, however,* That within ninety days from the effective date hereof (i) the lessee shall pay to the State or its grantee issuing such lease all rents, royalties, and other sums payable between June 5, 1950, and the effective date hereof, under such lease and the laws of the State issuing or whose grantee issued such lease, except such rents, royalties, and other sums as have been paid to the State, its grantee, the Secretary of the Interior or the Secretary of the Navy or the Treasurer of the United States and not refunded to the lessee; and (ii) the lessee shall file with the Secretary of the Interior or the Secretary of the Navy and with the State issuing or whose grantee issued such lease, instruments consenting to the payments by the Secretary of the Interior or the Secretary of the Navy or the Treasurer of the United States to the States or its grantee issuing the lease, of all rents, royalties, and other payments under the control of the Secretary of the Interior or the Secretary of the Navy or the Treasurer of the United States or the United States which have been paid, under the lease, except such rentals, royalties, and other payments as have also been paid by the lessee to the State or its grantee;

(d) Nothing in this Act shall affect the use, development, improvement, or control by or under the constitutional authority of the United States of said lands and waters for the purpose of navigation or flood control or the production of power, or be construed as the release or relinquishment of any rights of the United States arising under the constitutional authority of Congress to regulate or improve navigation, or to provide for flood control, or the production of power;

Rights of U.S. respecting navigation, etc.

(e) Nothing in this Act shall be construed as affecting or intended to affect or in any way interfere with or modify the laws of the States which lie wholly or in part westward of the ninety-eighth meridian, relating to the ownership and control of ground and surface waters; and the control, appropriation, use, and distribution of such waters shall continue to be in accordance with the laws of such States.

Surface waters west of 98th meridian.

Sec. 4. Seaward Boundaries.—The seaward boundary of each original coastal State is hereby approved and confirmed as a line three geographical miles distant from its coast line or, in the case of the Great Lakes, to the international boundary. Any State admitted subsequent to the formation of the Union which has not already done so may extend its seaward boundaries to a line three geographical miles distant from its coast line, or to the international boundaries of the United States in the Great Lakes or any other body of water traversed by such boundaries. Any claim heretofore or hereafter asserted either by constitutional provision, statute, or otherwise, indicating the intent of a State so to extend its boundaries is hereby approved and confirmed, without prejudice to its claim, if any it has, that its boundaries extend beyond that line. Nothing in this section is to be construed as questioning or in any manner prejudicing the existence of any State's seaward boundary beyond three geographical miles if it was so provided by its constitution or laws prior to or at the time such State became a member of the Union, or if it has been heretofore approved by Congress.

Sec. 5. Exceptions From Operation of Section 3 of This Act.—There is excepted from the operation of section 3 of this Act—

(a) all tracts or parcels of land together with all accretions thereto, resources therein, or improvements thereon, title to which has been lawfully and expressly acquired by the United States from any State or from any person in whom title had vested under the law of the State or of the United States, and all lands which the United States lawfully holds under the law of the State; all lands expressly retained by or ceded to the United States when the State entered the Union (otherwise than by a general retention or cession of lands underlying the marginal sea); all lands acquired by the United States by eminent domain proceedings, purchase, cession, gift, or otherwise in a proprietary capacity; all lands filled in, built up, or otherwise reclaimed by the United States for its own use; and any rights the United States has in lands presently and actually occupied by the United States under claim of right;

(b) such lands beneath navigable waters held, or any interest in which is held by the United States for the benefit of any tribe, band, or group of Indians or for individual Indians; and

(c) all structures and improvements constructed by the United States in the exercise of its navigational servitude.

Sec. 6. Powers Retained by the United States.—(a) the United States retains all its navigational servitude and rights in and powers of regulation and control of said lands and navigable waters for the constitutional purposes of commerce, navigation, national defense, and international affairs, all of which shall be paramount to, but shall not be deemed to include, proprietary rights of ownship, or the rights of management, administration, leasing, use, and development of the lands and natural resources which are specifically recognized, confirmed, established, and vested in and assigned to the respective States and others by section 3 of this Act.

(b) In time of war or when necessary for national defense, and the Congress or the President shall so prescribe, the United States shall have the right of first refusal to purchase at the prevailing market price, all or any portion of the said natural resources, or to acquire and use any portion of said natural resources, or to acquire and use any portion of said lands by proceeding in accordance with due process of law and paying just compensation therefor.

Sec. 7. Nothing in this Act shall be deemed to amend, modify, or repeal the Acts of July 26, 1866 (14 Stat. 251), July 9, 1870 (16 Stat. 217), March 3, 1877 (19 Stat. 377), June 17, 1902 (32 Stat. 388), and December 22, 1944 (58 Stat. 887), and Acts amendatory thereof or supplementary thereto.

5 USC 485; 16 USC 460d, 825s; 30 USC 35, 36, 38, 43, 46, 47, 51, 52, 33 USC 70 la-1, 701c, 701f, 701j, and notes, 708, 709, 43 USC 321-323, 325, 327-329, 372-498 passim, 661, 766.

Sec. 8. Nothing contained in this Act shall affect such rights, if any, as may have been acquired under any law of the United States by any person in lands subject to this Act and such rights, if any, shall be governed by the law in effect at the time they may have been acquired: *Provided, however,* That nothing contained in this Act is intended or shall be construed as a finding, interpretation, or construction by the Congress that the law under which such rights may be claimed in fact or in law applies to the lands subject to this Act, or authorizes or compels the granting of such rights in such lands, and that the determination of the applicability or effect of such law shall be unaffected by anything contained in this Act.

Sec. 9. Nothing in this Act shall be deemed to affect in any wise the rights of the United States to the natural resources of that portion of the subsoil and seabed of the Continental Shelf lying seaward and outside of the area of lands beneath navigable waters, as defined in section 2 hereof, all of which natural resources appertain to the United States, and the jurisdiction and control of which by the United States is hereby confirmed.

Resources seaward of Continental Shelf.

Sec. 10. Executive Order Numbered 10426, dated January 16, 1953, entitled "Setting Aside Submerged Lands of the Continental Shelf as a Naval Petroleum Reserve", is hereby revoked insofar as it applies to any lands beneath navigable waters as defined in section 2 hereof.

18 FR 405.

Sec. 11. Separability.—If any provision of this Act, or any section, subsection, sentence, clause, phrase or individual word, or the application thereof to any person or circumstance is held invalid, the validity of the remainder of the Act and of the application of any such provision, section, subsection, sentence, clause, phrase or individual word to other persons and circumstances shall not be affected thereby; without limiting the generality of the foregoing, if subsection 3(a)1, 3(a)2, 3(b)1, 3(b)2, 3(b)3, or 3(c) or any provision of any of those subsections is held invalid, such subsection or provision shall be held separable and the remaining subsections and provisions shall not be affected thereby.

Approved May 22, 1953.

"Policy of the United States With Respect to Coastal Fisheries in Certain Areas of the High Seas
"By the President of the United States of America

"A PROCLAMATION

"WHEREAS for some years the Government of the United States of America has viewed with concern the inadequacy of present arrangements for the protection and perpetuation of the fishery resources contiguous to its coasts, and in view of the potentially disturbing effect of this situation, has carefully studied the possibility of improving the jurisdictional basis for conservation measures and international cooperation in this field; and

"WHEREAS such fishery resources have special importance to coastal communities as a source of livelihood and to the nation as a food and industrial resource; and

"WHEREAS there is an urgent need to protect coastal fishery resources from destructive exploitation, having due regard to conditions peculiar to each region and situation and to the special rights and equities of the coastal State and of any other State which may have established a legitimate interest therein;

"Now, THEREFORE, I, HARRY S. TRUMAN, President of the United States of America, do hereby proclaim the following policy of the United States of America with respect to coastal fisheries in certain areas of the high seas:

"In view of the pressing need for conservation and protection of fishery resources, the Government of the United States regards it as proper to establish conservation zones in those areas of the high seas contiguous to the coasts of the United States wherein fishing activities have been or in the future may be developed and maintained on a substantial scale. Where such activities have been or shall hereafter be developed and maintained by its nationals alone, the United States regards it as proper to establish explicitly bounded conservation zones in which fishing activities shall be subject to the regulation and control of the United States. Where such activities have been or shall hereafter be legitimately developed and maintained jointly by nationals of the United States and nationals of other States, explicitly bounded conservation zones may be established under agreements between the United States and such other States; and all fishing activities in such zones shall be subject to regulation and control as provided in such agreements. The right of any State to establish conservation zones off its shores in accordance with the above principles is conceded, provided that corresponding recognition is given to any fishing interests of nationals of the United States which may exist in such areas. The character as high seas of the areas in which such conservation zones are established and the right to their free and unimpeded navigation are in no way thus affected.

"IN WITNESS WHEREOF, I have hereunto set my hand and caused the seal of the United States of America to be affixed.

"Done at the City of Washington this twenty-eighth day of September, in the year of our Lord nineteen hundred and forty-five, and of the Independence of the United States of America the one hundred and seventieth.

HARRY S. TRUMAN

By the President:
Dean Acheson
  Acting Secretary of State"

**"By the President of the United States
of America**

"A PROCLAMATION

"WHEREAS the Government of the United States of America, aware of the long range world-wide need for new sources of petroleum and other minerals, holds the view that efforts to discover and make available new supplies of these resources should be encouraged; and

"WHEREAS its competent experts are of the opinion that such resources underlie many parts of the continental shelf off the coasts of the United

States of America, and that with modern technological progress their utilization is already practicable or will become so at an early date; and

"WHEREAS recognized jurisdiction over these resources is required in the interest of their conservation and prduent utilization when and as development is undertaken; and

"WHEREAS it is the view of the Government of the United States that the exercise of jurisdiction over the natural resources of the subsoil and sea bed of the continental shelf by the contiguous nation is reasonable and just, since the effectiveness of measures to utilize or conserve these resources would be contingent upon cooperation and protection from the shore, since the continental shelf may be regarded as an extension of the land-mass of the coastal nation and thus naturally appurtenant to it, since these resources frequently form a seaward extension of a pool or deposit lying within the territory, and since self-protection compels the coastal nation to keep close watch over activities off its shores which are of the nature necessary for utilization of these resources;

"Now, THEREFORE, I, HARRY S. TRUMAN, President of the United States of America, do hereby proclaim the following policy of the United States of America with respect to the natural resources of the subsoil and sea bed of the continental shelf.

"Having concern for the urgency of conserving and prudently utilizing its natural resources, the Government of the United States regards the natural resources of the subsoil and sea bed of the continental shelf beneath the high seas but contiguous to the coasts of the United States as appertaining to the United States, subject to its jurisdiction and control.

"IN WITNESS WHEREOF, I have hereunto set my hand and caused the seal of the United States of America to be affixed.

"Done at the City of Washington this twenty-eighth day of September, in the year of our Lord nineteen hundred and forty-five, and of the Independence of the United States of America the one hundred and seventieth.

Harry S. Truman

By the President
Dean Acheson
 Acting Secretary of State"

INDEX